MAINELY LESBIANS

By

Alicia Langley

ISBN: 1-4107-3973-2 (E-book)
ISBN: 1-4107-3974-0 (Paperback)

Library of Congress Control Number: 2003092283

This book is printed on acid free paper.

Printed in the United States of America
Bloomington, IN

1stBooks – rev. 04/21/03

Book One

Alicia Langley

Chapter One

Almost midnight and the party was still going strong. The screen door opened with a squeak. Carolyn has been sent out on a mission to check the coolers on the back porch for more wine. Once outside she had forgot all about the wine. It was a beautiful Maine night; the sweet smell of fresh cut grass hung in the air and a full moon above the pine trees put its spotlight on the ripened gardens circling the porch. Carolyn could even see the house cats in the distance, checking out their land for anything that moved. She leaned against the railing and took a deep breath, knowing somehow it would help bridge any gap that may be between her and her surroundings. Lost in the feel of the night, she didn't hear the door squeak behind her, but felt Julie's arms slip around her waist. Julie's breath was warm on the back of her neck, "Too much for you in there?" She asked leaning into her, Carolyn replied, "Oh no, I was sent out to find more wine." Turning around in Julie's arms she continued "But once out here...I don't know what it is, it's almost magical." Julie had to chuckle, "I had no idea you were such a country girl." "Nor did I," she answered. Putting her arms around Julie's neck, she murmured, "I could stay like this forever." With that they moved into each other and shared a kiss as magical as the night that surrounded them.

When Julie looked up she saw Connie and Jean's silhouettes walking the path through the apple orchard to their 'special place'. Still holding on to each other Carolyn followed Julie's gaze. Julie said, "I'm so happy for those two. Who would have expected they'd be here, now, together." Carolyn added with a bit of wonder in her voice, "I'm just as surprised. In fact who would have thought only a year and a half ago, we would all be here now, celebrating our big day?" Julie just shook her head, as much as she had wanted to be here, in the beginning, she hadn't been so sure about Carolyn. Their thoughts were interrupted by a burst of laughter coming from inside the old farmhouse. Julie spoke up, "Are you ready to head back inside?" Carolyn said, "I'll be along soon, I just want a few more minutes." "Alright, but don't be too long." Julie found the wine on her way back in while Carolyn pulled up a chair and put her feet up on the railing. Slipping back to the connection she felt with the night, she couldn't get over the contentment she felt. It was hard to believe she had been one of the doubters, enjoying the idea of moving and starting a new life, but really thinking it was all just talk.

She was still lost in her thoughts, remembering how this all came about, when she caught sight of Connie and Jean making their way back to the house. Carolyn had known Connie and Jean before the "group" met them. She met Connie when she had given Jean Kennedy, one of her patients, a ride to her office for her weekly appointment. Carolyn didn't think Jean was gay but Connie definitely was and seeing the way her eyes rested on Jean, she knew she had feelings for her, but Jean…?

Jean was in a world of her own, laden with pills and booze. Carolyn didn't know what got her started but it was clear she wasn't ready to stop. Jean was court-ordered to see a psychologist and Carolyn had been recommended. This was Jean's third visit. Carolyn had learned she was a thirty-six year old woman from a well to do family in New Jersey, who expected a lot from their children. Much to her amazement, Jean had already been married three times! She had three children from her first marriage that lived with their father after he gained custody from the courts. The second marriage didn't produce any children, but she had two more from her third marriage. A custody battle was currently underway with her third ex-husband.

Carolyn also remembered the rough road Connie went through trying to help Jean. Jean's attitude was hopelessness. She had no control over herself. As long as she could get her drugs and booze, nothing else mattered. But there was another side to Jean that both Connie and Carolyn got a glimpse of, someone with high intelligence and quiet class that even the drugs couldn't diminish.

Chapter Two

While Jean and Carolyn settled into the next room for their session, Connie took a seat in the waiting room. She picked up a magazine but couldn't focus; her mind was on Jean. From the time she had first seen Jean hanging over her glass at the bar, she'd felt drawn to her. She couldn't see her face but saw enough to know she was disturbingly thin. Jean lifted her head looking for her glass. Finding it empty she reached for the glass beside her. Apparently she wasn't alone. Just then, the door to the men's room swung open hitting the wall with a thud, as a big burley, loud man came stumbling out. Heading for the woman at the bar, he bellowed, "Honey! Hey, lets go!" He slipped his arm around her waist and lifted her onto her feet as he spoke. The woman pulled back, looking for another drink, but he told her he had plenty to drink back at his place. Hearing that, she let him lead her out of the bar. As they passed by Connie, she lifted her head and their eyes met. Connie felt mesmerized as she looked into the most startling blue eyes she had ever seen.

Connie turning to Pete the bartender, whom she'd known for some time, asked about the woman. Pete shook his head, "I can't tell you much about her Connie except to stay away from her; she's not your type. She started coming in here about two weeks ago right after you went on vacation. Everyday the same time, same thing, even the same chair! She orders one drink and just sips it until some guy; any guy comes in and starts buying them for her. She drinks herself into oblivion and then lets the guy drag her away." Pete shrugged his shoulders, "Pretty pathetic really. She doesn't seem the hard core type." Pete left Connie with her thoughts while he mixed drinks for his other customers. Connie didn't know what compelled her, she didn't think Jean was a lesbian but there was something in those eyes that beckoned to her. Whatever the reason, Connie decided she wanted to be the one to buy her drinks.

It took awhile, but then one night Connie found Jean alone and bought her the first of many drinks together. For one brief moment, while Jean's eyes were able to focus, she realized Connie wasn't a man, but a woman. It was an easy mistake to make because Connie did look very masculine. Jean let her know right away that she wasn't into that kind of stuff. Connie just laughed it off, telling her she just wanted to share a few drinks and maybe some conversation, that's all. Connie didn't receive much back in the way of talk, but she didn't mind, she was a talker anyway and easily carried the conversation for both of them. Connie had to admit, with that thick, wavy black hair outlining sharp, but delicate features incased in olive toned skin and those beautiful blue eyes, that she found Jean to be very desirable. 'Well,' she thought with a resigned sigh, 'I should let this pass, it's going nowhere.'

It went on that way for three to four months. As many times that she told herself to stay clear of Jean…she couldn't. Rarely did Connie find Jean alone. As Jean's reputation got around, more and more men were coming around to "buy her drinks." Although Jean came to like Connie and even depended on her now and then, she still shunned her when a man walked into the bar.

Connie, unsuccessful in making Jean see what a dangerous lifestyle she was living, was helpless to walk away. The most she was able to do was steer Jean to the least threatening guy of the evening. It wasn't long before they became known as Beauty and the Beast. Most of the time it was a harmless joke from the guys Connie dispatched for at the highway department. Other times it was more serious from guys that she had a bad feeling about and had tried to keep away from Jean. She wasn't always successful keeping Jean out of harm's way. Many nights she would pace the length of the bar when Jean wouldn't show up for days at a time after going off with someone that she had asked her not to go with. When she finally did show up, the bruises from the abuse she had taken were obvious.

Nothing Connie, Carolyn, or the courts did, had any effect on Jean. Having seen the other side of her, Connie and Carolyn were helpless to do anything but stand back and watch while they hoped for a breakthrough. It was always just a brief glimpse, before Jean, bent on destroying herself, slipped back into her hiding place and became lost once again. Maybe today would be different. Connie was in court with Jean this morning when the decision to grant her ex-husband full parental custody of their children was handed down. 'Really,' thought Connie, 'how else could they have decided?' Even though Connie knew it was the answer they all expected, Jean was visibly upset about the outcome. Walking hurriedly out of the courtroom, she didn't say a word as she stood quietly by the car until Connie came around and unlocked the door for her. She remained silent on the ride over to Carolyn's office, blinking back the tears in a desperate attempt to maintain some dignity after the humiliation she felt in the courtroom this morning.

Carolyn had made sure Jean had an appointment right after she got out of court, hoping this may jar something inside of her. Jean didn't stay long and when she emerged from Carolyn's office she walked right past Connie, heading for the door without looking back. Carolyn stood in the doorway of her office, clearly upset for Jean. Connie caught up with her on the stairs but Jean didn't stop. With tears brimming over, she ran to the car. Once inside she broke down, crying uncontrollably. Connie got in, slid over to her and held her in her arms, trying to comfort her. Jean pulled back, "Connie, please, just leave me alone. All I need right now is a drink!"

Well there was no way Connie was going to take Jean to the bar tonight. Instead she stopped at the liquor store and picked up a bottle, then went next door to the grocery store, thinking if she got Jean something to eat, it may keep her from drinking too much. Once at Jean's apartment, Connie sat her down at the kitchen table with her drink and then went about making them something to eat. At first Jean told her not to bother getting her anything, she wasn't hungry, but the spaghetti sauce Connie was making smelled good and enticed Jean to pick at the rolls Connie had placed on the table. When the meal was cooked, Connie filled a plate and placed it in front of her. Jean was hungry and began to eat in earnest, but it was short lived and she soon pushed the plate away. She hadn't eaten as much as Connie had hoped, but it was probably the most she'd eaten in awhile.

Connie could feel her heart breaking as she looked at Jean. She looked awful. If Jean didn't do something to help herself soon, Connie was afraid she wouldn't survive. How long could she stand by and watch what was happening to her without being able to help? It tore her apart. Connie knew this was coming. She knew from day one not to pursue this relationship. She knew she would keep getting hurt, but it was too late. Connie was in love with Jean and there was no turning back. Her thoughts were interrupted when she heard Jean speaking to her, "I'm going to take a hot bath and call it a night, and Connie, thanks for being here." Not waiting for a reply, she turned away abruptly, poured herself another drink and headed for the bathroom. Connie finished cleaning up the kitchen and went into the living room, turned the radio on low and settled into a big easy chair in the corner. Even though it was still early, only 6:30, it had been a frustrating and stressful day and she immediately fell asleep.

Jean settled into the hot water, the steam blocking out the world. The soft music in the background was having an effect on her mind allowing her to think about the reality of her life. She hated the way she was, weak and useless. She had ruined three marriages and her children wanted no part of her, yet she felt powerless to change. She shook her head, trying to erase the thoughts and emotions filling her mind. Connie flashed in her mind and it seemed to have a calming effect on her. Finally she admitted to herself that she did care for Connie. She felt fortunate to have her for a friend, in fact her only real friend, although she couldn't understand why Connie would want to be around her. She had treated her badly from the start. Most of the time when they were together, she didn't even speak to her. She would just ignore her as she sat beside her at the bar and keep drinking the drinks she bought her. At first, Jean had thought Connie was a man. With her short sandy blond hair, muscular build and flannel shirts, jeans, and the work boots she always wore, she looked and acted like a construction worker. As soon as Jean realized Connie was a woman, she had told her she wasn't interested but Connie didn't seem to care and just shrugged it off. Taking another sip of her drink but finding the glass empty and the bath water starting to cool, it was time to get out. After toweling off and slipping into a robe, Jean headed to the kitchen for another drink. Noticing Connie asleep in the chair, she thought about waking her up to tell her it was time to go, but she decided to let her sleep. Somehow, she felt comforted and less alone having her close by.

After another hour Jean was feeling significantly drunk. Hugging the walls, she headed for bed. Lying alone in the dark room, she couldn't help but feel the sadness she had created in her life. Oh so quietly, she began to cry. In the next room Connie woke up feeling something was wrong. Turning the radio off, she could hear Jean in the other room. She was at her side in an instant. Slipping onto the bed behind her, she wrapped her in her arms, wanting to comfort her. Turning around in Connie's arms, Jean felt a soothing warmth that was all new to her. Trying to see Connie's face in the darkness, but not quite able to make it out, she reached out her hand. Connie held her breath and didn't dare move as Jean's hand nervously traced her eyes, nose and mouth. Connie's desire to help and comfort was rapidly changing and she knew she needed to get up away from Jean before she over stepped her bounds. Sensing this was about to happen, Jean slipped her hand around to the back of Connie's head, pulling her forward till their lips met. Connie felt the sensation of falling into this woman, never to be seen again. Swept up in the moment, she held her tightly as she returned her kiss. Jean's hands were timid yet demanding, helping Connie out of her clothes. Jean didn't think about what was happening, she was only connecting with the love Connie felt for her, something she had never experienced before. Connie, out of her clothes, slipped under the covers and as their bodies met, shock waves ran through them. They were suspended in time; fully in tune with each other, experiencing each touch, each sensation. Exhausted, they finally fell asleep around midnight, or rather Connie did. Jean was fully awake and completely confused. She had never entertained thoughts of being with another woman, but tonight, for the first time, she was both physically and spiritually awakened. She had never experienced feelings like this before. 'Am I a lesbian? Will I hurt Connie like I've hurt everyone else? Where is this going? I must be crazy!'

Jean's mind was spinning with questions without answers while she methodically dressed, careful not to wake Connie. Putting on her coat, she stood by the bed looking down at Connie sleeping and fought the impulse to touch her hair. Everything seemed unreal. It was just too much! She grabbed her pocketbook off the chair and quietly left the apartment. Connie awoke the next morning and without even turning over, she knew that Jean was gone.

Chapter Three

Although the curtains where closed, the morning sun still managed to find it's way in. Carolyn started to stretch but felt Julie curled around her, so she remained still, not wanting to wake her. She started to smile, remembering last night; it had been perfect. Both Carolyn and Julie knew it wasn't going to be easy keeping this relationship together, but they also knew they had to try. When they first met at Sally's, a local lesbian bar in Boston, they knew they had a lot in common. They were both coming out of a bad relationship and felt it was their fault that they had failed to keep it together. Carolyn, a state psychologist, was working late most nights and many weekends. Julie, who also worked for the state, was a social worker and understood the role that long hours had played in her past relationships. Both women had made a vow, not to put any one else, or themselves, through that again. But after seeing each other for three years and understanding the commitments to their careers, they felt they had a good chance of making things work between them. They didn't have much time together, but they made the most of it. Two years ago, they made a commitment to each other and it was working.

Every so often, they made an effort to do something special, like last night. Julie had mentioned a few times about a play she wanted to see and when Carolyn had the chance to get the tickets, she didn't hesitate. Giving Julie the tickets had made her day. She was so excited she immediately called someone to cover for her on the night of the play. With enough people in place, they decided make a night of it, planning to go to Sally's for dinner and drinks afterward. Finally, the big night came and off they went. The play turned out to be better than expected, taking hold of the audience till the very end. They emerged from the theater, their faces flushed with excitement, chatting about how wonderful it had been and looking forward to their dinner at Sally's. After a leisurely dinner they headed home, their spirits soaring, anticipating more. Julie had a bottle of wine chilled and waiting. Carolyn put on soft music and lit a few candles.

The shrill ring of the phone brought Carolyn back to reality. Reaching for it quickly, not wanting to wake Julie, she acknowledged the voice of her answering service. The operator was quick to apologize for bothering her on her day off, but a patient, sounding very distraught, was on the other line. Carolyn asked the operator who it was; the woman told her, "I'm not sure, her voice is slurred, but I think she said her name is Jean", Carolyn sat up in bed, she hadn't heard anything from her since the day she ran out of the office three weeks ago. "Put her through" she quickly responded. "Jean, Jean, are you all right?" Jean's voice was barely audible. "I'm ready." was all she said, sounding as if she were ready to fall asleep. Carolyn asked her, "Jean can you get to my office? No, of course not," she said, answering her own question. "Jean I'm coming to get you, tell me where you are." The phone was silent for a moment, then "I'm not sure, I think I'm at the bar…" her voice trailed off. Over the phone Carolyn could hear noise of cars driving by and figured Jean was in an outside phone booth. Searching her mind, she tried to recall the name of the bar where Jean hung out but all she could come up with was somewhere on Front Street. Carolyn spoke slowly, telling Jean to stay where she was "I'm coming to get you, don't leave, do you understand, can you hear me?" Jean said, "Yes, I'll be here."

By this time Julie was wide awake and listening to Carolyn's side of the conversation, she heard enough to know she would be leaving. Leaning over Julie kissed her shoulder and headed for the bathroom. Carolyn hung up the phone and dressed quickly. She was heading for the door when Julie came out of the bathroom. "I'm sorry Hon, I'll explain later," she told her as she picked up her keys and went out the door. "I'll call as soon as I can," her voice trailing behind her. Julie went about setting up the coffee and took a shower while it perked. She was disappointed that Carolyn had to leave. She was hoping they could sleep in together for a change, but that's the way it was.

Flying down the stairs, literally bouncing off the walls, Carolyn managed to make it to her car in one piece. Once inside she grabbed hold of the wheel and forced herself to stop for a moment and take a deep breath, knowing if she didn't, she would never survive the drive. She was surprised at how emotionally involved she'd become with Jean, she really felt compelled to help her.

Turning onto Boylston St. and down Mass Ave, Carolyn was feeling a little uneasy; afraid she wouldn't be able to find Jean. After what seemed like forever Carolyn saw the lounge where she hoped Jean would be. Pulling into the empty parking lot, she didn't see a phone booth so she drove around to the back. There it was, but it looked empty, 'Oh, God,' she thought, 'I hope I have the right place, where else would I even begin to look?' Getting out of the car Carolyn looked in the booth hoping at least to find a note. Pushing open the door she felt it hit something. Jean was on the floor squeezed into the corner. She looked lifeless with her head down on upraised knees and arms dangling down on the floor. Carolyn's hands where shaking when she reached out to touch Jean, looking for any sign of life. She was relieved to find warm skin and a faint pulse on Jeans wrist, "Oh, Thank God, Thank God," Carolyn whispered under her breath. "Jean, Jean," she said as she shook her gently. "Jean it's me, Dr. Adams!" Jean stirred and looked up with amazingly clear eyes. It was obvious she wasn't on drugs but…"Come on Jean, let me help you to the car," Carolyn gently urged. Helping her up, she put her arm around her waist for support. She was shocked at how thin she was. Jean had lost even more weight since Carolyn had seen her three weeks ago. Setting her gently on the front seat, making sure she was belted in, Carolyn got into the driver's seat and pulled out of the parking lot. "Jean, you're in rough shape, I'm going to take you to the hospital! "No…" Jean moaned, "please can't we talk first?" Giving Jean's hand a squeeze, Carolyn told her, "Of course we can if you feel up to it. We can go to my office. Just lean back and relax, it's a short drive from here." When they reached the office Carolyn helped Jean up the stairs and onto the couch. "Jean would you like something to eat?" she asked. Jean shook her head no, "Please, just coffee, I don't think I could hold anything else down." Carolyn made a pot of coffee and after taking a quick glance at the clock she saw it was 8:10, Julie crossed her mind. Carolyn made a mental note to call as soon as she could. Looking over at Jean, Carolyn couldn't help but wonder where she's been for the past three weeks. One thing's for sure; Connie will certainly be relived to hear she surfaced.

Carolyn brought them each a cup of coffee but instead of sitting at her desk, she pulled up a chair across from Jean and shared the footstool. Carolyn noticed Jean seemed to be holding her coffee more for warmth, rather than drinking it. It was then she noticed how chilly it was. She had turned the heat down yesterday, not expecting to be back till Monday. After turning up the heat, Carolyn gave Jean her full attention. "How is your coffee?" Jean didn't say anything for a moment as she tried to collect her thoughts. Finally, she said, "I'm sorry I bothered you so early..." Carolyn cut her off leaning towards her, "There is nothing to be sorry for. I'm glad you called, I want to help; it's what I do. Now tell me Jean, what's going on?" Taking a sip of coffee, Jean murmured, "It's time, I want some help and we both know I can't do it on my own. I need to be admitted to a hospital or something." Carolyn leaned over and took Jean's hands in hers, "Jean that's good news! There is a wonderful clinic not far from here. I'll get you in today!" Carolyn could sense Jean's nervousness and reassured her, "Remember, you're not alone, I will continue to see you, and of course Connie will be there for you too. She's a good person and you need to have friends around you now." Jean pulled her hands away from Carolyn shaking her head, "Connie doesn't know

I'm here and please don't tell her…I don't want her to know". "Oh," replied Carolyn, surprised by the seriousness in Jean's voice, "All right Jean, of course, I won't say anything if you don't want me to. Is there something you want to talk to me about?" Jean shook her head, "Not now, I'm sorry but I'm just too confused right now. I just need to get myself together." Carolyn could see she was getting agitated so she didn't pursue it further. "It's all right, just do what feels right for you." Jean visibly relaxed, "Thank you, I really appreciate your help. I don't mind telling you, I'm scared, I don't know what to expect." Carolyn went on to explain what would happen at the clinic and about the many programs available during and after her stay. She made sure Jean understood that although she would get a lot of support, if her stay in 'rehab' was going to work, it would be up to her. "Your system is used to the alcohol and drugs and will put up a good fight against getting help." Jean nodded that she understood. "Now you just stretch out and get some rest while I make a few phone calls and make the necessary arrangements to get you admitted."

Jean did just that, she was worn out and within a few minutes she was fast asleep. Carolyn took the afghan off the back of the couch and draped it over her. She stood for a moment looking down at her, shaking her head. She was amazed that this thirty six year old, child-like woman had already been married three times, had five children, and was probably on drugs and alcohol the whole time. She decided to let the clinic know that she may not be there for a while; Jean needed to sleep while she could. Once she started withdrawal, sleep would be hard to come by.

After making all the arrangements, Carolyn made herself another cup of coffee and while Jean was sleeping soundly, she sat down and called Julie. "Hi Hon," Julie said as she answered the phone. Carolyn was pleasantly surprised. "Oh, I hope you knew it was me!" Julie chuckled, "Of course," then asked, "How is everything?" Carolyn told her, "Good really, better then expected." Julie wanted to know if it was the case Carolyn has been so concerned with. "Yes it is, but I think there's been a break through. I'm at my office. She's sleeping on the couch right now and when she wakes up I'm taking her to a rehab clinic." Julie was surprised. Even though she didn't know the patient personally she and Carolyn had discussed Jean often, "She agreed to that?" Carolyn answered, "It was her idea and believe me, I am just as surprised." She paused for a moment, her voice taking on a more personal tone, "Julie, I really hated leaving this morning…" Julie answered, "I know that, and I also know if it had been one of my cases, I would of done the same. Last night was special and your leaving didn't take anything away from that." Carolyn answered, "I love you."

After finishing her conversation with Julie, Carolyn checked the time. The clock over her desk said 9:30. She would leave Jean sleeping until she woke on her own. Once at the clinic she planned on staying with her for a while. She was pretty scared right now and Carolyn wanted to make this as easy as possible for her. Looking at her, she noticed her body was faintly twitching as she slept. 'Just the beginning' she thought, 'I wonder where she has been these past three weeks, she looks awful.' Jean's face was bloated from all the alcohol in her system; Carolyn hoped she would be all right. Then her thoughts turned to Connie. She couldn't help but wonder what went on between those two. Jean was so insistent that Connie was not to be told anything about her. It was too bad, poor Connie has been so upset not knowing what happened to her. Carolyn knew it was going to be hard to see her and not say anything when she asked the inevitable question, "Have you heard from Jean?"

Carolyn busied herself rearranging her appointment book, making extra time so she could see Jean on a daily basis. She hoped Jean was going to be strong enough to see this through. Jean finally awoke around noontime. After straightening her clothes and freshening up, she turned to Carolyn saying with a strong resolve, "I'm ready!" On their way out the door, Carolyn gave Jean, a quick, warm hug, letting her know she wasn't alone. Jean gave her a shy smile in return. It was the first time Carolyn had seen her smile.

At the clinic, things went smoothly. Carolyn told the doctor about Jean's muscle spasms and he immediately prescribed a relaxant with a mild sedative. It had been a long day, but at last Jean was settled in. When Heidi, the nurse assigned to Jean, came in, Carolyn knew it was time to go. Taking Jeans hands in hers, Carolyn nodded toward Heidi saying, "I leave you in good hands. If there is something you need, Heidi will be here for you." Giving Jean a gentle hug, she assured her she would see her tomorrow and with that she got up and left the room. In the lobby Carolyn made a quick call to Julie. "I'm on my way, anything I need to pick up?" "No," Julie answered, "I ran out and got some things earlier, just come home." Carolyn answered, "Then I'm on my way."

About the same time Carolyn was heading home to Julie, Connie was turning the key and opening the door to Jean's apartment. The last time Connie stopped by, the landlord told her he couldn't wait any longer for Jean to come back and he needed to rent the apartment. He told her, "I'm sorry Connie, there's nothing else I can do. The first of the month is next week and if she's not back by then, I would appreciate it if you came by with the key." Well, this was the first of the month and still no Jean. As Connie pulled into the driveway, the landlord came out to greet her. "Hi Connie, how are you today?" Connie answered, "Oh, I've had better days. I have the key for you." He told her, "Listen, I'm sorry, I wish it didn't have to be this way." Connie knew that he meant it. He had liked Jean and hoped she was all right. "Connie, Jean didn't have much but you're welcome to take what's here and hold it for her till she comes back." Connie knew he said that more for her benefit then he probably believed. She thanked him, and agreed to take Jean's belongings with her.

Closing the door behind her and stepping into the kitchen, the memories of Jean came flooding in, hurting more than she could stand. With eyes closed, she said aloud, "Oh God Jean, where in the hell are you?" She was frozen to the spot. She had to physically shake herself until she could move again. Looking around the tiny apartment Connie saw that the landlord was right; Jean didn't have much. She filled two bags, containing all that Jean owned and left the apartment. She got in her car and headed for Sally's.

Chapter Four

Heidi came in with Jean's breakfast. It had been three weeks now and considering the years of addiction, Jean was doing remarkably well, except for her appetite. She was never a big eater to begin with, but now that they had removed the feeding tube, she knew that if she was ever going to be strong enough to make it on her own, she had to try. The most she could eat was maybe, a half of sandwich and a frappe. Anything else caused her stomach to feel nauseous. The doctor told her that would start fading soon.

Dr. Adams was right! The staff was wonderful; the clinic was steeped in a family atmosphere. Someone was always there if you needed anything or just wanted to talk. 'God! Talk! Everyone wants to talk!' she thought with a smile. 'This is the best thing I could have done for myself.' Without warning, Connie's face with her big warm smile flashed in front of her. Jean shook her head to rid herself of Connie's image. She wasn't ready to think about what happened between them. 'God, how Connie must hate me,' she said aloud. 'Enough of this,' she thought. 'I know I'll have to deal with this someday but now is not the time. I need to stay focused and get myself together. This means staying on the program. The medication is helping, but they will wean me off it with smaller and smaller doses until it is gone. I need to stay focused on this and only this, until I get well.'

Carolyn was in her office at the clinic, going over her notes from this morning's session with Jean. She has shown a lot of inner strength so far and she's been through a lot of tough battles. She's done remarkably well, focusing on getting through this, building a life for her self and a relationship with her children. Carolyn had hoped by now Jean would mention Connie, but she hadn't, and it really puzzled her. Something happened between them, but what? Jean was beginning to open up, talking more about her self. Maybe she'll get to the bottom of Jean and Connie yet. Glancing at the clock, Carolyn saw it was time to leave. Julie had phoned earlier to say everyone was meeting at Sally's tonight to plan Lillian and Anna's surprise anniversary party and she was looking forward to it.

Carolyn walked into Sally's, her familiar second home. Seeing everyone at their special table in the corner, she gave a wave and motioned she was stopping at the bar to pick up a drink. 'God,' she thought, 'this place is packed tonight.' Making her way to the bar she heard a familiar voice, although a little slurred, "Hey Doc, whatcha doing here? Seeing a few patients?" "Hello Connie, what a surprise seeing you here! No, I'm not here to work, I'm meeting a few friends for dinner." Carolyn said as a matter a fact. Connie thought for a moment, then with raised eyebrows replied, "Well, I'll be...I should'a known." Carolyn just laughed and asked Connie how she was doing. She replied, "I'm heartsick Doc, just heartsick. I can't stop thinking about Jean, not knowing where she is, or if she's all right. It's driving me crazy, I can't focus on anything else." Carolyn placed a hand on Connie's shoulder, "Connie, call my office this week and I'll figure a time for us to have lunch together. It might help if you had someone to talk to." Connie nodded her head, "Thanks Doc, I'd like that." They talked a few more minutes and then with drink in hand, Carolyn headed toward Julie and their friends.

Julie got up as she approached the table and greeted her with a kiss. "Hi, are you okay?" she asked, seeing something was on her mind. Carolyn nodded her head, "I just ran into a friend of one of my patients. I don't want to get into anything now, but on the way home, maybe you can help me with a dilemma I'm in." "Come on you two, we want to order," called Nancy, "we're starved." "All right", said Julie, "What are we doing, pizza?" Cathy, their friend and waitress came over and chimed in, "I'll go for that. I've only got fifteen minutes more before my shift ends, then I'll be back and we can plan the party. Now, is everyone having pizza?" Carolyn said she had been dying for one of Sally's Rueben sandwiches. Nancy said she would have the same, so that left pizza for Julie, Karen and Cathy and of course, another round of drinks. Julie spoke up with her glass raised to her lips, "What better way to plan a party, then while we're partying!" Cathy told them all, "Wait until I come back now before you start planning, I won't be long…" and off she went, orders in hand.

Karen said, "Imagine, Anna and Lillian…forty five years together! Really, for lesbians, it can't be that common." Julie nodded her head, "Yes it is quite an accomplishment, considering how much harder it had to be back then." Everyone agreed. Karen seemed to have a lot of questions on the subject. Turning to Carolyn and Julie she asked, "Look at you two, I don't know how you do it, living openly the way you do, with your jobs and family. What about your family?

25

What do they say?" Karen was on a roll. Nancy put her hand on her arm and said "Hold on for a minute!" Karen gave a short laugh and apologized for being so personal and was about to let the subject drop. Nancy spoke up again, "It's okay Karen, let's talk about it, maybe some one has some input for you." "Of course," everyone chimed in. Julie asked, "What's on your mind Karen?" Karen looked a little embarrassed, "Well, as you all probably know, Nancy wants us to move in together." Taking Nancy's hand she continued, "This openness is all new to me, so please bear with me. I just don't think I'm ready for it yet." Carolyn spoke up then saying, "Julie and I stopped the charade after we moved in together. We're no different than any other people in love who are sharing their lives together. We don't advertise it, but we do live our lives as a couple, and so far, we've been lucky. We haven't had any real problems in that area." "But," asked Karen, "what about your family, how do they feel?" Julie spoke up, "I have an uncle who is gay and lives openly with his partner. At first the family was shocked but in time they managed to get over it. When I told them about Carolyn and me I knew they would probably react the same way, and they did. It's only been the past couple of years that they've made the effort to get past it and accept us. Things have really been going well." Carolyn told her, "I wasn't so lucky, my family refused to hear it. They wanted things back the way it was, with them remaining in the dark about who I really am. We don't see much of each other anymore, but I'm still hoping." Nancy spoke up, "Karen, look, I'm sorry, I didn't mean to pressure you. I just want us to be together." Karen told her, "I've always felt that we would move in together some day, but I just don't feel I'm ready." "Okay!" they heard Cathy approaching the table, "make room, dinners here!" Every thing smelled so good they dove right in. Cathy, finished with work for the evening, squeezed in for her share of the pizza.

Standing by the bar, Connie couldn't help but feel drawn to the Doctor's table. Even though the place was packed, they didn't seem to notice any one else. She could hear their laughter above all the other noise in the bar while they ate their meal like a large, boisterous family. Connie felt envious, especially after seeing the kiss shared between the Doctor and the attractive woman who greeted her. Feeling sharp pangs of loneliness and longing come over her, Connie knew it was time to go.

Back at the table, every one was having a good time planning the party. There were only two people missing. Jamie, and whoever she might be with this week, hadn't shown up yet, and Susan had called Karen earlier saying her husband was home and she couldn't get away. They would have to plan around them. They all knew Lillian and Anna planned on celebrating their anniversary in Maine at the old family farm Lillian had just inherited. They decided to surprise them by holding the party there, but somehow they needed to get to Maine before they arrived. "How will we get in?" Cathy asked. Nancy answered, "Lillian mentioned once they kept a spare key next door at a neighbors house." "Great!" said Carolyn, "Now what about food, what should we plan on?" Nancy told them Lillian had mentioned that they had a big outdoor fireplace that they cooked out on all the

27

time. Nancy sat forward with an idea, "Hey lets have a cookout!" "In October? Won't it be too cold?" Carolyn asked. Julie spoke up liking the idea, "If it's too cold, we can always cook out and then eat inside."

They spent time on the menu, wanting everything to be perfect. Nancy spoke up asking, "Does anyone know where this place is? Everyone looked from one to another with raised eyebrows…then burst out laughing. They didn't have a clue! By eleven o'clock they were pretty well planned out. Nancy, seeing Karen looking tired, was the first to call it a night. Everyone else followed suit. They each took a list of what they had to do or bring to the party. They still had a month to go and planned on getting together once more to make sure everything was in place. It would be up to Carolyn to get directions to the farm. Leaving Sally's, they were surprised to walk out into a rainy night. Quickly saying their last good-byes, they ran for their cars. Cathy caught a ride with Carolyn and Julie. Her son was home from college for the weekend and had her car.

Nancy and Karen were soaked by the time they got to Nancy's car, "Well, that certainly woke me up," Karen said laughing. "Me too," Nancy replied as she wiped the rain from her eyes. "There, now where to? Do you want me to take you home?" "No," Karen answered, "I'd rather stay with you, but I want to stop by my place and pick up a few things." "Okay then, consider it done," Nancy replied. They were quiet during the drive to Karen's, both lost in their own thoughts and the rhythm of the windshield wipers. Nancy hadn't meant to pressure Karen; she just thought it was a step they should be taking. She knew she wanted to spend the rest of her life with Karen and knew Karen felt the same way. Karen just had this hang-up about everyone knowing about them. Nancy had no idea who 'everyone' was, nor did she care, but she would let it drop for now. She felt there had to be more to it. Karen was twelve years older then her and as often as Nancy told her it didn't matter, she was sure Karen thought it would be a problem later on. Karen was feeling bad, she certainly didn't want to do anything to hurt Nancy. She wasn't sure why she held back. It did seem rather foolish. They usually stayed together in one place or the other anyway. 'But,' Karen thought, 'Nancy is so much younger than me,' will she still want us to be together in ten years when she's only thirty-five and I'm almost fifty?'

Julie and Carolyn dropped Cathy off, watching to make sure she got in all right, and then headed home themselves. Cathy waved good-bye and closed the door behind her. It was going on midnight and she thought she might wait up for her son. She busied herself around the house for a short time then got ready for bed. Lying there with the rain hitting the windows, she couldn't keep her eyes open and decided she and her son could visit tomorrow over breakfast. Cathy smiled a mother's smile thinking about her son. It had been just the two of them since the divorce sixteen years ago. Tommy was only three at the time his father left and he and Cathy developed a real close bond over the years. His father never paid much attention to him and Cathy thought it was just as well. He could never be a good influence on Tommy. He was lazy and irresponsible and if it hadn't been for her working while they were married, they wouldn't even have had a place to live. She didn't know why she hadn't seen through him in the first place, but she was looking to get married, hoping it would stop the feelings she was having about women. As much as she hated her marriage, she was grateful to have her son. Cathy drifted off to sleep, content with her life. She had a terrific apartment, a job she liked, great friends, and, of course, her son. The only thing missing was a serious relationship, Cathy thought, 'Maybe its time to pursue that.'

Chapter Five

Connie left work early to keep her luncheon appointment with Doctor Adams. She really needed someone to talk to. They arrived at the restaurant at the same time and were seated right away. After ordering their meal, Connie started the conversation, "I'm sorry, but I have to ask, have you heard from Jean?" Reaching across to take Connie's hand, Carolyn truthfully told her, "Believe me Connie, I would love to tell you I have, but I can't," It was the answer Connie had expected, even so…"Thanks Doc and thanks for seeing me like this," Connie's eyes filled with tears. Carolyn felt terrible, she had the answer to ease Connie's pain, but she couldn't say a word.

Connie took a deep breath and regained her composure, "I'm sorry Doc. I just don't know what to do. I'm driving myself crazy. Jean has disappeared and it's all my fault!" Looking frustrated and scared, Connie added, "I don't even know if she's alive." Carolyn asked, "Why would you think it was your fault Connie?" Clearing her throat, Connie told her about their last night together, "I woke up suddenly and I heard Jean crying in the other room, I went to her." Connie stared at a distant point as if she were watching a movie; "There she was, hugging her pillow, rocking back and forth. My heart went out to her Doc," Connie shrugged her shoulders, "I put my arms around her to comfort her, but she turned to me and unless I was dreaming, she pulled me to her and kissed me." Connie, lost in the moment had to be brought back. Carolyn asked, "Are you all right Connie?"

"Yes...look, I don't deny the fact that I'm in love with her, but I would never take advantage of her like that. I honestly started to pull away, but she wouldn't let me go." Connie leaned forward when she spoke, "I have to tell you Doc, I haven't had a lot of relationships, but I've been around enough to know that night held something special. I have never made love to a woman before with such intensity and never have I been made love to with the same intense feeling." Carolyn let her professional demeanor drop, showing her surprise. Connie caught the look, "Believe me Doc, no one was more surprised then me". Carolyn said, "Then I don't understand, if Jean was willing, why do you think she left because of you?" "I don't know, but she did leave," Connie paused for a moment, "Maybe I imagined the whole evening, maybe she didn't want anything to happen. But then, she did kiss me first. I don't know; I'm so confused. That night I felt as if we were truly connected, that this was a beginning, not an ending." Carolyn's heart was breaking for her, but she had promised Jean she wouldn't say anything, "Connie, from what you've told me, you shouldn't be blaming yourself." Carolyn took a deep breath, "Maybe she'll be back and maybe she won't, but in the mean time you have got to take care of yourself. You look worn out! I'm serious Connie, depression is a killer!" Carolyn stopped for a moment to regain her composure, her voice took on a softer tone, "It's been, what, two months? Believe me Connie I'm not telling you to forget Jean but you need to make some time for yourself." Connie didn't say anything, so Carolyn continued more forcefully; "You came here to talk to me, now you need to listen to me!" Connie gave

Carolyn a hint of a smile. 'Well,' thought Carolyn, 'its a start.' Continuing, "I saw you at Sally's the other night. You don't usually go there do you?" Connie replied, "No, I'm not over in that part of town very often." Carolyn continued talking, "It's a warm, friendly place and you should make an effort to stop in once in awhile. You need to cultivate some friends and Sally's is a good place to do that. If you see me there, come over and join my friends at our table. I can guarantee you won't be feeling blue for long. They're a great bunch of women. It won't make you forget about Jean, but it will keep you from feeling so alone." "Well", Connie replied, "I'm sure your right," She paused for a moment, "I just miss her."

Chapter Six

Julie was on the phone with Susan, letting her know the plans for the anniversary party, Carolyn, just arriving home from work heard her saying "We all hope you can make it. We know it'll be hard for you to get away, but it's going to be such a good time. Maybe you could just come for the afternoon...all right Susan, but keep it in mind."

Hanging up the phone, Susan couldn't imagine how she'd ever get away. She would love to go, though. They were a wonderful group of women and the few times she was able to be around for one of their get-togethers, she came away feeling empowered, like she could be or do anything she pleased. Maybe she could go just for the afternoon. For the first time since she had married Jimmy, divorce popped into her mind. She immediately got rid of the thought; she would never break up her family. That was the one thing she was sure of these days.

Susan realized at a young age she liked girls much better then boys. She also realized from listening to kids and adults, that it was not the way to be. She had learned quickly not to be different. Later in high school Susan met Jimmy Chase. Jimmy was a little rough around the edges but he had a quiet nature. She thought he was much nicer then her friend's boyfriends. They were all loud, always telling dirty jokes while trying to grope the girls every chance they got. Jimmy was very shy and respectful, never looking for more then a goodnight kiss. Jimmy also had a secure future ahead of him. Once out of high school he planned on joining his father and brothers in the family's plumbing business. They have been married twelve years now with eleven-year-old twin daughters. They owned a nice house and while they weren't rich, they were pretty well off. Jimmy was always doing more then his share at work, coming home late and working most weekends. Lately he was cranky with Susan and the girls when he was around the house. In all fairness, Susan was fond of him and appreciated the long hours and hard work he did to provide for his family. She tried to stop him from working so hard, but he had something to prove to his father and that was that. As a result, they didn't share much of a life anymore, giving Susan more time to wonder what she was missing. And after meeting Nancy and Karen, she felt she'd found it.

Nature's Best was a small bakery/coffee shop located on the corner of her street. Susan stopped by weekly to buy her bread. She didn't know the owner, just enough to say "hi", and place her order. Even so, she was surprised when she went in one day, about two months ago, and saw that they had changed ownership. It really didn't matter to her; she just hoped the bread was as good as it had been.

Walking up to the counter Susan saw two women in the back. They seemed to be having a problem with an enormous roll of plastic wrap. As soon as one woman would get it in position on the rod, the other would drop it. This happened a few times. Unaware of Susan's presence, they struggled once more, sure they had it this time, but still the other end dropped. Instead of getting angry, they both burst out laughing! Susan couldn't help but laugh with them, bringing their attention to her. Putting a hand on her stomach to calm her laughter, Nancy extended her other hand over the counter, "Hi, I'm Nancy, and this is my partner, Karen." Trying to control her laughter, Karen said, "I'm sorry, "I guess we're just a little tired." "No need to apologize, I can always use a good laugh. I'm Susan, could you use another pair of hands?" The three of them liked each other immediately.

From that time on Susan stopped in more often. She enjoyed getting to know them. If they were too busy to chat, Susan would put on an apron and take orders. She really liked being around them. They were always upbeat and seemed to be able to handle whatever came their way. She was sure they were more then just "business partners," but, of course, she would never ask. In fact, she was embarrassed just to think it.

After a month had passed, Karen and Nancy mentioned a place in East Boston called Sally's. "Have you ever heard of it?" Karen asked. Susan's bright red face was all the answer they needed. Nancy spoke right up, "Oh, Susan, we didn't mean to..." Susan quickly told them, "No, no, that's okay, really, I was just taken aback a little. I've never been there, but I have heard stories." Karen spoke up, "Well, I don't know what you've heard, but it's a real nice place where you can relax and be yourself." "Anyway," Nancy added, "Karen and I try to go there a couple of times a month, just to unwind and have a few laughs. Would you like to come with us some time?" In a quite voice Susan answered, "I'd have to think about it, I mean, I'd really have to think about it."

And think about it she did. For one thing, for them to ask her, they must suspect she was like them. For

36

some reason this didn't bother her. It meant they were telling her about themselves and it gave her a nice feeling, a feeling of belonging. 'How can I go there and take a chance on being seen in such a place by someone we know,' she thought. 'I suppose it doesn't really matter anyway, I've never gone out without Jimmy and I can't start now.' It was easy to keep her morning visits at the bakery with Jimmy in work and the girls in school. In fact, it was always assumed she was home, cooking and cleaning. 'Well, not anymore!' she told herself. Suddenly being seen was not an issue anymore, the real question was, would she have the nerve to go? She felt a stirring in the very core of her being. She felt different, stronger, allowing her real self to emerge…'Hmm,' she thought, 'maybe I will find a way to go.'

Susan walked into the bakery around eleven o'clock that Friday. It was her usual time, just a different day. Things usually quieted down around that time. Nancy and Karen came from out back, greeting Susan with big hugs. "Hey!" Nancy said to Susan, "What are you doing here on Friday?" Susan answered, "Well, I just wanted to catch up with you before the weekend." Nancy asked, "Is anything wrong?" Susan answered, "Oh no. I was just wondering, are you going to Sally's this weekend?" "Oh," Nancy said, looking relieved, "do you want to go Susan?" Susan had a determined look in her eyes, "Yes, I think I'd like that." "That's wonderful, you'll love it!" Nancy exclaimed, giving Susan a big hug, as did Karen. They took advantage of the lull in the bakery and over coffee they made their plans for Saturday night.

All day Saturday, Susan drove herself crazy, 'Should I go, shouldn't I go? I want to go but it means people will know and what if it gets back to Jimmy?' She knew that was unlikely. By the end of the day Susan had made up her mind. Not only did she want to go, she needed to go. She planned to meet Karen and Nancy in the parking lot at Sally's at seven o'clock. That gave her plenty of time to drop the girls off at their slumber party. Susan's daughters were pretty excited about going and she was happy they were having so much fun. They were very popular, always being invited to go somewhere.

Susan pulled into the parking lot earlier than she originally planned. Looking around she didn't see Karen and Nancy's car, but it was only 6:30. She knew if she had waited at home after dropping the girls off, she would have found an excuse not to go. There weren't many cars there when she first arrived, but they were coming in now. Susan was parked so she had a clear view of everyone coming and going. She watched the women arriving, some were alone and others were holding hands with each other. They all seemed to know each other as they merged at the door to Sally's. Susan was so engrossed in watching them that she never saw Nancy and Karen until they poked their heads in the passenger side window. "Come on," Nancy said, "It's time." As Karen came around to open the door for Susan, she said, "Don't start worrying you'll be fine," 'Well,' thought Susan, 'there's no turning back now!' With a nervous smile, She allowed Nancy and Karen to lead the way. She felt like Dorothy being led to the Land of Oz.

Once inside Susan was surprised to see how nice it was. She really didn't know what to expect, but for some reason she thought it would be dark and dingy. Instead she walked into a big bright room. Actually big wasn't the word, it was huge. There were two pool tables off to the right, plenty of side booths and big round tables scattered through out the room. There were two enormous couches in front of a stone fireplace and card tables on either end. As they walked through, everyone they passed spoke to them. At the table more woman came by. Susan met so many women; she knew she would never remember all the names. What surprised her most was the fact that she wasn't a bit nervous, in fact she felt really alive. Being around all these lesbian women was the turning point in her life. By evening's end, she felt as if this had always been a part of her life. She let everyone know that she had a great time and promised to be back, especially after meeting Nancy and Karen's friends. 'And now they want me to be part of a surprise party they had planned for Lillian and Anna.' She was thrilled they had included her, but how would she ever pull that off?

The twins weren't a problem; they were going camping at Jimmy's parent's cottage that weekend. Jimmy on the other hand would be a problem, Susan thought, 'He's been watching me lately.' The last time Susan felt Jimmy watching her, she asked him if anything was wrong. "I'm not sure," he told her, "but there's something different about you. I don't know what it is, but you've changed." Susan felt her face turning red and tried to keep her voice steady, "Changed, me?" Jimmy started to say something but then shrugged his shoulders and went back to watching television. Susan wasn't sure how she'd changed, but she certainly did feel different. If Jimmy was watching her, the big party in Maine didn't look possible.

As it turned out, everything worked out fine. Jimmy and his father were on a job at the Cape for a few more days and the girls were going to a sleepover. She didn't have to make up any excuses to cover her tracks; she could just go. Now, would she have the nerve to drive to Maine by herself?

Chapter Seven

Carolyn couldn't shake the feeling of helplessness she felt about Connie; she was carrying around a lot of guilt over Jean's disappearance and she shouldn't have to. Carolyn believed whatever it was that happened between the two of them, had profoundly affected Jean. She was sure it was the reason Jean came for help.

When Carolyn got home Julie was on the phone so she went into the kitchen and poured a couple of glasses of wine. Coming back to the living room Julie greeted her. "Hi..." Julie said, taking her glass, "I was just talking to Susan. I wanted to see if she was going to Maine with us this weekend." Carolyn asked, "Will she be able to go?" Julie took another sip of her wine, "She doesn't know yet, but it doesn't look good. She catches her husband watching her. He senses something's different about her." Carolyn didn't appear to be listening. Julie asked if anything was wrong. "Yeah, kind'a...I'm really in a conflict between a patient and a friend and I'm not sure how to handle it." Carolyn answered as she changed her position on the couch to face Julie. Seeing the look of alarm on Julie's face Carolyn reached out and took her hand. "It's all right, I'm fine. Its about that patient I told you about before." Julie nodded her head remembering, "You mean Jean; I've been meaning to ask you about her." "Well," Carolyn told her, "Jean is actually doing very well, she seems determined to follow this through, but...," Carolyn paused for a moment shaking her head. Julie asked about the other woman. "That's the problem, Jean still hasn't mentioned her. The other woman's name is Connie. She's been torturing herself over Jean's disappearance and she blames herself for that. She doesn't even know if she's alive and there's nothing I can do to help. I promised Jean I would not disclose anything about her." Julie stopped her for a moment, "Look Hon, I understand why you are upset. Maybe you should talk to Jean again. She must care for Connie, otherwise I don't think that night would have happened." "Julie, I feel the same way, but she hasn't mentioned Connie in all this time. Then again at the same time I really don't feel Jean is ready to deal with this. I guess I was hoping to find a way to help Connie out of her turmoil." Julie reached out to her and said, "I think your doing all you can and I don't need to tell you that your first responsibility is to your patient." Carolyn didn't say anything for a moment, then, "I'm pretty sure you'll be meeting Connie soon. I saw her at Sally's the last time we were there and I invited her to come over to our table the next time she stops by." Julie said, "Then she knows..." "Yes, she apparently doesn't have any close friends and right now she could use some. Besides, she's a warm, likable person, I think she'll fit in nicely." Julie raised her eyebrows, "Gee, maybe her and Susan would hit it off." Carolyn was quick to say, "No; Connie believes she already met the one for her and I don't think Susan is ready to get involved. She's still getting used to all the new feelings she's allowed to surface." Julie knew she was right, it wasn't a good time for Susan to meet someone, and after all, she still was married to her husband.

Connie took Carolyn's advice and stopped by Sally's from time to time. After getting to know everyone, she began to feel better about things. They had included her into the group and made her feel welcome and not so alone. It had been three months since Jean had left and Connie knew she had to start facing the fact that Jean may not be back, although she really didn't want to believe that.

Chapter Eight

Karen and Nancy were getting ready to close up the bakery for the big weekend in Maine when the phone rang, Nancy answered, "Hello? Oh hi! Where have you been lately?" Nancy caught Karen's eye telling her it was Jamie. Karen had just finished putting things away. Gathering up the fresh bread and the anniversary cake they had made that afternoon, she took them out to the car. Coming back in, Nancy was just hanging up the phone, "God," Nancy said laughing, "that is one wild woman." Karen knew just what she was talking about, "Now what's Jamie up to?" Nancy answered as a matter of fact, "Women, what else! I told her she'd better be careful! She has all those women chasing after her and someday it'll be the other way around." They both had to chuckle as Karen said, "It would serve her right." Nancy continued, "She called to see if the party was still on and if she had the right directions. And," she added, "believe it or not, she's coming alone! She said she needed a rest!" They both chuckled over that. Making sure everything was secure, they put the lights out and closed the door behind them. Both women were excited about the weekend ahead of them and were hoping Lillian and Anna hadn't caught on.

Lillian came up behind Anna, putting her arms around her, "Forty five years Anna, it doesn't seem possible." Anna smiled hugging Lillian's arms against her, "No, Lil, it certainly doesn't. Do you think we can do another forty five?" Holding her tight, Lillian answered, "As long as I'm alive, I'll be at your side,"

Anna turned around in Lillian's arms and cupped her face in her hands, "You do know the way to a girl's heart." "I know my way to other places too," Lillian said tightening her arms around her, "You certainly do my dear, but now is not the time. We need to finish packing so we can beat the traffic to Maine, then we can stop and celebrate. I have a special bottle of champagne already packed." Lillian laughed, "Well then what are we waiting for woman, lets get going!"

After they'd finished packing and loading up the car Anna asked, "Lil, don't you think its odd we haven't heard from anyone?" Lillian replied, "Oh Anna, I meant to tell you I heard from Carolyn yesterday. She wanted to wish us a happy anniversary and said as soon as we get back she'd get everyone together and we'll celebrate." Anna was pleased to hear that and didn't think anymore about their absence. Anna hoped Lillian would like her gift. She was dying to see it herself. During their last visit in Maine, Anna secretly hired a carpenter to repair and screen in the big porch that wrapped around the house. Lil was always talking about doing that, but never got around to it. Anna couldn't wait to see her face. It will be a perfect place to open their bottle of champagne.

When Lillian and Anna first met through mutual friends, there was no doubt, no hesitation; they knew they were going to spend the rest of their lives together. It was a lot harder to go against society back then. All the young girls were expected to marry by eighteen. Anna was seventeen at the time and Lillian had just turned twenty-three, already considered an old maid. For a while, no one knew they were living together. Lillian had a small apartment in town near the hospital where she worked as a nurse in pediatrics. Anna was enrolled in a secretarial school in Boston, not far from the hospital. She was staying with Lillian most of the time instead of living in the dorm. With a little juggling and not many visits from the families, they were able to pull it off. When Anna finished school, she announced to her family that she had decided to live in Boston. Her argument was that she already had a job and someone to share an apartment with. They went back and forth for a while until her family finally relented. Anna felt her mother had known all along that when she went off to school, she wouldn't be back. Her mother told her, "I'm not happy about you living on your own in Boston. We don't want anything to happen to you." Anna reassured her, "Don't worry Mama, I have a good friend in my roommate. I'll be fine." They were both fine. Everyone in their small neighborhood just got used to seeing them together. They blended in and made a good life for themselves.

Everyone met at Carolyn and Julie's place hours before Lillian and Anna were expected to leave for Maine. There were two of them missing; one was Susan, who probably couldn't get away and the other was Jamie, who was probably on to her next adventure. After waiting an extra half-hour, they decided to head out without them. They wanted to get there early enough to make everything perfect before Lillian and Anna arrived. Besides, Jamie had directions; she may be there yet. They all headed to Maine knowing it was going to be a good time for everyone.

As soon as Jamie turned the corner she knew she'd missed them, but there was a car at the curb with a woman in it. Jamie pulled up behind her. As she jumped out of the car and stood up she quickly remembered her hangover. 'Oh God, when will I learn?' Holding onto her head, she knew there was no way she could drive to Maine. Susan was held up waiting for the girls to leave and by the time she arrived to meet everyone, they had already gone. Disappointed she resigned herself to a weekend alone when she saw a car pull in behind her, "Hi," Susan said getting out of the car. Jamie had a painful look on her face when Susan spoke. "Are you all right?" she asked tentatively. "Yes, just a hangover," Jamie answered, looking around, she added, "I was supposed to meet friends here, I guess I missed the boat." "Yes…" was all Susan could say, she was completely caught off guard by this woman. She was tall, with an athletic build and a very handsome face. Susan couldn't stop staring at her. Shyly, she held out her hand, "My name is Susan, I was supposed to meet the same group of people. Jamie gave Susan's hand a firm shake. Susan felt a contact shock, which lasted long after Jamie let go. Nodding gently, remembering her head, Jamie responded with "Names Jamie." 'Oh,' Susan thought, 'So this is the infamous Jamie.' Jamie vaguely remembered Karen and Nancy mentioning a Susan, "Well, no point hanging around here, I might as well go home, I'm in no shape to drive to Maine." Susan told her she had the same problem, "I was hoping I could catch a ride but…" looking around indicating she also was too late. Jamie, seeing the woman was as disappointed as she was, said, "Well, should I state the obvious?" Susan brightened up right away, her voice taking on an excited tone, "That I should drive your car? That would be great! I was so looking forward to this and..." But before Susan could go on Jamie held up a hand to stop the rush of words. "Look, as I said before, I have a hangover, if you want to do this you're going to have to be quiet. All I want to do is sleep it off in the back seat." Susan never swore, but right now she wanted to tell her to go to hell. She held her breath and slowly counted to ten, she did want to go and if Jamie slept in the back, she would deal with it. "I'll get my things," Susan said flatly.

Making herself comfortable in the back, Jamie could see the stiffness of Susan's back. 'Well,' she thought, 'maybe I was a little gruff, I should try to smooth things out, but when she started to sit up she caught sight of Susan's wedding ring as she grasped the steering wheel. 'Oh, one of those', Jamie thought, 'the bored housewife.' She knew the type all to well, afraid to live her own life, but not afraid to sneak around. If you were unfortunate enough to get involved, your life would never be the same. Sliding back down in the seat Jamie decided things were fine the way they were.

When Susan got in behind the wheel, she took the directions Jamie gave her and headed north on Rte 1. Concentrating on her driving, she soon forgot about the woman in the back seat. She was more concerned with getting out of Boston safely. She drove for almost forty-five minutes before seeing the sign indicating she was heading to Maine, and then she began to relax. She hadn't realized how tightly she had been holding the steering wheel until she reached for her directions again and found her hands cramped in place. Glancing at her directions Susan saw she had a way to go before she had to watch for the exit, 'There now', she thought, 'I'm on my way.' Reaching over she turned on the radio but quickly remembered Jamie in the back seat. Looking at her in the rear view mirror she could see she was sound asleep and she wanted to keep it that way so she turned the radio down low. 'As soon as I get there', she thought, 'I'll make arrangements with someone else for a ride home.'

Every once in awhile, Susan caught herself looking at Jamie in the rear view mirror. Grudgingly, she had to admit she could see why woman were attracted to her, she had such a physical presence it was hard turn away. But she was so arrogant Susan knew she would never be a follower. Instead of wasting anymore time thinking about Jamie, she turned her thoughts to the weekend ahead.

Coming out of the toll at exit #2, Susan pulled over and got out her directions. She placed them on the seat where she could see them and followed along until she reached the right road. 'Now,' she thought, 'I need to keep going until I see a large boulder on the side of the road with the name Hurley painted on it. That's it! I found it!' Susan almost woke Jamie in her excitement, but then thought better of it.

Turning onto the dirt road, she drove slowly and followed it over the bumps and little dips and turns it took. Surrounded by tall pine trees that gave off a wonderful fragrance, Susan was overwhelmed by the feeling of being in the woods. She smiled at the chirping of the birds announcing her arrival. 'What a wonderful place this is', she thought. As she rounded the corner she saw stonewalls on either side of the road that gradually led her to the farmhouse. Pulling up in front of the house, she didn't see any signs of life so she continued around to the back. It was there that she spotted the cars nestled in the shade under the trees. Pulling in beside them she heard a screen door slam then saw Karen and Nancy waving to her as they came off the back porch. Jumping out of the car, Susan slammed the door, not caring now if it woke the still sleeping Jamie.

Nancy called out, "Susan, is that you?" Then recognizing Jamie's car, Karen asked, "Where's Jamie?" Susan just laughed, giving them both a big hug as Jamie dragged herself from the back seat and came up behind them. "Hey guys, where's mine?" she asked holding out her arms. As the three of them exchanged hugs, Susan, ignoring Jamie, went back to the car to gather her things. Coming back, Susan could hear Jamie finishing the story of how they came to be together. "Well," Nancy said to Susan, "weren't you lucky to run into Jamie?" "Oh, yes, very lucky," she said with a tight smile. Nancy and Karen were so happy to see her, they didn't notice any tension, but it wasn't lost on Jamie, who looked a little bewildered, like, 'What'd I do?' They soon forgot all about the tension between them as they entered the house. Everything looked beautiful! It was full of balloons, laughter and warm, happy women engulfing them in big hugs.

Chapter Nine

Lillian and Anna arrived a short time later and much to everyone's delight, they were completely surprised and thrilled that everyone was there to share in their celebration. This was going to be a great time! They all headed outside, setting up tables, chairs, and blankets around the outside fireplace. Nancy, Jamie and Julie took over the grill duties while everyone else brought out the food and buckets of ice to keep the beer and wine chilled. Everyone was there except Cathy. She had an unexpected visit from her mother and couldn't get away. Even Connie managed to make it, although she said she might not stay the whole weekend. She still missed Jean and kept hoping she would show up again. Being around these women with their significant others sometimes depressed her so she decided to play it by ear.

At the grill Julie was ready for the corn but it hadn't been brought out yet so Nancy ran in to get it. Julie was glad to be alone for a moment, she wanted a private minute with Jamie. Turning to her as she spoke, "Jamie, I didn't know you knew Susan." Jamie was quick to reply, "Oh, I don't know her," and went on to explain what had brought them together. Julie didn't say anything, so Jamie asked, "Is something wrong?" "Look Jamie, I know it's none of my business," Julie hesitated, looking for the right words without offending her. "It's Susan, she's just starting to feel comfortable with herself. She hasn't been in a relationship with a woman before and, well, it's just that I'd hate to see her get hurt." "Look," said Jamie, "I don't even know her. Besides it doesn't matter anyway, bored housewives are not my type." They were so engrossed in their conversation; they hadn't realized that Susan was within earshot. Just then they heard Susan's voice coming from behind them, "That's enough, the two of you." They were both startled and very embarrassed. Julie started to speak, "I'm sorry Susan…" but Susan cut her off saying, "I appreciate your concern, but I can take care of myself!" and she meant it. Then turning to Jamie she spat out, "As for you, honey, what makes you think I'd be interested in an arrogant boar like you?" Jamie was so shocked, she wanted to laugh, but didn't dare. Susan took one last look at the two of them, shook her head and stomped off to the house, her face bright red. Jamie and Julie turned their attention back to the grill. When Jamie was sure Susan was in the house, she said in a stage whisper to Julie, "Well I guess we've been told!" Looking up tentatively, Julie saw that Jamie was smiling. Surprised that she wasn't furious, she whispered back, "We certainly have! I guess I don't have to worry about her being taken advantage of!" Then in a more serious tone she continued to say, "Jamie, I'm sorry, I was out of line." Jamie, never one to be concerned by trivial matters, replied "Forget it, I have."

Susan stood by the kitchen sink completely embarrassed that she was being discussed like that, especially to Jamie, of all people! 'This is all new to me, maybe I'm over reacting a little.' Then she thought of what Jamie said and got mad all over again. She took a deep breath and made her way back outside. Jamie and Julie heard the screen door slam and looked up to see Susan coming back out. Julie spoke to her as she came by, "Susan, I'm sorry. It was my fault. I hope we can get past this?" Susan, looking more composed than she felt, replied, "Sure Julie, I already have. Now let's get back to the celebration." Completely ignoring Jamie, Susan told Julie she was going to help Karen with the tables. Jamie stepped in beside Julie with just a hint of laughter behind her eyes, "I guess I haven't been forgiven?" Julie had to laugh, "No Jamie, I don't think you have." Luckily no one noticed what went on between them and the rest of the day went on with out incident.

The weather was spectacular, the crisp cool Maine nights had already brought out a beautiful display of fall foliage. Luckily the sun was warm that day, allowing them to stay out until dusk. It was a great time! Things finally began winding down and by the time everything was cleaned up and put away, it was well into the night. Everyone got out their sleeping gear and found a cozy corner for the night.

Lillian found Anna sitting alone on the porch and greeted her with a kiss, "Anna I still can't believe you had the porch done over. I love it! I couldn't have asked for a better gift, I love you." Anna took Lillian's hand, "I'm so glad you like it, Lil…" then stopped when she saw Lillian in a big yawn, saying, "I can see you're tired, we can wait and have our champagne tomorrow night." Lillian agreed, "Yes, I was thinking the same thing. What do you say we call it a night Anna?" Anna wasn't ready for bed; she was thinking of having a cup of tea first, "You go on in Lil, I'll be up shortly." Lillian bent down, kissing the top of Anna's head, "All right, but don't be long."

Neither Lillian nor Anna noticed Jamie sleeping in the lounge chair at the end of the porch, but Jamie wasn't the only one not inside with the rest. Susan was walking up to the porch when Anna saw her, "Susan dear, is anything wrong?" Startled, Susan jumped back a step. "Oh, Anna, you scared me," she said with her hand on her chest. Patting the chair beside her Anna said, "I'm sorry dear, here, come have a seat beside me." Stepping up onto the porch, Susan replied, "Thank you Anna, and don't mind me, I tend to be afraid of my own shadow." Anna gave a little chuckle, "Well there's nothing to be afraid of here. Now, are you sure there's nothing wrong?" Susan paused a moment, "To be honest with you, I was feeling a little awkward when everyone split up into couples and started getting ready for bed. I think Connie felt the same way. I saw her go for a walk a while ago. Maybe not awkward, lonely is the better word. You all seem to have such good relationships." Anna put her hand over Susan's, "Your not involved with anyone dear?" "In a way, I'm married." Anna showed her surprise, "I didn't know that, but then we haven't had much time to talk since we first met you. While we're both awake, why don't you tell me a little something about yourself? I was going to make myself a cup of tea. Would you like one?" Susan was quick to reply, "That sounds wonderful, I'd love it."

Tiptoeing through the house, they had to muffle their laughter, hearing all the snoring going on. Quickly they got their tea and Anna set a dish of cookies on the tray as they headed for the porch. Stopping at the hall closet, she pulled out two soft afghans to throw over their legs.

Settled down with their cookies and tea and the cozy afghans keeping their legs warm from the chill Maine night air, Susan began telling Anna about herself. "As far back as I can remember I knew I was different, but I never had anyone to talk to about it. Not wanting anyone to suspect that my girlish dreams were about women rather than Prince Charming, I did what was expected of me. When I was old enough to marry," Susan shrugged her shoulders, "I did. I was very successful in keeping all those other feelings buried, even from myself until I met Karen and Nancy at the bakery." Susan sat up excitedly remembering the day. Turning to face Anna, she said, "I knew it, I knew they were like me from day one. Oh, I wish there was a better word for it." Susan continued, "I just felt so connected, so open and relaxed around them. I have to tell you, it was a shock when I released all those old feelings again. I had completely lost touch with who I was. The more I am around all of you, the more I've been able to get to know and accept myself. I know this is going to make a big change in my life but I also know that I need to take it slow." "What about your husband, does he know?" Anna asked. Surprised, Susan answered, "No, not at all! Jim works all the time and believe me, being away from my family is a rare exception. I'm always at home with the girls. I have twin daughters." Anna smiled, "Oh, how nice for you. How old are they?" "Eleven," Susan responded, "they're great kids. I feel fortunate to have them." Anna agreed, both her and Lillian loved children. Lillian of course, got her fill of nurturing while working at the nursery. Anna often could be found there, helping out during her lunch breaks. Continuing,

Susan said, "So you see why I'm taking this slow; I don't want to upset anyone's lives. But someday I hope to find what you and Lillian have." Anna nodded her head in agreement, "I can understand that Susan, but life is based on loving and sharing with a partner who feels the same things you are feeling. When the love you seek doesn't conform within a patriarchal society, too many of us remain alone. Lillian and I were among the lucky ones. We knew from the time we met that it would be a life time commitment and no matter what, we would always be there for each other." Anna added, "Of course not having husbands and children made it a lot easier for us to move forward. What I'm trying to say is, you can't set a time for love; you could miss the one your looking for." Susan nodded, "I know Anna, I have thought about that. It must be wonderful to be in love, but like I said, my girls come first. I can't put myself before them." Anna patted Susan's' hand, "I do understand dear. It's good to take it slow, just leave yourself open to all your possibilities."

Susan was enjoying this quiet time with Anna. It was becoming more and more important to her to find the time to be herself, as long as it didn't interfere with her family. "Once the girls are older, I'll be able to do something about Jim." Susan went on to say, "I really don't see that as a problem. At this point we're just not together anymore. Working the late hours he does, Jim started sleeping in the guest room so he wouldn't wake me. It's just become a habit now." Shrugging her shoulders, "I don't think it matters to him anyway. We never had a good relationship in bed." Susan paused a moment taking a deep breath before continuing, "I do care about him though and right now I'm just working on being friends." Anna said, "So you are looking ahead?" Susan thought for a moment, "Yes, I guess I am."

Jamie still hidden in the shadows of the porch woke up during their conversation. Had it been anyone else but Susan, she would've popped right up and joined in the conversation. But knowing Susan didn't particularly care for her, Jamie knew she wouldn't have wanted her listening in on their private conversation. She was surprised Susan wasn't as 'flighty' as she expected her to be; in fact she sounded pretty sensible. 'Definitely not my type!' she thought. Jamie was used to women much like herself, just out for a good time, no ties, no tomorrows. Susan was attractive though; in fact Jamie thought, 'She is down right pretty.' Susan also had an innocence about her, not at all what Jamie was use to or for that matter wanted. Jamie would never admit this to anyone, but she was somewhat intimidated by her. She never felt that before and it was somewhat intriguing.

Susan turned to Anna, "Anna, why do you suppose we're different?" Anna shook her head and said, "My dear child, I do not for a moment believe 'we are different.' Looking into Susan's eyes she continued, "I have come to realize "truths" are always simple. So simply put, we are born who we are because it's an experience our souls need to learn from. That doesn't apply just to us, it applies to everyone; it's part of the soul's growth." Anna paused a moment looking for the right words, "I believe we are born many times over, living life in many different "suits," sometimes as a man, other times as a woman, experiencing different races or religious beliefs. I believe the ultimate goal is for the soul to grow and understand all aspects of life." Susan didn't reply, she seemed to be absorbing all Anna was saying. Warmed by the tea and getting to know each other, neither realized the time until Anna looked at her watch. "Oh my, it's after midnight! We need to get some sleep. I'm sure everyone will be up early tomorrow. Did you find a place to sleep dear?" "Yes Anna, thank you. Lillian set me up on the couch in the den and I can't wait to fall into it. Anna, it's been wonderful talking to you. You've certainly given me a lot to think about."

The next morning Susan woke up to the smell of fresh perked coffee and bacon cooking. She gathered her clothes and headed for the bathroom. Coming out of the bathroom she was surprised to find everyone still sleeping. Walking into the kitchen with a big smile, expecting to see Anna and Lillian, she was taken completely off guard to see Jamie at the stove. Susan still felt the sting of Jamie's remark about her being a bored housewife. So far their meetings hadn't gone well. Trying to regain her composure Susan mumbled, "Good morning, can I help?" "Sure," Jamie answered, "I need a plate for the bacon." It was obvious they were both feeling uncomfortable. Handing Jamie the plate she made an awkward attempt at small talk, "Boy it smells good in here. Is there anything else I can do?" Taking the plate from her, Jamie looked directly at Susan. It was the first time their eyes had met. She had such a bold look, Susan felt her face turning red and had to look away. Jamie said, "The coffee should be ready," nodding to the pot. Susan was thinking, 'Why do I feel so stupid?' She asked Jamie if she would like a cup. "Sure," she answered, "just black." Susan began pouring the coffee and much to her relief, everyone began waking up and piling into the kitchen to help with breakfast.

When Anna and Lillian came in, Karen had already set their place at the table and she steered them over to it, "Just sit and enjoy," she told them, and they did. Everyone was having fun working together. Connie made pancakes, Susan began a batch of scrambled eggs, Nancy was in charge of toast while Carolyn made home fries. It seemed obvious to everyone that this breakfast was special. The closeness they felt, the unity, even Jamie and Susan relaxed and shared a smile. It was a beautiful big old kitchen with a huge table that had sat many a family gathering, just like this.

Reluctantly around noon everyone began gathering their belongings, knowing it was time to head home. Amid warm hugs with everyone saying their good-byes, Susan and Jamie found themselves face to face once again. Although feeling awkward, they did manage a brief hug. Jamie said, "Susan, look I'm sorry, we got off on a bad start." Holding up her hands she continued, "I know it was my fault. Can't we start over?" Susan was surprised, not just from Jamie's apology, but from her sincerity. "Thanks Jamie, I'd like that." Standing there looking at each other, they were interrupted by Karen, "Come on Susan, we're off." "Okay, I'm coming," she answered, then turning back to Jamie, she said with more light heartedness than she felt, "Well, I guess I'll be seeing you at the next event." With that she turned and walked to Nancy and Karen's car. She could feel Jamie watching her as she walked away.

Connie was right in there with everyone else saying her good-byes. Already she felt bonded with these women. She hardly had time to think about Jean until the couples began to settle in for the night. Connie couldn't help but wonder what it would be like to have Jean at her side, but had to stop thinking that way; it just hurt too much.

Everyone headed home that day huddled in a warm glow. As Lillian and Anna stood on the porch waving good-bye, they felt the same way, knowing it had been a special time. As the last car drove out of sight, Lillian turned to Anna and said, "It's still early and such a beautiful day, would you like to take a drive and see more of this beautiful foliage?" Anna was quick to respond, "Yes dear, I'd love to. There's so much food left over, why don't we make up a picnic basket?" "That sounds even better," Lillian said laughingly, "and when we get back we can have our own celebration," she added with meaning.

Lillian and Anna loved their ride. The colors alone were vibrant enough, but when the rain clouds started rolling in, the colors intensified against the cobalt blue sky. They were sure they had never seen anything more beautiful. Wrapped in the colors of fall, Lillian and Anna headed back to the farm, where Anna had their bottle of champagne chilled and waiting. It turned out to be a memorable day, fitting for all the years they had been together.

Chapter Ten

Everyone else had to get back to the reality of everyday life while Lillian and Anna had the rest of the week in Maine. Anna called Julie during the week to say how much they had enjoyed the party, "Please let everyone know what a wonderful surprise it was; what a great time we had!" Anna went on to say, "Lil and I will be home on Saturday morning and we are planning on Sally's that night for pizza and beer. If anyone's going to be around, we'd love to see you all again." Julie thought it was a great idea and as far as she knew, her and Carolyn would be there. They talked a few more minutes and then Julie called Cathy to hold their table. After doing that, she called the others to let them know what was happening.

Cathy was happy to hear from Julie, she had wanted to get in touch to see how their weekend went but she hadn't had a chance to call. Even now, she was on her way out when Julie called. "Oh Julie, hi! I've wanted to call but I've been so busy. In fact I'm running late for an appointment right now. Can I call you later?" Julie replied, "That's okay Cathy, I just want to let you know that Lillian and Anna will be coming home Saturday morning and we'll all be at Sally's Saturday night," Cathy said, "Great. I'll be able to hear about the party!" After Cathy hung up, she headed straight for the deli where she had been meeting Carol for lunch on Wednesdays. Although Carol didn't show up last week, Cathy hoped she would today.

Cathy had first met Carol and Liz a couple of months ago at Sally's. After serving them a few times she took an instant liking to Carol, but she wasn't sure about her friend Liz. Instinctively, she knew there was something about her that made her feel uneasy. She realized why that was, about a week later, when she was at a local shopping center. She was pulling out of a parking space when a car crossed her path and stopped in front of her to pick up a woman coming out from one of the stores. At first she didn't recognize Carol, her face was partially covered with a kerchief. It wasn't until she turned her head as she got into the car that Cathy realized who it was. She started to wave and then noticed the bruises on Carol's face. She had no reason to think abuse, but somehow she knew. It was a shock to her and she couldn't move. Luckily, neither Liz nor Carol noticed her as they drove away. Cathy stayed where she was, unmoving until a car behind her beeped its horn. All that night during work, Carol's battered face would flash in front of her. She understood then why she didn't care for Liz. Later, during her break, she spoke of it to one of the other waitresses, "Chris, I realize battering goes on in some families by the husband, but have you ever heard of it among woman?" Chris leaned over, immediately concerned, "Cathy, are you all right?" "Oh, yes, I'm fine, but I've recently met someone that appears to be in that kind of situation; it really shocked me." Chris was obviously relived it wasn't Cathy, "Cathy, I don't know anyone personally, but I have friends that know of someone dealing with that." Cathy looked troubled, "Chris, I just can't understand why anyone would remain in a situation like that." Shaking her head she continued, "I mean would you put up with that?" Chris answered quickly, "No, of course not. I don't understand it either, with anyone, man or woman." Cathy agreed, "I feel the same way, but how do you help someone like that?" Chris just shook her head, "I don't know, it's beyond me. Wouldn't you think they would just leave?" Carol remained on Cathy's mind, although she didn't know what she could do about it.

Liz and Carol walked into Sally's the following week. Cathy felt herself getting a little anxious but quickly got herself under control. Walking over to the table she said, "Hi, what can I get you folks?" Liz answered, "Just a couple of drafts. Busy tonight?" "Yes," Cathy answered, "especially for a week night." That time she dared a glance at Carol, not that Liz intimidated her, she just didn't know how Carol would look. Most of the bruises had disappeared and she could only see a little yellowing around her eyes. Nodding to Liz, Cathy said, "Anything else?" Liz answered, "No, I guess we'll be fine for now." "Then I'll be right back with your drinks." Cathy brought them their drinks and left to wait on another table. When she came around again to see if they needed anything else, they were gone. 'Oh well,' Cathy thought, 'there's nothing I can do about it.'

About a week later when Cathy had some shopping to do, she saw Carol again, only this time she was alone. Cathy approached her, "Hey, how are you?" Carol looked a little startled to see her, "Oh hi, nice to see you. I'm afraid I don't remember your name." After Cathy introduced herself, she said, "I usually stop here on Wednesdays for lunch, it coincides with my shopping day, would you like to join me?" Carol looked hesitant at first, but then said, "Sure, that would be nice." And it was. The conversation was just chitchat and they seemed to enjoy each other's company. Carol never mentioned Liz so neither did Cathy. Cathy was not looking for this to be anymore than a friendship; she just felt compelled to try and help. After that, it became a weekly lunch date. As well as they got along together; the apparent abuse Carol was receiving was never mentioned. Cathy hoped some day she would open up and talk about it. Maybe then she would know what to do to help her. In the meantime she would be around just in case.

The last time they met it had run later then usual. Carol was the first to notice, "Look at the time, I'm late!" Cathy could see she was very upset about it, "Yes, how did that happen," Cathy said lightly, "Can I give you a ride?" "No!" Carol was surprised at how sharply she spoke and immediately softened her voice, "Thanks anyway, I just live down the street." Adding, "I will be back next week though, this has been great." With that they went their separate ways, Cathy heading back to work and Carol rushing to be home before Liz. Carol liked Cathy and felt if she could keep Liz from finding out about their meetings, she would have a good friend in Cathy, but if Liz ever finds out...Liz didn't want her to have friends, always telling her she was too naive, too trusting and people would just take advantage of her and that's the way it was. Carol had never done anything against Liz's wishes, until now.

Chapter Eleven

Saturday night arrived and Sally's parking lot was packed. Carolyn and Julie arrived just ahead of the others and after finding a spot; they parked and made their way inside. Stopping at the bar for a couple of drinks and a bowl of popcorn, they were greeted with a hearty, "Hey guys!" Cathy shouted out above the noise from the bar. She hurried out to greet them with a big hug, "I've missed you," Carolyn and Julie were just as happy to see Cathy and returned her hugs with equal enthusiasm.

Going to their table they met up with Lillian and Anna who were just sitting down. Soon Karen, Nancy, and Connie joined them. Amid all the hello's Cathy said, "It's so good to see everyone. I can't wait to hear all about the weekend I missed." "We had a ball!" Karen said, holding up her glass as she turned to Lillian and Anna, "Here's to many more get-togethers in Maine." "Of course dear," Anna said to all, "you will always be welcome." "Absolutely." Lillian agreed. "Wait a minute," Julie asked, "who's missing?" "Susan for one," Karen answered, adding, "I talked to her this morning. Her husband was going to be around so she couldn't get away." Anna said, "Oh, I'm sorry to hear that. She seems like such a lovely person. I enjoyed a quiet chat with her at the farm." "Yes Anna," Nancy said, "Susan mentioned that on the way home. She had enjoyed it too. And what about Jamie, did anyone hear from her?" Julie told them, "I talked to her the other day, she'll be here." Cathy had a puzzled look on her face, "You know, I haven't seen

Jamie all week. She's usually stops in a couple of times during the week." Carolyn said, "She must've met someone." They all laughed at that.

Karen began telling Cathy about the party and how they had managed to keep it a surprise. As she was talking, a voice interrupted from behind her, "Hey, where's Jamie?" It was Bobby, one of Jamie's "cruisin' buddies." "I don't know," answered Julie, "but she should be here soon." Noticing Bobby's serious tone, Lillian asked, "Why, is anything wrong?" Bobby answered, "I was hoping you'd tell me. I haven't seen her since she got back from Maine. She even canceled a double date I had lined up for us last night." Anna asked, with obvious concern in her voice, "You don't suppose she's sick?" "No," Bobby said, "she sounded okay. I've called her a couple of times this week to go out but all she said was she just wanted to stay home for awhile and get caught up on some work." Bobby paused a moment, then said, "That doesn't sound like her. Did she meet someone in Maine?" Anna told her, "No dear, it was just us." "Well," said Bobby, "there's something different about her." With a big sigh she turned away but not before asking "If she comes in, will you tell her I'm looking for her?" They assured her they would tell her. "Thanks, and nice to see you all again," and with that, Bobby stepped back from the table and got lost in the crowd. "Who was that?" Karen asked. "That's Bobby," Julie told her, "She's a friend of Jamie's. She's a bit gruff, but she's okay. I hope James all right though."

As if on cue, Jamie squeezed out of the crowd, "Hey everybody!" Anna asked, "Are you alright dear?" Jamie looked puzzled at the question, "Yes Anna I'm fine, why do ask?" Anna told her, "Your friend Bobby was just here looking for you. She seems concerned you haven't been going out." "Oh," replied Jamie, "I guess I have been staying close to home this week, but nothings wrong, I must be getting old. I'll stop by and see Bobby on the way out. So, catch me up on what's going on. Have I missed anything?" Lillian answered, "Actually, we were just reminiscing about the weekend, letting Cathy know all she missed. Anna and I just got back this morning. It was hard leaving there. I can't wait until we can stay for good." Connie asked, "When will that be?" Anna answered, "Not until next fall." Carolyn said, "I noticed part of the house was closed off. How many rooms do you actually have?" Lillian answered, "I'm not really sure. There are sections of that old house that had been closed off for years. My grandparents were old when everyone grew up and moved out, they could only heat and care for the four rooms we use now. In the spring, Anna and I plan on opening the back of the house and the upstairs. We need to see what repairs, if any, are needed." "That sounds like fun!" Connie said, "Would you like some help?" Anna replied enthusiastically, "Oh yes Connie, that would be wonderful!" Jamie was quick to say, "Hey you guys, I'd like to help too!" Before they knew it everyone was willing to help...Nancy said they should plan on Memorial Day weekend. "We could leave on Friday after work, and not have to be back until Monday afternoon!" And with that, they were excitedly planning their next trip to Maine.

Jumping up out of her seat, Cathy spoke up, "Before I forget, Sally's planning a New Years Eve party and it just happens to be their ten year anniversary. They're going all out to make it a huge celebration. It should be a great time! Is anyone interested?" As it turned out, they were all interested in going, so Cathy said she would reserve their table. Anna noticed Jamie was searching the crowd, "Are you looking for your friend dear?" "Who...? Oh no Anna, I was just wondering if Susan was coming tonight?" "No dear, she couldn't get away." Seeing Jamie was clearly disappointed Anna asked, "Did you want her for something?" "No Anna," Jamie told her, "I was just wondering."

During the course of the night, Cathy brought up the subject of Carol, asking Carolyn specifically, why someone would put up with a situation like that. Carolyn told her, "Believe me Cathy, you have no idea how manipulative and controlling these people are. They convince their 'victims' no one else would want them, totally cutting them off from friends and family, ultimately making them totally dependent." Cathy frowned, "But why would they stay, why not just walk out?" Julie spoke up, "Because they're convinced they can't and that's the way it is. They believe they are responsible for the abuse. It would happen in any relationship they were in." Carolyn added, "Most of the victims were raised in that environment, it's all they know." Cathy nodded her head slightly, "Well, that does shed some light for me. I just can't imagine putting up with that. My ex had that in him. I knew it was just a matter of time before the verbal abuse and pushing would change to punching, so my son and I packed up and left before it got worse." "I know Cathy," Julie said, "but you're not the type to take it. These women usually go into relationships with low self esteem, in fact, they're preyed upon because of it." Then Lillian asked, "Does she talk to you about this Cathy?" "No, it's never mentioned. I have a strong feeling that if I were to bring it up, she would deny it and then what? So for now I'm just trying to keep things light." Pausing for a moment in thought, Cathy said, "You know she does seem shy, unsure of herself. I suppose she could be intimidated, it's too bad." Carolyn said, "Yes it is, Julie and I see it all too often." Carolyn then asked, "Do you think she'd open up to you for help?" Cathy shrugged her shoulders, "I'm hoping she will. If it reaches that point, can I call on you for help?" Carolyn never hesitated, "Of course." Both Carolyn and Julie worked with battered women, not only with their jobs, but they also volunteered at a local shelter.

The rest of the evening went by quickly. Everyone was talking about the upcoming holidays. Lillian and Anna were having Thanksgiving dinner at home this year. Everyone was invited to come for dinner or just drop by for a drink; they'd love to have them. Connie was quick to accept. She had no contact with her family at all so she usually spent her holidays by herself. Nancy and Karen already planned on going to Nancy's sister's house, but they definitely would stop by. Jamie said she was going to her parents for dinner but would stop by on the way back. Everyone else would be out of town for the weekend.

Jamie turned down quite a few women that night who were trying to get her attention or buy her a drink.

Even the more aggressive ones, asking if she'd like some company at the end of the evening, were turned away. No one at the table paid too much attention, but Anna did.

Both Anna and Lillian had a special place in their heart for Jamie. They had known her since she was a teenager, searching for answers about herself. On their twenty-fifth anniversary Lillian and Anna wanted some professional pictures taken of them. They were looking for someone that would be sensitive to their relationship. They were introduced to a very young photographer named Jamie. They hit it off right away. Jamie was looking for some one to talk to about the feelings she was having about women. They had grown close over the years, in fact they thought of Jamie as a daughter, so they paid extra attention to her. Anna asked, "Jamie, aren't you going to look for Bobby?" Jamie shook her head no, "I'm tired, and I think I'll just head for home." She gave Anna and Lillian a kiss on the cheek and said her good-byes to the others, promising to stay in touch. By then, everyone was ready to leave. On the way out, Connie caught Carolyn's eye, "I know it's a waste of time, but have you heard anything about Jean?" Carolyn said, "Connie, I wish I had some news for you," and she clearly meant it.

On the way home Carolyn was preoccupied, thinking about Connie and Jean. Julie reached over taking her hand, "Hon, is anything wrong?" "Its Connie, she asked me tonight about Jean. I can see the pain in her eyes...and I can't help her." Julie asked, "Have you mentioned Connie to Jean lately?" Carolyn answered, "No I haven't, but I think its time that I do.

I'm supposed to sign her release on Monday but I probably won't have time to talk to her then," Carolyn thought for a moment then, "Julie, do we have anything planed for tomorrow?" Julie said, "No, the only thing I had in mind was some Christmas shopping in the afternoon, other than that, it's open." "Then if you don't mind, I'd like to go over to the clinic in the morning and visit with Jean." Julie thought it was a good idea, "Sure Hon, that's fine with me, I feel bad for Connie too."

Sunday morning Carolyn woke early, showered and left to visit Jean. Walking into the clinic, Carolyn went over to the nurse's station before seeing Jean, "Good morning Pat." "Well good morning to you Doctor, what brings you here today?" Pat gave Carolyn her full attention. Pat had known her for almost ten years now and had come to admire the down to earth attitude she had with all her patients, treating everyone as her equal. Carolyn told her, "I just stopped by to visit with Jean. I'm sure she's feeling nervous about leaving here." "Yes she is, but you know," Pat said with confidence, "I think she can handle it." Carolyn looked at her, nodding her head in agreement.

Carolyn tapped lightly on Jean's door before stepping in, "Good morning Jean." Jean flashed Carolyn a bright smile, "Oh Doctor Adams, good morning, what a surprise," but Jeans smile quickly faded, "Is anything wrong?" Carolyn was quick to reassure her, "No Jean, not at all. I know you're leaving tomorrow and I thought we could visit for a while. Have you had breakfast yet?" Jean looked relieved, "No, I was just going down to the cafeteria," Carolyn asked, "Well then, may I join you?" Jean said,

"Of course, that would be wonderful." Carolyn took Jean's arm as they headed for the stairway leading to the cafeteria.

After filling their plates they found a table at the far end of the room away from everyone where they could talk without being overheard. "Jean, I must say, you look wonderful," Carolyn said and meant it. Jean rewarded Carolyn with a real blush, "Thank you, I do feel so much better. I don't know how I'll ever repay you for all you've done to help me." Carolyn quickly replied, "Jean, don't under estimate yourself, you, and only you did this, all I can do is help guide." Jean thought for a moment, "Like an angel." Carolyn laughed and replied, "Okay, I like that." Jean took a deep breath before speaking again, "I'm nervous about tomorrow." Carolyn leaned over taking her hand and told her, "I know you'll do fine. You're a strong woman Jean. You need to recognize that and remember you won't be alone." Jean looked unsure, "Thank you, I hope your right. Tomorrow, a woman from the boarding house is coming by to pick me up. She'll help me settle in and meet everybody over there." Seeing Jean's apprehension, Carolyn quickly said, "Jean, you know your parents did offer to help." Jean paused for a moment, "Yes, I know that and don't misunderstand me, I'm glad we are at least talking again. I know how hard it's been on them, but right now I know I would not be able to measure up to their standards. I don't think I can handle the extra pressure of trying to be all that they expect me to be right now. It would also mean moving to New Jersey." Jean shrugged her shoulders, "This seems to be where I should be, to work out my life." Carolyn leaned over,

"Jean, can we talk for a moment, off the record?" Jean looked right into Carolyn's eyes, "This is about Connie," she said, more as a statement, than a question, which caught Carolyn off guard. She was quick to reply, "Yes it is, but if you don't want to talk about her, we won't." Jean told her, "Well, I don't know if I'm ready for this yet, but lets give it a try."

Having finished their breakfast, they decided to walk to the solarium. Jean asked, "Have you seen Connie?" Carolyn nodded her head, "Yes I have." As they stepped inside Jean asked, "How is she?" Carolyn took a deep breath before answering, "She's doing all right, except for not knowing what happened to you. Jean, I have to tell you, Connie blames herself for your disappearance." Jean became visibly upset, "Oh God, how she must hate me for the way I've treated her." Carolyn could see the tears filling Jeans eyes, she quickly put her arm around her, "Believe me Jean, Connie cares deeply for you, there's no room in her heart or mind for anything else. Come, let's sit down over here." Carolyn led Jean over to some chairs by the windows. All of a sudden it dawned on Jean that Carolyn knew about the last night she spent with Connie. Carolyn knew instinctively what Jean was thinking and let her know she was not there to judge, but to help. She told Jean how she and Connie had become friends; then she completely revealed her personal life to Jean.

Driving home Carolyn felt pretty good about her visit with Jean. After talking for a while, Jean promised to give some thought to Connie. Although at this time, she felt she had more than enough to deal with. They had ended their visit on a lighter note, talking about a couple of job interviews Jean's social worker had lined up for her. Jean had a good eye for art and one of her interviews was with a local gallery, she was hoping for a job there. Turning into her driveway, light snow began drifting down. The weatherman was right for a change, the forecast called for snow showers today. 'Good,' Carolyn thought, 'this will make it a great day for Christmas shopping!

Across town Jamie was at a loss on what to do with the day. She really didn't have any desire to go out, but at the same time her apartment was feeling pretty lonely. Jamie had never felt this way before. She usually appreciated her solitude, choosing not to bring dates home, but rather staying at their place, or getting a room elsewhere. Now she was beginning to feel there should be more out of a relationship. Of course, knowing Lillian and Anna and her other friends, she knew relationships could last for years, but she had never considered it for herself, until she met Susan. 'I must be out of my mind,' she thought, 'How can I let someone have this much of an effect on me?' Walking over to the phone Jamie decided to call Bobby, line up a couple of dates, and go out and have some fun, 'I need to get past this woman!'

Chapter Twelve

Nancy was in the bakery at five o'clock on Monday morning, unable to sleep after the argument she and Karen had last night. The tension had been building over the past few weeks and had culminated into a shouting match between them that ended when Karen walked out on her, slamming the door as she left. Nancy was feeling bad about it, but at the same time she wanted a change. Keeping separate apartments was getting old, especially when Karen was at her place most of the time anyway. All this time they had been together Nancy couldn't understand why Karen would even hesitate to make a commitment. They had been over this a hundred times before. Nancy usually let the subject drop when Karen got upset. Well not this time! Nancy was pouring herself a cup of coffee when Karen came in. "Want a cup?" Nancy asked. "Yes," Karen answered with a sheepish grin, "and I'd like to talk to you." "All right," Nancy said as she headed to a table, "Sit down and we'll talk."

Karen began, "Nance, you know that I love you, and I want to spend the rest of my life with you." She took a sip of her coffee before continuing; "I've been up all night thinking about this, wondering why I keep holding back." Karen stopped speaking and took Nancy's hands in hers, "When we first got together, I honestly thought it would be short lived." Nancy started to say something but Karen held up her hand, "Look, I know what you are going to say, but let me finish. You are a lot younger than I am and so pretty, I honestly didn't think we would be together this long. As much as I dreaded the thought, I expected one day that you would come to me saying you met some one else, more your age." Nancy interrupted her, "Karen I love you and there is no one else for me." A smile began to appear on Karen's lips, "I realize that," She paused and took a deep breath, "and I know I've been really happy sharing my life with you, so if you still want me…" before Karen could finish, Nancy was on her feet pulling her up to her, "Do you mean it Karen, are you sure?" "Very sure." Nancy grabbed her in an excited hug. Karen started laughing, "God Nance, I can't breathe!"

Julie walked into Carolyn's office, she was going to surprise her and take her to lunch. Just as she got there, two women ahead of her were going in. Not wanting to disturb anyone, Julie took a seat in the empty waiting room. 'Everyone must be at lunch', she thought. She hoped she hadn't missed Carolyn's lunch time by not calling first. 'Oh well,' she thought, 'I'm bound to see her before too long.' Picking up a newspaper lying on the table, she decided to hang around and get caught up on the news while waiting for Carolyn.

It was only a few minutes before Carolyn's door opened again and an older woman came out carrying a briefcase. Julie thought she recognized her, perhaps another social worker. Following behind her was Carolyn with a younger woman who was holding tight to her arm. 'God,' Julie thought, 'she's beautiful!' Walking to the door Carolyn caught sight of Julie and gave her a wink, but kept her professional demeanor. Carolyn continued speaking with her patient as they walked behind the social worker. The beautiful woman turned to face Carolyn as she spoke, "Well, I guess this is it." Carolyn gave her a warm smile, "Don't worry Jean, you'll be fine and you'll still be seeing me on a weekly basis. If you want to come in more often all you have to do is call." Jean looked relived, "Thanks, I needed to hear that. Well, I guess we'd better get going, and doctor, please remember what I said about Connie." Jean smiled her good-byes and left with the other woman.

Julie stood up looking amazed, "Carolyn, was that Connie's Jean?" Carolyn nodded "Yes". Julie said, "Well, no wonder Connie can't forget her, she's beautiful!" Julie followed Carolyn as she walked back into her office. Carolyn asked her, "Are you here to take me to lunch?" Julie had to laugh, she'd almost forgot, "Well, yes, now that you mention it, but you have to fill me in on Connie and Jean." Carolyn reached for the phone, "Let me make a quick call to Connie, I want to see her after work. Then I'll explain over lunch."

At lunch Carolyn explained that Jean was not beautiful like she is now when she first met her. "She was so pathetic looking, I wasn't even sure she would survive." Carolyn went on to explain that she had let Jean know of her friendship with Connie. Julie interrupted…"Then she knows about you." Carolyn told her, "Yes, I thought she would be more at ease if she wanted to talk to me about Connie." Julie nodded her understanding and asked, "Is she going to see Connie again?" Carolyn shook her head, "That I really can't say. She has agreed to my letting Connie know what happened to her and more importantly, to impress upon her that it wasn't her fault that she left that night. She also told me not to give Connie any false hopes." Julie asked Carolyn, "What do you think will happen?" "I don't know, Jean has a lot of battles ahead of her and I'm not sure there's going to be room in her life for Connie, or at least not in the near future.

Chapter Thirteen

News Years Eve day was finally here and Susan's mother-in-law was there to pick-up Carrie and Jen for a couple of days. She told Susan she hoped Jimmy and her would take advantage of this time without the girls to have a good New Years Eve together. Susan replied, "Thank you, but with Jimmy's back still bothering him, I think we'll just end up staying home for the evening." "Well," said her mother-in law, "that can be nice too." She had a feeling they were having problems but didn't want to pry. With more cheerfulness than she felt, she turned her attention to the two girls who were jumping and squirming with anxiety, "Well girls, I have a lot planned for us, so say good-bye to your mother. Susan don't forget, you and Jimmy are coming for dinner tomorrow." Susan smiled at her, "I'll be there, but I'll have to wait and see how Jimmy's feeling," As the girls got into the car to leave with their grandmother, Susan looked at the time, it was two o'clock, 'Jimmy should be back from the doctor's any minute now.' She'd have to see how he was feeling before she would know if she could get away to Sally's.

It wasn't long after that when Jimmy drove in. Coming into the kitchen he said, "Did the girls leave already?" Susan answered, "Your mother picked them up a little while ago, they were pretty excited about it. How did you make out at the doctors?" Susan asked, but could plainly see he was uncomfortable. Sitting at the table, Jimmy told her, "It still hurts like hell, but the Doctor said it wasn't as bad as last time. He gave me some pills but told me to wait until I was home before I took them." Susan got him some water, "Here Jimmy, take your pills while I make you something to eat." "Thanks," he said as he took his pills. He ate the lunch Susan made him and before long, he was getting drowsy. Seeing him looking tired and uncomfortable, Susan began feeling guilty about her plans for the night and asked, "Can I get you anything else Jimmy?" Pushing back from the table he answered, "No, thanks, I just want to lie down and let these pills work," then added, "I'm sorry about tonight, this was just lousy timing." Susan felt another jab of guilt, but she felt she had to move forward, "That's all right Jimmy, we didn't have any plans anyway. If you're feeling better tomorrow, your mother invited us over for dinner." "That sounds good," he said and added, "I'd like that." After he went into the den, Susan busied herself around the house trying not to think about the party tonight. Finally around six o'clock, she poured herself a glass of wine hoping it would relax her a little bit. She had never done anything like this before. She was feeling anxious about sneaking around like a teenager. 'This is a dangerous game I'm playing.' she thought, 'I'm risking a lot here,' but even realizing that didn't stop her from going. Finishing her wine she went in to take a shower and began getting ready for Sally's. No doubt about it, she had made up her mind, she had to go.

It turned out to be a frigid night, the kind when the snow crunches under your feet when you walk on it. Everyone arriving at Sally's ran from their cars to get inside as quickly as possible. As they opened the door, the cold winds followed them in, causing the decorations and balloons to dance with the merriment of the season. Greeted with familiar hellos, loud music, party hats and balloons everywhere, it was clearly a party in full swing! Carolyn and Julie were just coming off the dance floor when Jamie came up from behind grabbing them both around the waist, "Your not done already are you?" she asked laughing. "No." Julie said, "We're just taking a break. Why don't you come over…" but before Julie could continue, one of Jamie's many "admirers" grabbed her hand. She flashed them a big grin as she disappeared on to the dance floor.

As Carolyn and Julie made their way back to the table, they met Lillian and Anna who were just coming in with Connie, who they met in the parking lot. Sitting down Connie said, "I'm starved, are we ordering anything?" "No need to." Cathy said as she joined them, "Look!" She pointed to the wall by the fireplace where two long tables had been set up with all kinds of food. Julie said, "It looks wonderful! I hope Karen and Nancy get here soon, they're not going to believe this." Anna spoke up, "They should be right along. They were stopping to pick Susan up on their way." Connie looked surprised, "Susan's coming?" "Yes," Anna answered, "I don't know how she managed it, but it will be nice to see her again." Everyone agreed.

Lillian couldn't help but notice a grin on Connie's face that just wouldn't quit, "Connie, aside from the party you seem quite jovial this evening." "That I am," said Connie, "I feel as if a big weight has been taken off my shoulders." Connie went on to tell everyone that she finally had heard something about Jean. Although no one knew Jean, they were all familiar with her story. "Are you going to see her again Connie?" Cathy asked. She was quick to answer, "I would love nothing better, but I'm afraid it's not what Jean wants. Knowing she's alright is the best Christmas present I could ever have asked for, it has done wonders for me." Turning to Julie she said, "Why don't we get in line at the food tables. Well bring back enough munchies for everyone!" Julie laughed and said, "Lead the way!"

Susan was nervously watching the clock, 'They should be here soon,' Slipping on a robe over her clothes, she went in to check on Jimmy. Looking into the den she could see he was asleep on the couch. She went into the bathroom for a glass of water, putting it on a table next to Jimmy, just in case he woke up needing his pills. Seeing that he was sleeping soundly, she went to get her coat. Pausing in front of the hall mirror, she liked what she saw. She had decided on a plain black dress with thin straps and a low, but modest neckline. With her ash blond hair, it made a striking impression. She added a strand of pearls to finish it off, 'There,' she thought, 'dressed up, but not overdone.' She knew most of the women at the party would be wearing pants, but for her, a dress was what she felt most comfortable in. She threw a short black jacket over her shoulders; picked up her coat and with a deep breath she headed out the door. It was freezing out, but Susan didn't even notice.

Everyone entering Sally's that night were greeted by colorful balloons rippling across the ceiling each time the door opened and the wind found it's way in. It became routine for everyone to look to the door when the balloons began their dance. Carolyn was the first to spot Karen, Nancy and Susan coming through the door, "Oh, look, here they come now!" Weaving their way to the table, Susan caught the attention of more than a just a few women as she passed by. Some were very vocal of their appreciation of her, while others were content to openly stare at her. Susan was more than happy to get the table and out of "the limelight," so to speak. Standing up Anna gave her a welcoming hug, "Oh my, Susan, you look lovely," Susan wasn't so sure, "I don't know Anna, I think I may have overdone it." Everyone thought she looked terrific, perfect for a night like this. Lillian said, "Just relax and enjoy the evening, you look beautiful." And then added, "We're happy you could come. We haven't seen you since we were in Maine." Susan went on to explain how she managed to get away, still feeling a little guilty about leaving Jimmy in his moment of crisis.

With everyone together again, they began filling each other in on how they spent the holidays, it wasn't long before they were out of food. Lillian asked Susan, "Why don't you come with me and we'll get some more food for the table?" "Alright," Susan answered, "but I'd like another glass of wine when Cathy comes by," she said to no one in particular. Once she was on her feet, she could feel the energy of the party. She had been so caught up talking with everyone; the noise of the party had faded into the background. Feeling nervous and excited, Susan followed Lillian through the crowd. Aware of the bold looks she was attracting, she slipped her hand into Lillian's. Lillian responded by giving her hand a reassuring squeeze. As they approached the tables lined with food, they each took a plate and started filling them up. Lillian seemed to know everyone there. Women kept coming up to her to engage her in conversation. Feeling a little self-conscious just standing there, Susan was about to make her way back to the table when she turned and saw Jamie. She was laughing loudly while being hand-fed a sandwich by a pretty redhead, who definitely had too much to drink. Turning quickly, not wanting Jamie to see her, she felt her face getting hot and made her way back to the table. Julie asked, "Susan, are you all right, your face is bright red?" "I'm fine Julie, I just got a little warm in the crowd." Susan was surprised at her reaction to seeing Jamie with another woman, but quickly brushed it off. She was determined not to let it become anymore than a minor annoyance. A handsome woman that had been checking Cathy out all evening finally caught her eye and came over to ask her for a dance. This started the ball rolling and seeing that Lillian was still making the rounds, Anna asked Susan to dance.

Bobby saw Jamie at the bar and worked her way over, "Hey, Jamie, what's going on, I just got here." Jamie had to yell to be heard over the music, "The place has been hopping since I got here, in fact I'm in need of a rest. I think I'll go over and sit for awhile," Jamie said indicating the table where Carolyn, Julie and Connie were sitting. Bobby asked," What about later, anything lined up?" Jamie was quick to reply, "Yes, as a matter of fact I do. Remember that red-head I went out with a couple of times last spring?" At first Bobby wasn't sure, then it seemed to dawn on her, "I remember her, a real beauty, that one," she replied. "And still is," Jamie said, and added, "She's looking for some fun tonight, if you're interested." Bobby looked surprised, "You wouldn't mind?" "Nah," she answered, "come on I'll introduce you." Following Jamie past the dance floor, she suddenly stopped dead in her tracks. The music was so loud Jamie had to yell, "Bobby, what's wrong?" Still looking toward the dance floor, Bobby asked, "Who's that dancing with Anna?" Bobby was obviously smitten by whoever she was looking at and Jamie had to laugh until she followed her gaze and saw it was Susan. Jamie immediately felt a jolt run through her. Bobby nudged her arm, "Hey Jamie, do you know her? God, she's a knockout, is she with anyone?" Jamie was reluctant to talk to Bobby about Susan, trying to be vague, "I really don't know her," she said while trying to steer her back to the redhead, but Bobby's gaze was fixed on Susan. Bobby then turned to Jamie asking, "Are you interested?" Jamie hesitated for a brief moment then said, "No, not me, I think she's married." "Married?" said Bobby, "That's my favorite kind!" Slapping Jamie on the shoulder, leaving her with mixed feelings, Bobby headed for Susan.

Tapping Anna on the shoulder, Bobby asked, "May I cut in?" Susan had noticed her with Jamie and she had a feeling Anna was hesitant to let her go, "Its all right Anna," Susan told her. Turning to Bobby she said, "Hi, I'm Susan," flashing her a beautiful smile. Bobby was over-whelmed. Anna, on the other hand, went back to the table feeling very uncomfortable leaving Susan with Bobby. Although she knew that Bobby was a friend of Jamie's, but she never really cared for her. She was a user, not caring about the women she dated, just a game to be played. Back at the table she shared her concerns with the others. "Don't worry Anna," Julie said, "Susan has already made it clear that she can take care of herself." Karen spoke up, "She's right, look at her, she seems to be enjoying herself." Anna had to admit Susan did seem to be having a good time.

After the dance Bobby guided Susan to the bar. She wanted to go back to the table with everyone else, but when she saw Jamie watching them she went along with Bobby. By the time they finished their drinks Susan was feeling very warm and her face was flushed. Bobby wanted to go outside with her to get some fresh air but Susan thought that was a bad idea. She slipped off her jacket, revealing her bare shoulders and modest cleavage, making Bobby more determined than ever take her home. Taking Susan's hand, she led her back to the dance floor. Knowing Susan was feeling the effects of the wine, she took full advantage of her. Holding her tightly against herself, she ran her hands up and down her back. By this time, Susan had enough of Bobby but couldn't seem to get away. Lillian happened to look toward the dance floor and saw Susan's discomfort at being pawed over. It was obvious, whether anyone else believed it or not, Susan needed help. Across the floor Lillian could see that Jamie was watching as well. Lillian whispered to Anna, "Susan looks uncomfortable up there. I'm going to see if I can get Jamie to cut in and bring her back to the table." Anna was glad to hear that, she felt Susan was much too sweet to be with the likes of Bobby.

Making her way over to Jamie, Lillian asked, "Jamie, be a dear and go rescue Susan from Bobby." "What?" Jamie said, sounding surprised, "Looks to me like Susan's having a good time." The sarcastic tone in her voice caught Lillian off guard. She instinctively wanted to ask her if something was wrong, but Susan needed help now. "Jamie, I've caught a couple of looks from Susan and believe me, she really wants to get away from Bobby. Won't you please cut in on them?" Jamie had more than enough to drink and was obviously irritated about something, but she couldn't say no to Lillian. Looking uninterested Jamie told her, "All right, I'll do what I can."

Jamie knew she couldn't just walk over and cut in on Bobby. She decided to enlist the help of her redheaded friend. Finding Debbie at the bar, Jamie told her that Bobby was very interested in meeting her. She knew if she could get Debbie into Bobby's arms, she would keep her very busy and very happy.

Karen and Nancy noticed that Lillian and Anna looked troubled and went over to where they standing. Nancy asked, "Is anything wrong?" Lillian explained that Susan got in over her head with Bobby, "But don't worry," she told them, "Jamie's handling it." Karen spoke up, "I'm going to see if Susan wants to go home." But Anna was quick to stop her, "Not now dear, Jamie will take care of her, besides the count down will be starting soon." Anna had sensed Jamie's feelings for Susan and steered everyone back to their table.

Debbie had successfully cut in, steering Bobby to the other side of the dance floor, leaving Susan standing awkwardly in front of Jamie. Taking hold of Susan's hands, Jamie could feel her trembling, she immediately felt bad she hadn't seen her distress sooner, "Susan, are you all right?" With a slight nod,

Alicia Langley

Susan said, "Yes, thank you." Jamie stepped in closer so she could hear her above the noise. Taking Susan's hand she said, "Come on, I'll take you back to the table." Susan pulled back, "Please Jamie, not yet! Just give me a minute to regain my composer." She took a deep breath and continued, "God I feel so stupid! I guess I can't take care of myself." "Susan, I know Bobby, she can be pretty overwhelming when she's coming onto someone. Believe me, she's not your average suitor," Jamie said with a smile trying to coax one from Susan, and succeeding.

As they were standing at the edge of the dance floor, Jamie could see Susan was still upset. Making sure Bobby was nowhere in sight, Jamie guided Susan back to the dance floor as the next dance began. As Jamie put her hands on Susan's waist, Susan rested her hands lightly on Jamie's shoulders. Swaying gently to the music, she began to relax. Jamie was being so nice and caring, a side of her that Susan never expected. One song ended and another began but neither one said a word. They were caught up in the new feelings they were experiencing as a warm vibration engulfed them. Jamie could have held Susan all night. Susan moved in closer and her arms circled Jamie's neck allowing their bodies to melt into each other. Resting her head on Jamie's shoulder Susan felt Jamie's arms tighten around her. In the background, the last song was being played, 'A Sunday Kind of Love'. Although they had both heard the song many times before, tonight they felt it had been written for them, 'I need a love that lasts past Saturday night,' hit Jamie hard, connecting her with the inner feelings she had been trying to ignore. Susan's breath caught in her throat when she heard, 'I'm hoping to discover, a certain kind of lover, who will show me the way.' Jamie stopped moving, cupping Susan's face in her hands, both surrendering to the moment, neither one heard the count down begin. Amid loud horns, balloons, confetti falling from the ceiling, and while everyone was singing, "Auld Lang Syne," Susan and Jamie shared their first kiss.

The New Year held a lot of promise and change for many of the women in the "group." Karen and Nancy announced that they were moving in together. Karen was giving up her apartment in favor of Nancy's, although they both agreed it was still too small. They planned on looking for a house in the spring. Lillian and Anna were excited about all the changes that would be happening in their lives. This was the year they were to retire and move to Maine for good. The only draw back was leaving all their friends. Connie was also looking forward to the New Year. Knowing that Jean was all right, she couldn't help but think she would be seeing her again. And Cathy, although taking it slow, had met a woman on New Year's Eve named Ronnie, definitely somebody she wanted to get to know better. Jamie and Susan hadn't seen each other since that night on the dance floor. They would have liked more time together, but in the excitement of the "count down," with people running around wishing each other "Happy New Year," they had become separated, only catching a glimpse of each other as everyone was leaving. They both went home that night unable to sleep and unable to forget that kiss.

Alicia Langley

Book Two

Alicia Langley

Chapter One

Anna was just taking the chicken out of the oven when she heard a faint knock on the door. She could hear Lillian say, "Jamie, what a nice surprise, come in." Lillian raised her voice to call to Anna, "Anna, Jamie's here." Anna came in from the kitchen wiping her hands on her apron and greeted Jamie with a kiss on the cheek, "Jamie dear, you're just in time for dinner, I hope you can stay." Jamie, looking a little sheepish, "I didn't mean to interrupt your dinner." Lillian was quick to say, "Oh Jamie, your not doing anything of the kind! We'd love for you to stay, we haven't seen much of you lately." Jamie had to smile at the warm welcome, "Thank you, I'd love to stay, it smells wonderful in here." It was warm and cozy in their apartment, quite a contrast from the blustery cold outside. Lillian took Jamie's coat, "Have a seat Jamie and I'll go get us a beer. Anna would you like anything?" "Yes dear, a glass of wine would be nice."

Returning with their drinks Lillian took a seat beside Anna on the couch. Both Lillian and Anna sensed something was on Jamie's mind. Lillian asked, "Is anything wrong Jamie?" Taking a deep breath, Jamie said, "I need some advice. I've met someone I can't seem to stop thinking about." Both Anna and Lillian knew it was Susan, but didn't say anything. Jamie continued, "I've only seen her a couple of times and already I feel something for this women, a connection I can't explain." Jamie looked confused, "This isn't like me." Anna spoke up then, "Jamie dear, it sounds like your falling in love."

Chapter Two

"Mom, Mom," Susan's daughter Carrie, was standing in front of her trying to get her attention. "I'm sorry honey, what is it?" Carrie asked, "Can me and Jen stay over Allison's for supper?" Of course the inevitable question, "Is your homework done?" "Yup, mine is done and Jen's just finishing hers," Carrie answered with a big smile. Susan returned the smile, "All right, but it's a school night, I want you both home by eight o'clock, no later." Carrie gave her a quick hug then ran to tell Jen.

Once the girls left, Susan tried to stay busy to keep from thinking about Jamie, but it didn't work. It had been two weeks since New Years Eve and all she could think about was that kiss. She had never experienced anything like it before.

On New Years day Susan and Jimmy went to his parents for dinner, it was a disaster. She could still feel Jamie's lips. It was hard for her to concentrate on anything else. At one point Jimmy followed her out to the kitchen, "Susan," he said, keeping his voice low so his family in the other room couldn't hear him. At first Susan hadn't heard him, stepping in front of her, he grabbed her by the shoulders, "What's the matter with you?" he asked through clenched teeth. "Everyone thinks we're fighting!" Susan was taken by surprise, "Oh, Jimmy, I am sorry, my head is just a little fuzzy. I must be coming down with something." Jimmy didn't appear to buy it. Susan managed to pay more attention and finally got through the rest of the day.

When they got home and the girls were in bed, Susan continued her excuse about not feeling good and went to bed early. Of course she couldn't sleep. Her mind was going over every sensation she felt in Jamie's arms. That kiss had been so much more than she ever expected. She couldn't help but wonder if Jamie felt anything, 'I shouldn't kid myself,' she thought, 'Jamie has plenty of women, all single and available. All she has to do is pick up the phone. Do I really want to be one of those?'

Chapter Three

Cathy noticed the time; it was ten minutes to one. She had left a little early for the Deli, just in case Carol showed up. Driving over Cathy was still hopeful, even though it had been five weeks since she'd last seen her. She feared the worst as each week passed. This time though, Carol was there. "I was beginning to wonder if I was ever going to see you again," Cathy said with a relieved smile. "Well," Carol began, "clumsy me had to slip on the ice. I've been laid up with a sprained back. I should have called, but I lost your number." Carol didn't tell Cathy the real reason why she hadn't called. Liz always checked the numbers on the phone bill, saying she was just looking for mistakes, but Carol knew better. "How awful for you! Did you see a doctor?" Cathy asked. "Oh no," Carol replied, "that wasn't necessary, Liz always takes care of me." Leaning across the table, Cathy felt the need to let Carol know about her suspicions that Liz was abusing her. "Carol…," she started to say, but seeing the frightened look in her eyes, she finished lamely with "I'm glad you're alright."

Later that night, Cathy was still mulling over her conversation with Carol as she mixed drinks at the bar, not knowing what she could do, if anything, to help. She was glad to see Connie approaching the bar; she sure could use a distraction. "Hey Connie, I'm playing bartender tonight, so what can I get you?" "Just give me a draft beer." Connie said and then asked, "Why are you tending bar…, where's Annie?" Cathy set the beer down in front of Connie and answered, "She asked me to cover for her tonight. She has a long weekend planned with her new girlfriend," "Speaking of girlfriends" Connie said, "you were awfully cozy with that good looking brunette New Years Eve, anything going on there?" Cathy smiled, "Well, we're just getting to know each other right now. Her name is Ronnie. I really like her and lucky for me, I think the feelings are mutual." Cathy paused, shrugging her shoulders, "We'll see what happens." In the meantime, she had to get back to work; a waitress was waiting to turn in an order. Walking away, she noticed Jamie walking in the side door, "Connie, Jaime's just coming in," she told her. Connie turned to where Cathy was pointing and waved to Jamie. Connie thought, 'It would be good to have a couple of beers together.' Jamie returned the wave and indicated she would be over in a minute.

Connie watched Jamie weave her way through all the women trying to get her attention. Most seemed to know her, and those that didn't...wanted to. Finally reaching the bar, she took a seat beside her and said, "Hey Connie, nice to see you here." Cathy came over with Jamie's usual beer and another one for Connie and then rushed off, as the bar was getting busy. Connie and Jamie held up their glasses in a mock salute to each other before taking a drink. Setting her glass down Connie said, "God Jamie, it must be nice having all those women throwing themselves at you." Jamie laughed wistfully, "Oh yeh, it used to be, but things seem to have changed a lot lately." Connie looked at Jamie remembering New Years Eve. Putting on an innocent smile Connie asked, "It wouldn't have anything to do with that kiss between you and Susan would it?" Jamie looked at her and with a hint of laughter in her eyes answered, "Don't tell me you noticed that one kiss! There must have been over a hundred women kissing each other that night." Connie nodded her head in agreement, "That's true, you weren't the only ones, but you haven't answered my question." Jamie gave Connie a scrutinizing look and decided in that split second that she really liked her. "Well okay, how about another round and we'll talk about that kiss," she answered. Connie was all for that and waved to Cathy for two more beers and a bowl of popcorn. Cathy was back in a flash with their beers, "Hey you guys," she said, looking at their empty glasses, "that was quick!" Looking up at Jamie, she asked, "Is it going to be one of those nights?" Jamie in turn asked Connie, who replied, "Why not?"

Long before the night was over, Connie and Jamie were 'best buddies.' Much to Connie's amusement, while Jamie was moaning about Susan, saying, "One kiss and I can't think about anyone else," women kept coming up to her at the bar, trying to get her attention. Before long they finally left her alone after she turned them all away. "So go figure," Jamie said with a wave of her hand, her voice a little slurred, "I could be with someone tonight, or any night for that matter," "Yes," Connie said smiling, "I can see that." Jamie just shook her head, "That one kiss…"

After yet another round, it was Connie's turn to talk, telling her story about Jean. Jamie was a good listener and sensitive enough to realize that Connie was going through some real heartache. It may have been 'one of those nights,' but it was one they both needed. When Cathy's shift was over, she didn't mind driving them home.

Chapter Four

When Jean entered the office, Carolyn came around the desk to greet her, "Come in Jean, have a seat. How are you doing?" Sitting down Jean paused for a moment before answering, "I'm not sure how I'm doing. There seems to be more stress than I can handle or I'm just not handling it right." Carolyn looked at her with real concern and said, "Give me an example Jean." "Well between working, having to be at the AA meetings, coming here and trying to set up a time to see my kids," Jean took a deep breath before continuing, "I just feel overwhelmed and I've been craving a drink." Carolyn leaned forward, thinking for a moment before she spoke. Jean had been doing so good, she hated to see her loose it now, "Jean, first of all, anytime, day or night, you feel that urge, call your house mother. She's always there for you. Even more important, have you made any friends?" Jean shook her head, "No, I haven't," she answered. "Look," said Carolyn, "I really feel it would help if you had someone else to talk to besides your doctors and social workers, someone you could just talk with." Jean nodded in agreement, "I know your right, but it's not easy for me." Carolyn didn't say it, but she was hoping she'd talk to Connie. Jean looked at Carolyn and said, "I know what you're thinking, that I should call Connie. Don't think I haven't wanted to, but I just can't do that. I've already put her through enough." Carolyn was quick to reply, "Believe me Jean, Connie cares very deeply for you and would be more then willing to help you any way she could." Jean, looking irritated with the way the conversation was going, said in a voice louder than normal, "Tell me something Doctor, will the courts let me have my kids back when they find out I'm in love with a woman?" Shocked, all Carolyn could say was, "Are you?"

On the bus ride back across town, Jean was going over her conversation with Dr. Adams. She was just as surprised as Carolyn when she said she was in love with Connie. She hadn't allowed those feelings to surface before. 'Now what?' she thought. 'I can't think about Connie right now, I have to concentrate on my kids and my job.' She was really feeling the stress of having so many demands on her and she felt ready to come apart at the seams. She did like her job though; it was the one she had hoped to get at the art gallery. During her interview she had been escorted around and shown the paintings. The gallery director was very taken with her, not only did he find her charming and beautiful but he saw that she had a good eye for art. He hired her on the spot. She started out being a receptionist, just answering the phones and taking messages. She hadn't held a job in years and this seemed a good way to start, there wasn't too much expected of her. Gradually though, the director of the gallery wanted her to get more involved, especially when they were having a special showing. Among other things, he felt she added a lot of style and class to the place. Secretly, he liked having her around because he was attracted to her. Jean liked becoming more involved; she loved being connected to the art world. The only draw back, was all the drinking that went on. It was becoming harder and harder to say no when someone poured her a glass of wine. And now, on top of everything else, she had finally admitted to herself and Doctor Adams how she really felt about Connie. She thought, 'How will I ever be able to deal with all of this and stay sober?' She was gazing out the window on the bus, lost in her thoughts. The shops they passed were just a blur. Suddenly Jean's breath caught in her throat, her eyes focused, Connie was coming out of one of the stores. It opened a flood of emotions that she had been fighting to keep down. It took all her strength not to stop the bus and run after her. She was so confused; if she wanted to continue gaining the trust of her kids and the courts, she just couldn't enter into a relationship with a woman.

Walking into her apartment, Connie was keenly aware of the quiet empty feeling it held, 'God,' she thought, 'will it always be this way?' It had been two months since Carolyn had told her about Jean. At first, Connie had been optimistic, feeling Jean would be in touch with her when she got things under control, but now with no word, she was losing hope of ever seeing her again.

Chapter Five

The last time Cathy had lunch with Carol, she had felt something was very wrong. Concerned, she asked, "Carol is everything alright?" Carol answered with an apologetic smile, "I'm sorry Cathy, I guess I'm not very good company today." Hoping this may be the time that Carol would finally open up, Cathy pressed on, "Carol if there's anything you want to talk about, I'm a good listener." Carol appeared to consider that, but said, "I'm just feeling confused lately, but," she went on, meeting Cathy's eyes, "it's something I have to deal with myself." That was six weeks ago and Cathy hadn't seen her since.

Chapter Six

It was seven o'clock in the morning; Karen and Nancy were getting ready to open the Bakery when Susan knocked on the door. Nancy welcomed her with a big hug, "Susan, what are you doing here so early? We've been thinking about you and wanted to call but...," Before Nancy could continue their customers started coming in for their morning coffee and pastry. Nancy gave Susan an apologetic look, but Susan just smiled and grabbed an apron. Within ten minutes the place was packed and stayed that way until ten thirty, then everyone seemed to vanish at once. Finally they were able to take a much-needed break. Sitting down with their coffee, Susan looked a bit over-whelmed, "My God you guys, I had no idea you got so busy! Don't you think you should get some help?" Karen and Nancy exchanged a knowing look, Karen said, "It's just what we've been talking about, but we're not sure we want to do that." Nancy went on to explain, "We're afraid it would change things. We like working here together and we're not ready to share our space with someone else. All we wanted was a small town bakery we could run by ourselves. It's nice, in a way, to be successful, but we didn't want it to become more than what we could handle by ourselves." Susan, looking surprised, asked, "What will you do? You can't keep up this pace by yourselves!" Karen laughed, "We have no idea! But enough about us, we haven't had a moment to sit and talk in months, what's going on?" Susan looked a little embarrassed; she hadn't realized it had been that long. "I wish I knew, well that's not true, I do know, I'm just afraid to admit it." "Susan," Karen asked, "what's wrong?" Taking a deep breath, Susan said, "Its Jamie. I know you'll both think I'm crazy, but we kissed on New Years Eve and I can't think of anything else. I've never felt this way before. What should I do?" Nancy said, "Susan, don't get me wrong, we love Jamie, but we've never known her to get involved in a committed relationship." Karen interrupted, "As long as we've known Jamie, she has never been with anyone for more then a few dates. And to be honest with you Susan, she's always made it clear she would never get involved with a married woman. You are still married, aren't you?" "Yes, I'm still married. I know I shouldn't be thinking this way, but…"

Susan and Jamie did see each other a couple of times over the winter months, although only briefly and always in the company of others. During those quick, awkward, moments, it was clear to everyone present what was happening between them. Karen and Nancy had conceded between themselves that there seemed to be a big change in Jamie's attitude, but they didn't say anything to Susan about it. They didn't want to encourage her to get involved with Jamie and she was, after all, still married.

Connie, along with everyone else, had watched Susan and Jamie trying not to pay particular attention to each other. She knew that Susan was married, but she thought she should at least know how Jamie felt about her and vice versa. It was painful for Connie to watch without interfering. Finally at a get-together at Julie and Carolyn's, she decided to approach Susan about it. Susan gave Connie a big smile as she made her way over to her; she always enjoyed Connie's company. After a warm hug and some small talk, Connie watched as Susan's eyes followed Jamie making her way around the room. Taking on a serious look, Connie took a deep breath and said, "Susan, I know it's none of my business, but I think you should know, Jamie has feelings for you."

Sitting up in bed that night with an open book laying beside her, Susan couldn't keep Jamie out of her thoughts. When Connie first told her that Jamie had feelings for her, she was completely surprised. She couldn't believe it, but oh how she wanted to. Her thoughts carried her back to the night Jamie held her in her arms...Susan jumped when she heard a knock on the bedroom door. "Susan?" Jimmy's voice came through the door, "Are you awake?" Susan sat straight up, "Yes, come in." When Jimmy entered the room Susan asked, "Is there something wrong?" She was immediately anxious and concerned. Jimmy wouldn't bother her unless there was a problem. As he sat down on the edge of the bed, he seemed to find it difficult to start speaking, which was making her all the more nervous. Finally, in a rush of words he blurted out "I was thinking of having my mother pick up the girls for Memorial Day weekend, it would give us some time together, just me and you, what do you say?" Susan was silent, realizing what Jimmy was implying, "Jimmy, we're going to your family's camp, it's a tradition." Susan knew it was a lame answer, but it was all she could think of.

Early the next morning Susan sat with her coffee, still stunned about last night. Jimmy had told her he realized how much they had drifted apart. He accepted full responsibility for it, feeling that it was his fault because of all the hours he put in on the job. He told her, "Susan, I'd like to do something about it, but I need to know how you feel." When Susan didn't answer, she could see the hurt look on his face. "Jimmy, it's been so long, I really don't know what to say." Jimmy went on in a positive note about how much fun they could have together and that he planned on being home more so he could spend more time with his family." All the while Susan's head was spinning as she tried to keep herself from screaming, "No!"

The big Memorial Day weekend was fast approaching and Susan was facing it with dread. She had finally talked Jimmy into all of them going away to the lake. So far, he hadn't tried to sleep with her, but she knew it was just a matter of time. 'Now what', she thought, 'I don't want to loose myself again. I like where I'm at, but at the same time, can I risk breaking up our family? And what about Jimmy? He doesn't deserve this. He's going along, thinking everything's fine and we'll be together forever.' It wasn't too long ago that she had thought the same, but not any more. Her need to be with Jamie was growing stronger with every passing day. Lost in her thoughts, Susan jumped when she heard the phone ring. Picking it up she heard, "Mom?" "Jen, is everything alright?" Her daughter very dramatically explained how she forgot to bring the game that everyone at the slumber party wanted to play. Susan laughingly agreed to bring it over to them. She could use some time out. Maybe the drive would clear her head. Once there, she stayed for a cup of coffee and managed to push her problems aside for a while. But that was short lived, alone again in her car, her thoughts turned to Jamie once again as she relived that kiss. She began driving aimlessly around, or so she told herself, until she found herself turning onto Jamie's street. She knew where she was going because she had secretly driven down the street many times before, hoping to catch a glimpse of her.

Jamie had been on the phone with Connie, making last minute arrangements to ride up to Maine with her for the Memorial Day weekend. They were becoming good friends. Jamie really enjoyed their talks. It wasn't late, only nine o'clock, but Jamie knew if she stayed up, she would just end up thinking about Susan. She was confused about all these new feelings she was experiencing, so with a busy day looming ahead of her, she decided call it a night and go to bed. As she crossed the room, putting out the lights as she went, she heard a faint knock on the door.

Chapter Seven

Lillian and Anna were all packed by Wednesday night in preparation of leaving for Maine early the next morning. They wanted to be there ahead of the others to make sure everything was ready for a great weekend. They were more excited than usual, not only because of all the company they would have, but this was the year they planned to retire and leave Boston for good. This time when they packed the car, they were bringing along things to set up housekeeping at the farm in preparation of their move to Maine in the fall.

They left Boston in the wee hours of the morning on Thursday and arrived in Maine a couple hours later. So anxious were they to get to the farm, they had not made their usual stop for breakfast and they were starved. All the furniture and appliances had been covered with big sheets of plastic to keep out the dust, prior to closing the house for the winter, so it didn't take long to get the kitchen in shape and the stove ready for cooking. The house felt empty and damp so Lillian quickly went about starting a fire in the wood stoves and the fireplace. Soon the house was warm and cozy and the smell of bacon cooking in the kitchen brought back comforting feelings, much like she felt as a child whenever she visited the farm. 'How nice this is,' she thought, 'it feels like home. Anna and I are going to be very happy here.'

The first thing Anna did upon entering the kitchen was to plug in the refrigerator and make sure it was running properly. As she set about filling it with the perishable food they had brought with them, she thought, 'this is the last time this old refrigerator will have to be shut down and emptied out, now that we are soon to be permanent residents.' The thought made her smile with contentment, as they had been planning this move for a long time. They had packed plenty of food for everyone to last the long weekend, including all the fixings for a turkey dinner on Sunday. 'It's already beginning to feel like home,' she thought as she set the table for breakfast. She felt all along, this was where they belonged. Instinctively she knew this move would bring about a big change in their lives and she was looking forward to their future in Maine.

After breakfast Lillian finished unpacking the car. It was loaded down with cleaning supplies. They knew there would be plenty of cleaning to do after they opened up the back rooms of the house and they wanted to make sure they wouldn't run out of anything. That part of the house had been locked up for so long, Lillian couldn't even begin to remember what was in there. Meanwhile Anna prepared a chicken for roasting. She had already made a potato salad the night before, making it an easy supper for the two of them tonight. As much as they were looking forward to everyone arriving tomorrow, they were glad they had this time to themselves and they were planning to make the most of it.

Early Friday morning Julie rolled over in bed expecting to find Carolyn beside her, instead she was coming through the bedroom door, all dressed and carrying two cups of coffee. Julie had to laugh, Carolyn looked bright eyed and ready for adventure. Taking her cup, Julie said, "Hey, I'm looking forward to leaving early, Hon, but it's five o'clock in the morning! If we leave now, Lillian and Anna will probably just be getting up when we arrive!" Carolyn smiled, "I know, but I thought we could take our time driving up. We could go Route One instead of the highway and stop somewhere along the way for breakfast." Julie was surprised; this was out of character for her. True, Carolyn did enjoy any time they had been able to get away, but there was always a part of her missing, still connected to her job. "Alright," Julie said, "I'll take a quick shower, then we'll leave." Leaning over Carolyn gave Julie a kiss and simply said, "I love you."

Julie was glad Carolyn had thought of this, it was a fun ride. They waited until they got to New Hampshire before stopping for breakfast. Carolyn's upbeat attitude had caught up with Julie early on. They had a great time, talking and bantering with each other during their ride and took their time over breakfast. Traffic was much slower than expected; it seemed as if everyone was heading to Maine, but they didn't mind, they were able to take in all the sights and smells of the many shops and restaurants along the way. This was especially true when they came to a small town not far from Lillian and Anna's turn off. Carolyn was concentrating on the traffic, until it slowed down to a crawl. Julie, realizing they couldn't be more then ten minutes from 'the farm,' couldn't believe what she was seeing. This was a whole different world from what they perceived "Maine" to be. Throngs of people were everywhere. Neither of them minded the slow pace as it gave them a chance to be tourists and really look around. Entering the tiny village, they were completely enchanted by the beautifully decorated stores, each one framed in tiny white lights. They were so engrossed in the quaint little shops that at first, they hadn't noticed the people. Then Julie said, "Carolyn," as she started to pay more attention, "do you see what I see?" Carolyn was watching two women walking down the street with their arms around each other, it was obvious they were a couple, "I'm beginning to." Then before they knew it, they had passed through the town. Both agreed they would have to ask Lillian and Anna why they had never spoke about this place. They definitely wanted to know more about it.

Lillian and Anna were awake early this morning in anticipation of everyone's arrival and were bustling around getting prepared for their weekend guests. Anna, standing on a chair in the kitchen said, "Lil, be a dear and hand me up the rest of those cups." Having done that Lillian asked, "Anything else Anna?" "No, I think we're done," she said turning around to admire how good the kitchen looked. They knew everyone would be spending a lot of time in here and decided it was the best place to start. While Anna washed all the dishware, Lillian wiped down the shelves and removed the old curtains, washing the windows as she went along; taking special care with one in particular that graced the wall behind the old pot-bellied stove. Lillian had wonderful memories from her childhood visits of sitting on the floor by the stove in front of her grandmother's rocking chair as she brushed her hair and imparted her wisdom upon her. While gazing out the window into her past, something caught Lillian's eye, 'Oh it's a car,' she thought, bringing her back to reality, "Anna, I think Carolyn and Julie are here!"

After Carolyn and Julie had unpacked the car it was about eleven o'clock. Julie had brought along a big pot of chili for their supper and while Anna helped her put things away, Carolyn went in and changed into some warmer clothes. Although the sun was shining brightly, true to Maine, there was a crisp chill in the air. As she came out of the room, heading to the kitchen, she came across Lillian coming through the door with more firewood in her arms than she could handle. Carolyn said, "Here, let me help!" Gladly handing over half of her load, Lillian went into the kitchen to add a couple more logs to the wood stove while Carolyn added more to the living room fireplace, then she rejoined everyone in the kitchen. Anna was asking Julie if she'd heard from anyone. "Yes, I talked to Karen last night. They were going to close the bakery at three and then head up. They already packed the car so they should be here around four thirty, five o'clock. Same with Ronnie and Cathy, they'll be getting here a little later, maybe around six thirty." Then Lillian added, "I spoke to Jamie a few days ago. She and Connie are supposed to ride up together. Connie was leaving work at noon, so everyone should be here by dinner time."

Chapter Eight

Jamie was coming out of the shower when she heard the phone ringing. Wrapping herself in a towel, she rushed to answer, thinking it may be Susan. "Hello?" "Hi." It was Connie, "I just wanted to let you know I'm getting out earlier then I thought, can you be ready to leave at eleven instead?" Jamie didn't say anything at first, trying to collect her thoughts. "Jamie, are you alright?" "Yeh Connie, I'm fine and sure, I can be ready then."

Jamie tried to concentrate on getting ready for the trip, but all she could think about was last night when Susan arrived at her apartment. It had been the last thing she expected and she was filled with mixed feelings. It had been quick and intense, like nothing she had ever experienced before. She could still feel the heat of Susan's body.

Jamie was unusually quiet on the ride to Maine, prompting Connie to ask again if she was all right. Jamie told her all about last night. Connie was surprised that Jamie didn't appear to be happy about it. "Is something wrong?" Jamie paused a moment in thought before answering, "There is no denying I've been thinking about Susan for awhile now, but to tell you the truth, I just can't picture myself being able to deal with her being married." Connie answered, "Jamie, as you know, I haven't done very well in matters of the heart, but I do know you care for Susan, and its obvious she feels the same. Give it a chance."

Susan had laid awake all night, her emotions going from the joy she experienced with Jamie, to the dread of having to deal with Jimmy at the lake. How will she handle this? She tried to stay 'chatty' with the girls on the way up to the camp, wishing the ride would never end.

At her in-laws cabin, Susan was in the kitchen helping her mother-in-law with lunch. She was still finding it hard not to get lost in the images of her and Jamie's lovemaking last night. On top of that, she still didn't know how she was going to handle Jimmy. Her daughter, Carrie came into the kitchen, "Mom, can we go out in the boat with Kelly's family?" Susan replied "Oh honey, your grandmother and I have lunch all ready, can't it wait until after we've eaten?" Carrie was quick to ask, "Can Kelly eat with us?" Susan answered, "Of course, now go get her and your sister while we put lunch on the table." Carrie gave Susan a quick hug before she flew out the door. Susan's mother-in-law had to smile, "They're sweet girls Susan. Ed and I would love to have them come up after school gets out for a little vacation." Susan told her, "They would just love that, but they can be pretty demanding." Her mother-in-law chuckled, "We know, but they're older now, I'm sure we can handle them."

Jimmy, his brothers and father were coming in from fishing as the girls were finishing their lunch. Jimmy made sure they had their life jackets on as they ran by him out the door. Susan, trying to keep busy, was clearing the table when he came up behind her, putting his arms around her waist and kissing her on the cheek. He felt her stiffen, but chose to ignore it. He figured she just wasn't used to him anymore; he planned on changing that.

After lunch the men had some work to do on the boat's motor and her mother-in-law wanted to do some shopping, asking Susan if she would like to come along. Susan declined, saying she had brought a book along with her and she would like to start it while the girls were gone. It wasn't long before everyone had left, leaving Susan alone with her thoughts. Before she could decide what to do about Jamie, she first had to figure out what to do about Jimmy. Jimmy said he wanted her to go to a marriage consular with him. When Susan asked him, "Why Jimmy, why now after all this time?" He told her he wanted more out of life then work. He loved her and wanted to work on their marriage, asking, "Don't you want the same thing?"

Chapter Nine

At the farm, Lillian, Anna, Carolyn and Julie had just finished a light lunch and were ready to get started. Lillian got out the keys to the back of the house. As they came to the locked door, the only sound to be heard was the jangle of the old keys she was carrying. Finding the right key, the door quietly swung open to reveal a doublewide staircase leading to the second floor. The thick layer of cobwebs and dust couldn't hide the beauty of the old wood beneath it. Anna was the first to speak, "Lil this is wonderful, but we need more light. Are there any lights in here?" Lillian shook her head, "No Anna, I don't believe this part of the house was ever wired for electricity." Little by little their eyes began to adjust to the dim light filtering in from the end of a long hall. They were all excited caught up in the adventure of exploring a place where time had stood still for so many years.

As they walked around the staircase and headed down the hall towards the light, they could see it was coming through two big panels of old drapes against the back wall. As they each took a panel and pulled, the sunlight spilled into the room. They were astonished to see the beautiful doors that had been hidden beneath them. They were made up of dozens of small panes of old glass. As they were admiring the doors, Anna got a glimpse of the other side, "Oh my, it looks like a garden out there." She attempted to open the doors, but they were locked. Lillian moved in front of Anna with her assortment of keys and after trying a few, she found the right one. The knobs turned, but

117

the doors wouldn't budge. "I think they're just stuck. It's damp in here and the wood's probably swollen. Anna lets try tapping the edges." Anna helped Lillian as Julie and Carolyn gently pushed until the doors gave way and swung open. Julie, who had always wanted a place where she could garden, was absolutely giddy as she followed Anna out into the old garden. She exclaimed "This must have been a beautiful flower garden at one time! Look Anna, you can see new shoots growing up through all that dead brush!" She went on excitedly, "And look at all these old rose bushes. I'm sure it would be a lot of work, but this place could be brought back to life." Anna agreed and was already on her knees pulling away the dead brush. Both Julie and Anna had found all they wanted to see for the moment so Carolyn and Lillian headed back into the house; they weren't done exploring yet.

Back inside it was easier to see with the sunlight streaming in from the garden doors. They were anxious to find what was behind the doors that lined the hallway on either side of the staircase. Each door was opened to reveal a small bedroom, a total of four in all. The rooms looked as if they were furnished, but it was hard to tell as they were packed with boxes. Lillian thought the rooms might have been used years ago for the field hands when this was a working farm. Heading upstairs they found three big, unfinished attic rooms, cluttered with boxes and old furniture that had been put in storage years ago. Yet, in spite of that, they could see a lot of potential for two of the rooms to be made over as guest rooms. Both of the rooms had a big fireplace with huge windows looking out over the farm. The third room had the same windows overlooking the farm, with an opening for another fireplace, though unfinished. Lillian was trying to take in everything at once as she flitted from room to room, deciding what needed to be done first. They spent quite a while moving boxes out of the way; Lillian wanted to see everything. Noticing stains in a corner of one of the ceilings she knew the roof would be the first priority. As she stood with her hands on her hips, she could see it was going to take a lot of money to get the old place renovated. They had been saving a long time for their retirement, building up a good nest egg and neither of them wanted to sink it all into repairs. Carolyn must have picked up on her thoughts, "This is going to be an expensive project, but you have the rest of your lives, just do a little at a time."

Heading down stairs, Lillian explained to Carolyn that on the far northern corner of their land was a small cottage that they were thinking about selling. "It's a nice little place, but Anna and I won't have time for it and we hate seeing it just sitting there, neglected. Now that I've taken a look around and have an idea what we have ahead of us, I can see that selling it would be the thing to do. The money from the sale would help defray the costs. Carolyn put a hand on Lillian's arm, thinking out loud, "Maybe Julie and I would be interested in buying the cottage Lillian. We have been talking about looking for a little hide-away to escape to. You'll have to show it to us." Lillian thought it was a wonderful idea and couldn't wait for them to see it. She knew they would fall in love with it, just as she and Anna had.

They were about to join Anna and Julie in the garden when they heard a car horn announcing Connie and Jamie's arrival. "Hey guys," Jamie greeted them as she bounded up the porch steps catching them both in a big hug. Connie was right behind her waiting for her kisses and hugs. They wanted to know right off what they found behind the locked door, but Lillian said they would have to wait until they hooked up with Anna and Julie so they could all take the tour together. Walking out back to the garden where Anna and Julie were working, Lillian and Carolyn were amazed at the transformation that had already taken place, telling Connie and Jamie it looked a hundred percent better than it had just a couple of hours ago!

As Anna lead the way, conducting the tour around the garden, Julie lagged behind, catching Carolyn's hand, "You are not going to believe what Anna showed me," Julie told her, her voice filled with excitement. "Come on!" Still holding Carolyn's hand, Julie led her out of the garden and down a tree-lined path where she came to a stop before a small footbridge. The bridge led over a rushing brook that ran through the property. Standing there, Carolyn's eyes followed the path beyond the bridge and saw a little cottage nestled in the trees. Carolyn thought, 'This must be the cottage Lillian was talking about.' She started to tell Julie that her and Lillian were just talking about the cottage, but decided to wait and see what she had in mind. Still holding Carolyn's hand, Julie led the way over the bridge and down the path to the cottage steps. Giving Carolyn's hand a squeeze, she said, "Lets go in!" Following Julie's lead, Carolyn stepped inside and liked it right away. Julie immediately saw beyond the dirt and clutter and pointed out the big flagstone fireplace that took up one whole wall in the big room they had just entered. There was a fairly good size bedroom with a small wood stove and glass doors that led out to a garden similar to the one at the big house. They saw a big, open kitchen with plenty of cabinets and shelf space and a tiny room off to the side, which was probably a sewing room at one time. Watching Carolyn as she looked around, Julie held her breath as she said, "Anna told me they were thinking about selling this, what do you think?" Carolyn stood looking around, "I love it Julie, but it's going to take a lot of work to fix this up. What about electricity and plumbing?" Julie felt her heart sink, "It doesn't have either, but we could work on it…couldn't we?" Carolyn didn't say anything at first, prompting Julie to finish her sales pitch. Julie's voice raced on, "Carolyn just give it some thought. We don't have to fix it up all at once. We could just work on it a little at a time. This could be our retirement home, and in the meantime we could use it on long weekends and vacations." Carolyn had to laugh as she raised her hand to slow down Julie's rush of words. Carolyn's smile was the only answer that Julie needed; she caught her in her arms and gave her a big 'thank you' kiss that surprised Carolyn so much she couldn't catch her breath. When they finally stopped laughing, Carolyn asked facetiously, "So what do you think, did you say you liked it?" Still giggling like schoolgirls, wrapped in each other's arms, they left the cottage and headed back to the farm where they caught up with the others as they were finishing their tour. They were just in time to head to the kitchen for a cup of Julie's chili.

Chapter Ten

Cathy ran to phone and answered breathlessly, "Hello? Oh Ronnie! Are you through work yet?" Ronnie could hear the excitement in Cathy's voice. Feeling bad she said, "No Cathy, I'm running a little late, I'm really sorry. I have a girl out tonight and I need to find someone to cover her shift. In the meantime I have to stay on the front desk." Cathy knew Ronnie was in administration at the hospital, but didn't really know what it entailed. Cathy could hear the disappointment in her voice, so she tried to stay upbeat, "That's not a problem for me. I could use the extra time to get some last minute things done." Ronnie replied, "Look Cathy, don't feel you have to wait for me, I wouldn't mind if you went on to Maine…" Cathy interrupted her, "I wouldn't think of doing that! I would rather wait and go with you." Ronnie was quiet for a moment, and then said, "You know Cath, I think I'm falling in love with you." When Cathy hung up she knew her face was bright red and she began talking to herself. 'I'm not good at this,' she thought. 'What a fool I am! Here we are, on the verge of spending some real time together, she tells me she's falling in love with me and all I can say is 'Oh?' Maybe I should call her back, but what will I say?'

She finished packing and thought about what she would say if she called Ronnie back, but then decided to wait until she came by to pick her up and just let things play out. As it turned out, Ronnie was going to be a lot later then she had thought. Calling Cathy again she urged her to go ahead, telling her she would drive up as soon as she could. But by then Cathy already had other plans, "Ronnie, it's alright, really, I just saw the traffic report and I think it would be a better idea if I make us a late dinner and you stay here tonight. We can leave tomorrow morning instead." It was Ronnie's turn to say, "Oh?"

Ronnie hadn't planed on getting serious again, but when she met Cathy on New Years Eve, it just happened. Ronnie, now in her early forties, had been married at an early age. It only lasted about a year; both were too young to really know what they were looking for in a relationship. After the divorce Ronnie decided to go to college, as she had planned on doing before she got married. She had a good head for business and wanted to learn more about it. During her first year in college she dated a little, but for some reason she had never experienced the excitement or passion her girlfriends always talked about. It had been the same during her marriage, she didn't know what was missing, but she knew there had to be more. She decided to forget about men for a while and just concentrate on her studies.

One Saturday night a few of her friends talked her into going to a party on campus. Ronnie really wasn't into going but they talked her into it anyway. Once she was there she was glad she went; she was having a great time and needed an escape from her studies. She hadn't had any liquor in quite awhile and it didn't take too many drinks before the room started spinning. Making her way outside for some fresh air, she found a bench off to the side and sat down, trying to keep her head still. After a while she began to feel better. Contemplating going back inside and looking for a ride back across campus, she heard a women giggle. Ronnie was sitting in the shadows and couldn't be seen but was able to see two women leaning against one of the big maple trees by the corner of the building. At first Ronnie didn't think too much about them, then she recognized one of the women as Peggy. She had heard rumors around campus that Peggy was a lesbian. She was embarrassed seeing the two women kissing and wanted to look away but there was an excitement stirring in her belly that she'd never felt before. As she continued watching them, she saw Peggy's hands slip underneath the other woman's sweater. She was shocked, not by what they were doing, but by her reaction to what they were doing. She felt her own body responding as she connected with feelings she never knew she had. Spinning around she went back to the party and got a ride back to her dorm.

A couple of weeks later, Ronnie's mind was still in a turmoil, unable to shake the feelings that had bubbled to the surface as she had watched Peggy with the other woman, and admittedly, she was not all that sure she wanted to shake them. She found herself seeking Peggy out on campus, always turning up wherever Peggy was expected to be. Peggy on the other hand was very much aware of the looks she was getting from Ronnie and finally asked her out. It was a brief, but intense affair that opened Ronnie up to all that had been missing in her relationships with men.

After the affair with Peggy, Ronnie met a woman and fell in love. It lasted almost ten years, until one night she told Ronnie she had met some one else. Ronnie was devastated; it was the last thing she had expected. After that she threw herself into her job and eventually bought a small house not far from her work. She dated off and on with several women, but never seriously, until Cathy. She had felt an immediate attraction to her from the moment she saw her. As time went on and she got to know her better, she allowed herself to dream of Cathy during quiet times when she was alone. For the first time in many years, she knew she was in love. Admitting that to herself, she vowed to put the past behind once and for all and move on with her life.

Meanwhile in Maine, Julie, still euphoric after their visit to the cottage, was putting the finishing touches on the chili while Carolyn and Connie set the table. Anna was mixing the dressing for the salad when the phone rang. It was Cathy calling to let them know that they had a change of plans and wouldn't be arriving until sometime Saturday morning. Lillian was bustling around, adding more wood to the fireplace and wood stoves. Jamie had her camera out recording everything on film. She had taken quite a few pictures since they had all started coming to Maine and was planning on giving everyone a photo journal for Christmas this year.

After helping themselves to a bowl of chili, they took their seats around the old wooden table in the kitchen, but before they could take a bite, Karen and Nancy arrived, loaded down with fresh bread they had made before they left. "Hey, just in time," Connie said as she helped them in. Everyone started talking at once, telling the newcomers what they had seen and done since they had arrived at the farm that morning. Above all, they were all excited about being together in Maine once again. The meal was long and leisurely with everyone content to just relax around the table making plans for the following day.

With some prompting from Connie, Jamie told everyone about Susan showing up at her door last night. Karen and Nancy were surprised, but didn't say anything. They had just talked to Susan the other day and she had told them she how she felt about Jamie, but she hadn't said anything about pursuing it. In fact she was more concerned with how she was going to handle her husband. He was looking to renew their relationship this weekend at his family's camp. They were sure Jamie didn't know anything about it, and they weren't about to be the bearer's of bad news. Jamie felt a little better after talking about Susan, even though nobody could give her any real advice, except to say, "Go with your feelings."

As they were finishing their meal, Nancy asked if anyone had heard from Cathy? "Yes," Anna answered, "she called earlier saying Ronnie had to work late so they wouldn't be able to leave until tomorrow. But," she added with a smile, "I don't think Cathy was too upset about it. I think she had plans for them later." "Well," said Karen, "I'm happy for her. She wouldn't get involved in a real relationship until her son was out on his own. It's about time she started thinking of herself." They all agreed with that.

As they continued their plans for the weekend, Lillian spoke up saying, "After we finish the work around the house and garden, Anna and I want to take everyone sight-seeing Sunday. There's a quaint little town just down the road that we think you'll find very interesting." Before she could continue, both Julie and Carolyn said in unison, "We drove through there this morning!" Carolyn explained. "Julie and I took the long way up this morning instead of taking the interstate. What a beautiful little village, with so many shops to explore, I can't wait to go back there." She held up her hands in amazement and continued, "I couldn't believe how many people were milling about on the sidewalks and into the street." "But," added Julie, "as we started noticing the people, we saw lesbian women, just like us, holding hands or just walking with their arms around each other right out in public. Gay men too and no one even seemed to notice, except us," she laughed, "we were gawking at them like we had never seen anything like that before." More serious now she said, "Funny thing though, there were families with young children among them as well and everyone just blended in together." Connie spoke up, "Yeah, I heard about that place. I've always wanted to go there. I didn't realize we were so close. Well isn't this going to be an interesting weekend?"

Chapter Eleven

Saturday morning, Cathy opened her eyes to find Ronnie looking back at her. Cathy had to laugh, "I take it you've been waiting for me?" Ronnie answered without hesitation, "All my life." Although they were both looking forward to meeting up with everyone in Maine, they weren't anxious to leave their new found intimacy. They would be driving up today, but not just yet.

At the farm everyone was up early in the morning as usual. After enjoying a big breakfast together, they split up into two groups to tackle the work ahead of them. Julie, Anna and Nancy headed to the garden shed to see what they could find for rakes and hopefully a wheel barrel. Carolyn, Lillian, Karen and Jamie headed to work on the house, while Connie flittered back and forth between them, helping out wherever she could.

Karen took on washing all the windows, including the glass doors. Connie and Jamie removed all the bedding and pulled the mattresses outside in the fresh air. Lillian and Carolyn swept out the dust and cobwebs that had collected in the old rooms. Lillian came across boxes and boxes of bed linens and handmade quilts, all in good condition, although very musty smelling. They would just need a good washing and airing. Connie found an old clothesline that needed to be re-strung, which she did while Carolyn started the wash. After all the rooms were stripped and swept out, Jamie and Connie began washing down walls and floors. Karen joined in and helped them when she was done with the windows. It was mid afternoon before they all took a break for lunch, but it was short lived, everyone was anxious to get back to work and finish the major workload before the day ended.

The bedding Carolyn and Lillian washed and hung out came back soft and fluffy with a fresh, clean air smell. One by one the rooms were put back together. All the boxes were removed and stored upstairs until Lillian and Anna had a chance to go through them. As small as the rooms were, they looked cozy and inviting. The pictures were back on the walls and the beds were made up fresh, each with a bright, cheery hand made quilt draped over them. Jamie was the first to lay claim to a room for her visits and Connie was quick to follow, claiming hers. Carolyn said she and Julie were fine with the sunroom off the kitchen, so Karen laid claim to the room across from Jamie, leaving the last room for Cathy and Ronnie, if they ever showed up.

It wasn't until two o'clock in the afternoon before Cathy and Ronnie finally emerged from the apartment. Cathy wanted to stop by the deli and pick up a couple of sandwiches that they could eat on the ride up to Maine. She had been pretty busy lately with Ronnie and hadn't had much time to think about Carol, but as they turned into the parking lot she felt a sadness come over her as she remembered the last time she had seen her. Ronnie picked right up on it, her voice was full of concern, "Cath, are you all right?" Cathy replied, "I guess I'm feeling a little guilty, I haven't given much thought to Carol lately. I hope she's alright." They sat in the car for a few moments talking about Carol until Cathy said, "Well I guess there's nothing I can do but pray she gets some help." Ronnie squeezed her hand just to let her know she understood. Cathy returned the gesture, "I think I'm feeling bad because I'm so happy. I wish she could find someone like you." On a more upbeat note she said, "Now let me get those sandwiches, I'm starved!" As she walked into the Deli, she couldn't help looking over at the empty booth she and Carol used to share. She wished she could have been more of a help to her. She paid for her order and headed out the door, her thoughts on Ronnie waiting in the car, when she heard a soft voice calling her name. Turning around, Cathy's bag fell to the sidewalk as her hands flew to her mouth.

Chapter Twelve

Nancy, Anna and Julie continued their work in the gardens, raking and cutting down the old vines that seemed never ending, but all in all, things were beginning to take shape. Slowly it was becoming the beautiful extension of the old farmhouse that it once was. As they worked, they uncovered an intricate network of old paths that eventually linked everything together. Like a maze, they led the follower from the house, to the barn, to the tractor shed and on to the tool shed and the old chicken coop, then through the gardens back to the main path behind the house. The old garden shed was of great interest and in relatively good condition. It had a wall of windows where seedlings could be started in early spring. They found three old benches that were stored in the back under mounds of junk. With great effort, they pulled them out cleaned them up. One needed some repairs and they put it back until another time. Setting the other two benches in the garden they stepped back to admire their work. They decided it was a nice touch. While they had accomplished a lot, there was still plenty left to be done.

After checking on each other's progress, it was time to call it a day and start the grill for supper. Connie and Jamie had brought steaks for everyone and Carolyn had made potato salad earlier in the day. Karen and Nancy were working on shucking the corn they had bought at a farm stand, on the ride up. After seasoning them with salt, pepper and butter, they carefully wrapped them back in their husks and set them in the grill to roast. The cool night air kept everyone from eating outside, but no one minded; the fireplace and wood stoves filled the house with a warm glow. As usual the meal went on for some time with everyone talking excitedly about what they had found and how much work had been done so far. They were a "mutual admiration society" giving credit to each other for the tasks completed. Carolyn and Julie were especially excited this evening and couldn't stop talking about "their cottage," as they now referred to it, now that they had agreed to purchase it. They all made plans to take a tour of the little village tomorrow and were eagerly looking forward to that. With all the camaraderie and good feelings between the couples, a deep sadness and longing for someone to share her life with, came over Connie. Not wanting her mood to cause a downer for anyone else, Connie excused herself after dinner, saying she was going for a walk. Anna gave her a flashlight to take with her. Jamie asked, "Connie, do you want some company?" Connie declined, "No thanks, I won't be long." Jamie caught a glimpse of the sadness in Connie's eyes and went over and gave her a quick, hard hug. After Connie left, Anna, picking up on Jamie's concern, asked her if everything was all right. Jamie, looking after Connie with a frown, didn't hear her at first. "Jamie dear," Anna was quick to put her hand on her arm, "Jamie, what's wrong?" "Oh, Anna I'm sorry. Connie's missing Jean. I just feel bad for her."

Connie was missing Jean. Even up here away from the familiar places, she could feel her presence. It started about a month ago, Jean coming into her mind so strong it felt as if she were standing beside her…if only she were, but no sense thinking that would ever happen, it was becoming apparent even to her that she was not to be in Jean's future. During her walk, Connie came upon a knoll with a big Oak tree on it. In the moonlight she could see the new buds coming out after a long winters nap. Connie stayed for a while feeling a kinship to the tall oak, standing alone.

Jean was confused about how she should feel. There had been many changes in her life since she had sobered up; she wasn't complaining, she was happy with the way things were working out. Now that she was on her own, she had gained confidence in herself, feeling strong and healthy, greeting each day with anticipation. She excelled at work and eventually was responsible for setting up the art shows. She had even started painting on her own again, something that had always just come natural for her. Her boss, Ted, had told her that she had real talent for art. Jean wasn't sure if he really meant it or was just trying to score points with her. She knew from the way he looked at her that he was attracted to her. He had asked her if she was in a relationship and she told him no, but quickly added it was her choice. Her life was complicated enough right now without adding him to the mix. He hadn't brought up the subject since and she was happy about that; she liked her job and didn't want his interest in her to conflict with it. She liked things just the way they were. Aside from that, things were going remarkably well. She was amazed at the progress she was making with her kids and she felt they were beginning to trust her to be there when she said she would and to be sober. They were happy to see her now, feeling relaxed enough to be themselves and not treat her like company. Even her ex-husbands were friendlier and more considerate of her, allowing her more time to be with the kids. Best of all, she was having fun with them, listening to their banter, laughing at their jokes. It was a good time in her life, one she could only dream of just a few months earlier. But, there was one draw back; something Jean hadn't given any thought to before, though she should have. She saw that her kids were happy with their lives the way they were. Their fathers were doing a good job raising them; they were great kids. Jean was beginning to realize that her hopes of having custody one day wouldn't be the right thing to do. Seeing how happy they were, how could she expect them to leave their homes, their friends and their lives? Right now their visits were great, but would it remain the same if she tried to get custody? She had to ask herself if they would end up hating her if she tried to get them back. She didn't know the answer and felt she needed to talk to Carolyn. She decided to call her office and see if she could get an earlier appointment this week. She had come to admire and respect Carolyn's courage to live her life the way she did and was grateful that she had someone as capable as her to turn to when having to make difficult decisions. Carolyn had allowed Jean to see past her 'professional demeanor,' and get to know who she really was because she knew it would help Jean get back on track. For this Jean would be forever grateful. She picked up the phone and called Carolyn's office. The receptionist told her Carolyn was out of town for the long weekend, but she would make her an appointment for Tuesday afternoon. After she hung up, she made a cup of tea and put her feet up to relax.

Connie flashed in her mind again, only this time she didn't try to shake the image, 'Yes,' she thought, 'everything is working out good for me but there is one other thing…I wish I could see Connie again, but wouldn't she just send me away?'

Connie came back from her walk to find everyone sitting in the living room, enjoying the crackling fire that Lillian was tending to. She grabbed a cold beer on her way in and found a spot on the couch beside Anna. "Did you have a nice walk dear?" "Oh yeah," she answered, "You guys are so lucky to have this place." Anna replied, "Thank you dear, and please know that you'll always be welcome here. Now tell me, have you heard anything from your friend Jean?" She saw a flicker of sadness in Connie's eyes, "No Anna, I haven't, but for some unexplained reason, I'm still hopeful that will change." Anna and Connie continued to talk about Jean while Carolyn, lying on the floor with her head on Julie's lap, pretended to be asleep, not wanting to be drawn into the conversation. She couldn't add anything to it and she honestly didn't know if Connie would ever see Jean again. It wasn't long before she did fall asleep. It had been a very physical day, not at all what she was used to, yet she had enjoyed every minute of it.

Chapter Thirteen

Carolyn awoke quickly from Julie urgently shaking her shoulder, "Carolyn wake up!" When Carolyn looked up she saw Cathy and Ronnie entering the room supporting someone between them. Whoever it was seemed to be hurt. It dawned on Carolyn right away, 'This must be Carol.' Everyone sprang into action as if they'd done this many times before. Anna immediately set about getting her a cup of tea which, she muttered more to herself than anyone else, had medicinal qualities and would help calm and sooth her. Connie gave Carol her seat on the couch and someone got a blanket and a pillow to rest her head on. While Carol didn't know anyone or even where she was, she immediately felt comforted by their nurturing and concern for her. Cathy caught Carolyn's eye as she sat down next to Carol on the couch and nodded towards the kitchen. Carolyn reached for Carol's hand and gave it a gentle squeeze, "Carol, I just want to check on that tea Anna is making you. I'll be right back but in the meantime; I want you to sit here in front of the fire and just relax for a little bit. We are all here for you so please, just concentrate on your own needs for the moment," then she motioned to Julie to take her place beside Carol, "Julie will tend to you and get whatever you need."

Anna was in the kitchen making the tea when Cathy and Carolyn came in. She turned to them and said, "Cathy, don't you think she should have gone to a hospital? She is obviously in pain and she may have some serious injuries." Cathy was understandably upset, "We didn't know what to do. We tried to talk her into going to the hospital but she wanted no part of it. We couldn't let her go back to her..." Carolyn stopped her with a wave of her hand, "Of course Cathy, you did the right thing, but we need to make sure she's alright." Anna spoke up, "Perhaps after she has some tea, we'll get her into a hot tub." Carolyn said, "Yes, that's a good idea Anna, now let's bring her that tea." Turning to Cathy, Carolyn saw how stressed she was. She stopped and put her arm around her and said, "Don't worry Cathy, I'm sure she'll be fine. Come on now, she'll probably have to be rescued from being helped to death in there." Cathy had to smile in spite of the situation. By the time they had everything under control, it was close to eleven o'clock. The tea and the warm fire did a lot to help Carol relax. Anna asked, "Carol dear, why don't I run a hot bath for you? I'd say we're about the same size so I'll find something for you to sleep in." Anna had said this in a very matter of fact way, so there was no room for any argument. While she prepared the bath, Jamie went into the room she had set up for herself and removed her things. Finding Anna in the bathroom, she said, "Anna, let Carol sleep in my room, I'll crash on the couch." "Thank you dear, that's very thoughtful of you," she said, giving Jamie a kiss on the cheek. "Now, everything's set in here. Would you let Carol know her bath is ready?"

Cathy and Anna helped Carol into the bathroom. Anna excused herself to look for something for Carol to wear, thinking she would be more comfortable with only Cathy in the room. Cathy tried to keep her emotions in check as she helped Carol out of her clothes, but it wasn't easy. She was horrified at all the bruises she saw before Carol slipped into the bath. Cathy asked again if she was all right, "Yes," she answered, "I'm okay and thank you." After a few minutes of silence as her aching body was comforted by the warm water she spoke again, "Cathy?" "Yes," Cathy answered as she pulled up a chair beside the tub. Carol kept her head down to avoid eye contact, "I don't know what to say, everyone's being so nice…" Carols eyes began to tear. Cathy reach over, cupping her face in her hands, "Its alright honey, you don't have to say anything, believe me, we're all glad we can be of some help." A soft knock on the door announced Anna's return, "I have a nightgown and a robe that I think you'll be comfortable in. I even found a pair of slippers for you. Is there anything else I can do?" Anna kept her voice light but Cathy saw shock flicker in her eyes as she noticed the bruises on Carol's breasts. Cathy answered, "No thank you Anna, I think we're all set for now." "Well then I'll leave you to your bath and there's a room all set up for you down the hall. I hope you sleep well my dear." Anna bent down pressing her cheek to Carol's, "Please try to have a good night."

As Anna made her way to the kitchen, she couldn't stop the flow of angry tears. Lillian was on her feet and by her side as she entered the room, "Anna, are you alright?" Anna laid a hand on Lillian's arm, "Yes Lil, I'm just so angry and disappointed that anyone, especially another woman, could abuse someone like that." "We all feel the same way Anna," Julie said standing up to pull a chair out for her. Carolyn added, "There's more of it going on then people realize." "That's right." Julie said, "I see a lot of it in my work too." Ronnie agreed shaking her head, "We see it in the emergency room all the time, women coming in all beat up, but mostly from men, although I've seen a few women that I'm sure were victims of other women. The sad part for them is no one knows how to handle it. Most programs are not sympathetic to lesbian women." Carolyn nodded in agreement, "Your right, I have a few clients that I'm working with and I'm sure the only reason they're allowing me to help is because I can relate to them. I'm sure there are more women out there that could be helped but have no where to turn." Karen said, "There should be a safe house where gay women can go for help." They all agreed with that. Jamie asked Carolyn, "What can we do to help Carol?" Carolyn told her, "Well, I would like to admit her to the clinic where she would be safe until we found out more about her situation, but from what Cathy says, she would refuse any help like that." Nancy said, "She's probably too ashamed and embarrassed to let people know what's going on." "Well," Anna spoke thoughtfully, "She could stay here with us, couldn't she Lil?" Lillian said, "Of course she can Anna." And then she asked, "But doesn't she need professional help?" Julie answered, "Yes she does and once the bruises go away, she may not be so reluctant to seek counseling." Anna looked at everyone around the table, "She has more bruises than you can see." "She's right about that." Cathy said, as she entered the room and stood by Anna laying her hand on her shoulder. Ronnie spoke up, "How is she Cath?" Cathy shook her head, "Well, between the tea and the hot bath, I think she'll sleep okay tonight, but Anna's right, there's more then you saw. She has been battered frequently

139

by the look of her. There is hardly a place on her body that doesn't have welts and bruises." Carolyn asked Cathy, "Should she go to the hospital?" "I don't think so, she is pretty banged up, but nothing appears to be broken…except her spirit." Cathy went on to tell them about the bruises on her breasts, her back and even on her arms and legs. They were all outraged to think that a gay woman could treat another woman like that. Connie stood up and began pacing the floor, "I had no idea this was going on, I wish there was something I could do to help." Cathy began to apologize again for bringing Carol with them but everyone interrupted her saying, "You did the right thing!"

Carol, lying in a strange bed in unfamiliar clothes, felt like she was in a dream state, not sure what was going to happen from here. Although she couldn't understand what they were saying, the sound of voices coming from the kitchen was comforting to her. It wasn't long before she fell into a deep sleep.

Jamie, along with everyone else, found it hard to sleep that night. 'I thought I had problems,' she thought, but nothing compares to what Carol has been going through.' She hoped things would turn out good for her in the end. Then her thoughts went back to Susan, remembering how good it felt to hold her in her arms. Comforted by that thought, she finally fell asleep. It had been a long day for all of them.

Chapter Fourteen

As Jimmy rolled off Susan and turned to go to sleep, Susan couldn't keep the tears from spilling down her face and onto her pillow. She had tried to ignore his advances all evening, knowing what he had in mind, but when it was time for bed, there was no way out. There had been no response from Susan, which reminded him why he had stopped making love to her in the first place, but he didn't care. Susan had to clench her teeth to keep from screaming when Jimmy removed her nightgown.

After a restless night, Jamie decided to get up early and get into the day. She wanted to see what she could do to help Carol. Thinking she was the only one up, she very quietly gathered her clothes and took them with her into the bathroom for a quick hot shower. All dressed, she headed for the kitchen to get the coffee started, but the aroma wafting through the house told her someone had already beat her to it. Nancy and Karen were in the kitchen getting breakfast started. "Good morning," Jamie whispered, "I didn't know anyone else was up." Nancy replied, "We haven't been up long." Karen added, "We thought we'd get up early and make breakfast for everyone." Jamie said she would lend a hand after she had her coffee. They talked awhile about Carol, hoping she would be all right.

The smell of fresh coffee and the biscuits baking in the oven found it's way through the house. It wasn't long before everyone was up and hungry, including Carol, who to everyone's amazement, looked much better. As soon as she sat down they began piling food on her plate until she had to hold up her hands in protest. Connie couldn't help but laugh, which was highly contagious; it even brought a smile to Carol's bruised face. Breakfast went on smoothly with everyone talking and making plans while including Carol into the group. The conversation stayed light; they just wanted Carol to feel relaxed, not pressured into talking, unless she wanted to. It was a good way for her to get to know all of them. She kept her eyes on her plate, feeling embarrassed and unsure of herself. Gradually she began to feel the energy of the women surrounding her. She liked listening to them share their thoughts and ideas with each other, their voices strong and confident. She was sure that none of these women would ever allow themselves to be in a situation like she was in. They talked about anything and everything, but the only thing they didn't talk about was their visit to the village they had planned for that morning. Of course Carol wouldn't want to go and they certainly weren't going to go off and leave her behind all alone. Cathy, knowing of their plans, brought up the subject and said very diplomatically, "Ronnie and I know you all have plans later, but if you don't mind we'd just like to stay here and putter around." She looked at Carol, "Later on with Carol's help, we could cook that turkey dinner Anna had planned for tonight." She also thought if she and Ronnie had some time alone with Carol, she might want to talk.

After the table was cleared and everyone was ready for a second cup of coffee, Jamie commented that it was too nice to stay inside and picked up her coffee and headed for the porch. Following her lead, the others did the same. Cathy hooked her arm through Carol's and followed along. Jamie patted the seat beside her on the porch swing for Carol. Sitting down, Carol took a deep breath then quietly told everyone how grateful she was. Anna spoke up, "Carol dear, there's no need to thank anyone, we're happy to be of help." Anna walked over and gave her a motherly hug, adding, "Dear, we all feel as if we know you." Carol looked a little confused. Cathy leaned forward in her chair facing Carol and she explained what Anna meant, "Carol, I had my suspicions about your relationship with Liz for some time. I didn't know what to do, so I discussed it with my friends to see if they could advise me on how I could help." Carol's eyes began to widen. She looked around at all the faces, "You knew…you knew all along?" Carolyn could see that this was a lot for her to absorb, along with everything thing else that had happened, and told her, "Carol, we just want you to know that we care, and that we all want to help." Carol, unable to think of any thing to say, took Cathy's hand and gave it hard squeeze.

No one was anxious to leave the porch. It was a beautiful Maine morning. A gentle breeze was blowing, bringing with it the fragrance of Lilacs that were just in full bloom. For a change everyone was quiet, lost in the scented air and their own thoughts. After a while Connie stood up stretching, "Well, I don't know about the rest of you, but I'm ready to do some sight-seeing." She turned to Carol giving her a wink, "I just want you to know that I'm saving my appetite for that turkey dinner." Carol smiled at her. Nancy looked at her watch; "It's almost noon time already! I guess we should get going if we want to have time to see everything." Everyone agreed. The eight of them, chatting about taking in the sights, piled into two cars and headed down the road, waving goodbye as they left. Back on the porch, no one appeared to be in any hurry to do anything but enjoy the tranquil feelings that engulfed them. Carol, swinging gently on the porch swing, let her mind drift with the sounds around her. The rustle of the leaves brought to life by the gentle breeze along with the chirping and calling of the many birds, lulled her into a relaxed state that she had not experienced in a long time. It wasn't long before she was dozing in the warm sun. Ronnie and Cathy tiptoed off the porch so not to wake her and agreed it was good that she get as much rest as she could.

"Carol?" she heard Cathy call her name as she woke from her nap, "I'm going to make some lunch. Would you like a chicken sandwich and a glass of ice tea?" "Yes, that would be nice. I must have dozed off, I'm sorry, can I help?" she asked starting to rise out of the chair. Cathy gently stopped her by putting her hand on her shoulder, "I'm fine Carol, and there is nothing to be sorry about, I'll be back in just a minute." Carol felt shy around Ronnie at first but Ronnie set her mind at ease just chit chatting until Cathy returned. As they ate their lunch, Carol wanted to know more about everyone. She tried putting a face with the names and she was getting pretty good. She was quiet for a moment before speaking again, "I'm glad to be here. I don't know what else I could've done." Cathy told her, "We're just happy we were there for you. We both feel it was meant to be." Ronnie spoke up, "Cathy's right, it was more then just a coincidence." Carol gave them a brief smile and then changed the subject, "Shouldn't we be making a turkey dinner?" she said light heartedly. "Oh, your right!" Cathy said, "We'd better get going." Ronnie said she would start the turkey while Cathy and Carol cut up the vegetables. Cathy said, "After we're done we should all go for a walk and get a better look at this place."

In the village, the women were having a ball on their outing. They had parked their cars in the municipal lot and joined the throngs of people walking on the sidewalks, taking in the sights and sounds of the small resort village. Everyone, with the exception of Lillian and Anna, were surprised at how close the farm was to the ocean, "This is wonderful," Karen said, adding, "you guys have the best of both worlds here!" Anna suggested they have lunch and then start at one end of the village and work their way through to the other end so they wouldn't miss anything. She guided the small group to a delightful little outdoor café that she was sure they would all enjoy. During lunch, they enjoyed watching as gay women and men passed by on the sidewalk, walking arm and arm or holding hands with their partners. While they were not familiar with each other, the passerby's seemed to recognize that they all shared a secret between them and they smiled and nodded to them as they sat eating their lunch. "This place is great, I love it!" Jamie said, as she nodded back. She even smiled back at a few of the winks that were sent her way. As much fun as they were having, they hadn't forgotten about Carol. They decided to pick out some clothes for her while they were shopping. They knew she would probably feel uncomfortable with them buying things for her, so Anna said she would put them in her bureau and just give her a couple of things when they got back.

While Carol was helping with dinner, she noticed a shared look that was special between Cathy and Ronnie and that a touch tended to linger. Sensing that theirs was a new love unfolding, she was sure they would like some time alone. "There," Ronnie announced, "the turkey's in the oven and should be ready around six." "Good," said Cathy, "Carol and I are just finishing cutting up the vegetables. It's too early to start them, so lets go for that walk." Ronnie said it was fine with her, "I'm looking forward to it. How about you Carol, are you ready for a walk?" She replied, "If you don't mind, I think I'd like to lie down for awhile." Cathy was quick to ask if she was all right. She assured them she was fine, just a little tired.

As soon as she was alone and lay down on the bed, Carol felt the tears begin. Everyone was so nice, but she needed to figure out what she was going to do. She was still in love with Liz and all along she had hoped things would go back to the way it was when they were first together. Instead things just kept getting worse. Liz just became more and more angry as time went on. She would explode in a fit of temper over the littlest thing, blaming everything on her. Carol remembered back to a time during their first few years together when Liz was so kind and gentle. She was always thoughtful and considerate, before their age difference became a problem. Liz was twenty years older than Carol, and in the beginning it wasn't an issue. She was in good physical shape, never feeling or looking her age, and then she got sick. She'd had a battle with pneumonia that had severely damaged her lungs. It completely changed her lifestyle. She was no longer robust and ready to tackle everything. As time passed she became angry and distant, convinced that Carol would end up leaving her for a younger woman. As much as Carol tried to reassure her that all that mattered to her was their being together, Liz didn't believe her. She believed that Carol pitied her, and that's when the beatings started.

Ronnie and Cathy were surprised and delighted to find themselves alone. After a long walk around the farm, they took a bottle of wine and a blanket out on the front lawn and relaxed in the afternoon sun. Cathy, relieved that Carol was finally safe, asked Ronnie her opinion, "Ron, what do you think about Carol, do you think she'll go back with Liz?" Ronnie pondered a moment as she opened the wine, "Cath, I really don't know the answer to that anymore than you do. I certainly hope not! No one should be in a situation like that. I have to say it really surprises me how much of this abuse is going on. I know one thing for sure, if Carol stays around this group, its bound to have a positive effect on her.

Driving back to the farm, everyone in the sight seeing party was in high spirits. They were all looking forward to a turkey dinner with good conversation about their latest adventure. Nancy and Karen were particularly animated after Lillian took them to the village bakery. They loved the place and bought some bread and a couple of apple pies. Nancy told everyone excitedly "It's a small shop, just like ours and can you believe this, the owner is thinking about selling it! When she found out that we had a bakery in Boston that we were thinking of selling, she thought it must have been fate that brought us together today. Maybe she's right! Karen and I are going to stop by and see her on our way home tomorrow." Julie asked, "Are you thinking about buying it?" Nancy shrugged her shoulders, "Well it wouldn't hurt to find out more about it. Karen and I haven't really settled on what we're going to do with our bakery and we're still looking for a place to move." Karen said, "That's right, and we've both fallen in love with Maine. This may be our answer." Pulling her car up to the front door of the farmhouse, Jamie was the first one out, bounding upon to the porch and into the house, "Oh God, it smells great in here!" she exclaimed in a theatrical voice. "Hold it," Cathy said laughing, "we're not ready yet. We just took the bird out of the oven so it will be a while longer, but we have some appetizer's set up in the living room." One by one they looked for Carol and found her in the kitchen helping with the preparations for supper. As they hung around her making sure she was okay, she rewarded them with a shy smile and a warm hug.

In the living room Ronnie had set up a couple of trays of crackers and cheese along with a couple of large, chilled, bottles of wine. Jamie sat down in a big comfortable, overstuffed chair, reached for her huge camera bag and got busy unloading the film from her camera. Carol's interest was sparked immediately, "Jamie," she asked, "Could I look at your camera?" Jamie had spent a lot of money on her equipment and as it was the only way she earned her living, she usually didn't let anyone handle it, but seeing Carol's eyes light up that way, she was more than happy to hand it over to her. Carol was properly impressed and told Jamie so, making her glow with pride. She had always been interested in photography, but Liz had never let her pursue any interests of her own. As everyone settled down with the munchies and wine, they regaled Cathy and Ronnie about their afternoon adventures while Jamie showed Carol how to use the camera and before long Cathy called out that dinner was ready. After a succulent turkey dinner, they retired with coffee and desert onto the back porch and began showing off the treasures they had bought, along with gifts for Cathy, Ronnie and Carol. In addition to the tee shirts they had bought for the three of them, they bought Carol a couple of sweatshirts and pants for those cool Maine nights. Carol thanked them all, "I don't know what to say, you all have been so kind, thank you." Anna said, "Well dear, you are very welcome. Now…these poor souls," she said indicating to everyone sitting around her, "have to head back to reality tomorrow, but Lil and I are staying here until Saturday. If you'd like, your more then welcome to stay with us, it would give you some time to plan on what you are going to do." Carol hesitated a moment before answering, "Yes, that would be wonderful, I'd like that, thank you." They sat out on the porch laughing and talking until the sun went down and the chill night air drove them back into the living room to bask in front of the warmth of the fireplace. It was well past midnight before they finally called it a day and went to their rooms.

As tired as they all were, once in bed their minds wouldn't shut down. Karen and Nancy were talking about the little bakery in the village. Carolyn and Julie were talking about the cottage they had decided to buy and Jamie was thinking about Susan. Connie didn't stay awake long. Two very busy full days, along with the sleepless nights she had spent thinking about Jean had finally caught up with her and she fell into a deep sleep. Lillian and Anna were exhausted. It had been a full weekend and they were pleased with all that had been done around the place. They were happy that Carol planned on staying with them for the rest of the week. It felt good to be able to help someone in need. While everyone else was sleeping or pondering their thoughts, Cathy and Ronnie were quietly making love in their room.

Chapter Fifteen

Carol was the first one up. She hadn't slept very well. Her mind kept screaming at her, 'Now what are you going to do, fool? You don't expect these people to take care of you forever, do you?' Listening to her own thoughts, she shuddered, she sounded just like Liz…and what about Liz? In just a few short days, under the influence of her newfound friends, she had found the dignity, strength and determination to make a better life for herself. 'But,' she thought, "after all these years together, I need to let Liz know I'm alright so she won't be worried about me. She'll work herself into a frenzy and that's bad for her breathing.' The thought flitted through her mind, that even this far away, Liz still had control over her. Old habits are hard to break but she knew she'd never go back to that situation. With a sigh, she sat up in bed and found a notebook and pen in the nightstand, determined that once and for all she would cut the tie that binds. Very quietly, so as not to wake anyone, she put her thoughts to Liz in a letter. Right off, she let her know she was all right, that she still cared about her and hoped she'd get some help, but she wasn't coming back, that much she knew. She had already changed and was no longer that same person who allowed herself to be degraded and beaten. She let her know that she would be back to remove her things from the apartment, but it wouldn't be right away. She told Liz she was planning her future and the life they had shared, was not the direction in which she was going. 'I am, from now on, free-thinking and independent,' she wrote, 'someone you definitely wouldn't want to be with.' In the end she wished her well and reminded her again that she would be in touch sometime. After she sealed the letter and addressed it, she felt a cleansing and sense of relief flow through her very being reaffirming that she was changed. Writing that letter had put that part of her life behind her now and while she still wasn't sure what the future held in store for her, she instinctively knew it could only get better.

Carol decided while she was the first one up this morning, she would start earning her keep. She went to the kitchen, started the coffee and went about making breakfast for everyone. Nobody seemed anxious to get up that morning; they all knew they would be heading back to Boston and wanted to prolong it a little bit longer. Carolyn and Julie, awake in the sunroom, were planning their day. The smell of fresh coffee brought them quickly to their feet and into the kitchen. "Good morning Carol," Julie greeted her, that coffee smells awfully good." Carol looked surprised to see them up so early, "I hope I didn't wake you." "Oh no," said Carolyn, "Julie and I have been awake for a while. We just didn't have the inclination to get up until the smell of that coffee wafted in." Julie went over and poured a cup, "I think I'll take this and head for the shower before the line forms," she said, as she rolled her eyes. Both Carol and Carolyn had to chuckle, understanding just what she meant. Without further ado, they got busy making breakfast, before everyone got up. As they worked together, Carol talked about her relationship with Liz. Once she began reminiscing about what her life was like as Liz's partner, her whole body shuddered as all the pent-up emotions began pouring out. It felt good and once again she felt that sensation of being cleansed. Carolyn saw first hand that Carol had indeed, changed. Exhilarated by their talk, they threw themselves into preparing the 'best damn breakfast north of the Piscataqua,' and it wasn't long before everyone was up and eager to eat, shower and enjoy the rest of their time in Maine.

After breakfast Karen and Nancy were the first to leave. They had to get back and get things ready to open the bakery in the morning. They hated leaving so early but they wanted to stop in the village and check out the bakery one more time. Cathy and Ronnie weren't long after that, wanting to beat the heavy traffic heading south. Cathy spent some private time with Carol before leaving and felt comfortable that she would be all right. Carol thanked her for being there and said, "I still can't believe you knew what was happening between me and Liz all along." Cathy then told her about the time she saw her at the shopping center, covered with bruises. Carol looked at her in astonishment that Cathy had been waiting all this time just to help. She just put her arms around her and held on tight. After they left, Carolyn and Julie, along with Lillian, walked down to the cottage. Lillian wanted them to see all the land that went with it. Julie couldn't have been more excited. She was talking a mile a minute about the renovations they had planned to make. Carolyn was excited as well but the best part for her was seeing Julie so happy.

Connie and Jamie weren't in any hurry to leave. Connie had nothing to go home to and Jamie wanted more time to think, she was still confused about whether to pursue a relationship with Susan. While they remained behind after the others left, they wanted to help out by doing some more repairs around the house. Remembering Carol's interest in the camera, Jamie struck up a conversation with her. Jamie loved her camera but she handed it over to Carol with complete trust that she would not misuse it. She said "Carol, take a walk around the grounds and shoot whatever catches your eye." She wanted Carol to go off by herself so she wouldn't be distracted or inhibited by her. After Carol went on her way, Jamie went over to the old barn where Connie and Anna were. Walking in, she heard Anna saying "Oh dear, Connie that's awfully heavy! I don't want you to hurt yourself." "Hey," said Jamie, "I'm here to help. Let me give you a hand with that." "Jamie," Anna said, "that old trunk is heavy! Be careful both of you that you don't get hurt! I would never forgive myself!" Jamie waved her aside and grabbed the leather strap on the side of the trunk and pulled it out of the way. "Great!" Connie said, "I needed that out of there so I can fix these shelves for Anna." Anna replied, "That will be a big help. Neither Lil nor I are very good with tools but I suppose we'll have to learn." "Well," said Jamie, "I'm pretty handy. Is there anything else you need fixing?" Before Jamie knew it, she had a screwdriver in hand and was replacing the hinges on the smaller barn door. From then on, Anna kept them busy with what seemed like an endless list of repairs. They were more than willing to do all they could to help out and as the day wore on, they were beginning to feel that this was their home too.

Walking back from the cottage, Lillian, Carolyn, and Julie ran into Carol. It was encouraging to see the smile on her face and the light in her eyes. Carol clicked off the last picture in the camera, catching the three as they walked towards her laughing at the antics of a couple of chipmunks running to get out of their way. She told them about her interest in photography and how sweet Jamie was to let her use the camera. They thought it was a wonderful, knowing it was good for her to focus on something other than her troubles with Liz. It was coming on lunchtime so they headed back to the farm for some of those delicious turkey sandwiches that Anna had promised. "God," Carolyn said, "it seems all we do when we're up here is eat. I'm going to be huge if this keeps up!" With a chuckle, Julie grabbed her in her arms and said, "That gives me a whole lot more of you to love!" To which Carolyn responded by giving her a menacing look.

Jamie, Connie, and Anna were busy in the kitchen preparing lunch and already had the turkey out, slicing it up for the sandwiches. Carolyn and Julie sat down at the table and began talking about their plans to buy the cottage. They were pretty excited about it and planned to come up to Maine whenever they could and work on fixing it up. As they finished their lunch, bellows of dark heavy rain clouds started rolling in. Carolyn and Julie thought they'd better pack it up and head on back to Boston before the storm hit. They knew the traffic would still be bad at this time of day, but they wouldn't mind, they had a lot to discuss about the cottage. Saying their goodbyes to everyone, they piled their overnight bags and souvenirs in the back seat of their car and headed down the road just as the rain began.

After a beautiful and productive day, it was almost seven o'clock before Connie and Jamie reluctantly decided to head for home. It was hard for them to leave the warmth of the farmhouse for their empty apartments, but all the excuses 'not to go' were used up and besides, the traffic should have thinned out by now. Giving Lillian and Anna big hugs and kisses goodbye, Jamie turned and gave Carol a hug and promised as soon as she got her pictures developed, she would mail them up to her. They waved goodbye to the three women standing on the porch and drove down the lane out of sight.

On the way home, both Jamie and Connie were quite. The rhythm of the windshield wipers lulled them into their own deep thoughts. Jamie's thoughts went immediately to Susan and the night they spent together. Connie was thinking about the bench she repaired and had set down beside the Oak tree on the knoll. As she set it down, she had a strong feeling that one day Jean would be sitting there beside her. At this time though, it seemed impossible; she hadn't seen Jean in eight months.

It was dark and dreary when Connie dropped Jamie off and in the few minutes it took her to reach her own place, the rain had turned into a cold drizzle with the fog rolling in. She pulled into the parking lot behind her apartment building and parked the car. Instead of getting out, she sat for a moment allowing Jean's face to appear in her mind. A sad longing came over her that turned her inside out. She got out of her car abruptly, trying to shake it off. Head down against the wind swept drizzle; Connie made it around to the front of the building. She was startled to see a small dark figure sitting on the steps. Connie took a step backwards then stopped…her breath caught in her throat and Jean's name came out as a whisper. Connie's big smile melted right through the fog into Jean's heart and she knew everything was going to be all right. There's a rhythm that connects two people in love. Connie and Jean experienced that as they ran to each other. Ever so gently, with Jean's face cupped in her hands, they kissed, their tears mixing with the rain.

Chapter Sixteen

Susan had said goodnight to the girls and went into the kitchen to clean up after their late supper. They got stuck in traffic coming back from camp, arriving home, hot, tired and hungry. All they wanted was food, a shower and bed. Jimmy came into the kitchen after the girls went to bed looking for her. Susan stiffened as he approached. It didn't go unnoticed, instead of putting his arms around her he turned and went to his room. She was relieved; she was determined never to sleep with Jimmy again. She was glad there wouldn't be a scene. She wished she had never let it happen. She finished up in the kitchen, poured herself a glass of wine and went to her room to call Jamie. Jamie was glad to hear Susan's voice on the other end of the phone. Any doubts she had about pursuing this relationship quickly vanished.

Back at the farm, Carol said goodnight to Lillian and Anna and made her way to her room. She knew they would probably like some time alone. She had hoped her and Liz could've had a relationship like theirs, but it just wasn't to be. She missed the "old Liz," but she was glad she was able to get away from her. If it hadn't been for Cathy, she would probably still be there. There was no one else to turn to. Thanks to Liz, she had no friends. Her family had disowned her when she told them she was in love with a woman, and she hadn't heard from them since. When she fell asleep that night, she slept soundly for the first time in ages. She knew, some how, this was where she belonged.

A couple of days later, Lillian, Anna and Carol headed into town to do some errands. Carol had told them about the letter she wrote to Liz and she wanted to get it in the mail without delay. Lillian dropped Anna and Carol at the grocery store and went along to the post office and mailed Carol's letter along with some things of her own. She came out carrying a package addressed to Carol from Jamie. She ran into the hardware store for some supplies they had ordered and then picked up Anna and Carol at the grocery store. Carol climbed in the back seat and before Lillian could tell her about the package, she had it in her hands. The two women observed how wide-eyed and childlike she was as she opened it. In that instant they felt a deep sadness within themselves; the thought of anyone being abused for so long, the way she had, struck a cord way down deep and they knew then that they would do all they possibly could to keep her from going back to her tormentor. Inside the package was a photo album with her pictures, a note from Jamie taped to the back of the album, along with a camera that she didn't use any more. Jamie wrote that she thought the pictures were very good, telling Carol she had a good "eye" with a camera. She added that she particularly like the picture she took of Carolyn, Julie and Lillian, catching them in a shared moment of laughter. Carol was shocked; she had never been praised by anyone for anything she had ever done. Even as a child growing up, her parents never took enough interest in their kids to know where their talents may lie. They were too busy fighting with each other; there hadn't been room for anything else.

Chapter Seventeen

Carolyn and Julie were finding it hard to get back into the swing of things, especially now that they were the proud owners of a home in Maine. They knew that they would be at the cottage most weekends and holidays and what fun they were going to have making it their home away from home. Already Julie was planning the flowers she wanted to plant and she had plenty of ideas for landscaping the grounds and the area around the bridge. Carolyn was more concerned with the repairs that needed to be done. The cottage itself seemed in good shape, but it needed wiring and plumbing before they could stay there, so that was the first priority. They would also need a phone installed. It was going to be an expensive project, but together, they were financially well off and it wouldn't be a burden on them. It was something they could do gradually.

Karen and Nancy were envious of Julie and Carolyn. They had fallen in love with Maine as well. They did a lot of daydreaming and envisioned themselves in the new bakery. After all, they both agreed, "We are at a time in our lives that calls for a change, are we not?"

Susan dropped the girls off at school and headed over to Jamie's. She had managed to see Jamie almost every day since she got home Monday night. She had a radiant smile on her face as she pulled up in front of Jamie's apartment. Never before had she felt such passion, her body had never felt so alive!

Lillian and Anna awoke to the smell of coffee and bacon coming from the kitchen. Carol had taken it upon herself to take over most of the household chores. They told her it wasn't necessary, but she needed to feel useful and she was a big help to them. She turned out to be a terrific cook and they enjoyed having her around. She had begun opening up to them as the days went by. She talked a lot about Liz. It seemed to release the heavy burden she had been carrying around. Lillian and Anna saw a big change in her. She was energetic and had a bright bubbly personality and she loved the sights and sounds of the farm. She even made friends with the two elderly sisters that lived next door. It seemed everyone that met Carol was enchanted by her endearing personality.

As good as things seemed to be going, Lillian and Anna felt it was time to talk to Carol about her plans, if she had any. They had discussed between themselves the idea of letting Carol stay on at the farm as a caretaker. She seemed to love it and now that she had made friends, she wouldn't feel alone up here. "Besides," Lillian and Anna assured each other, "We will be up here almost every weekend from now on, getting ready to move in the fall." When they approached Carol with their idea, she couldn't have been happier, she loved the farm and had never felt as free anywhere else, to be herself.

Now that the decision had been made for her to remain at the farm, she asked Lillian and Anna how they felt about cats. "We love them dear but they don't allow pets in the building where we live. As soon as we move up here for good, we plan on getting a couple of cats and a flock of laying hens. The chicken coop is in need of a good cleaning and some repairs first, though." "The reason I asked about the cats," Carol continued, "the cat next door at the Sister's place, had a litter of kittens and they're looking for homes for them. Now that I'll be here to take care of them, I'd love to have a couple of them, if it's all right with you." Without hesitation Anna said, "I think it's a wonderful idea! Could we help pick them out?" "Sure," Carol replied, "let's go over there now and get them. Without further delay they all went next door and over a cup of tea they picked out two adorable kittens they named Micki and Maude.

That night in bed Lillian and Anna lay awake talking. Anna was glad Carol was staying on at the farm. She had a feeling Carol would not only be a big help to them, but the experience would help her grow into a strong individual. Anna was not an overly spiritual person but she always felt a strong sense of spirituality from this land. Everything seemed to become more alive and stronger here. She believed Carol could only benefit from being in these surroundings.

The next morning as they prepared to leave, they hated the thought of leaving Carol up here by herself, but in their hearts, they knew she would be fine. Lillian had made sure the phone was hooked up earlier in the week so they could all stay in touch with her. Cathy and Ronnie bringing Carol to the farm that night had brought all of them closer together. Helping Carol get through her trauma was a common goal they were all a part of. As she helped Lillian and Anna pack their car, she felt tears escape from her eyes. She was sad to see them leave; she had grown very fond of them. She felt as though she had gained the family she had always wished for. Spending this past week together was like none other she had ever known. Unlike being with Liz or even her own family, she was expected to make her own decisions as to what was best for her. She felt she was on the right path.

Chapter Eighteen

When Jean woke up Sunday morning, she stretched out in the bed like a contented cat. Connie was up early, cooking breakfast for her. Jean had been there ever since Connie got back from Maine on Monday evening. Hearing Jean stirring, Connie stuck her head in the door greeting her with that big smile of hers, "Breakfast is ready Madam," she announced, "and just in case you forgot, we have a busy day ahead of us!" Connie was up early in anticipation of picking up Jean's belongings from the halfway house and moving them over to her place, permanently. After that, they were going over to Lillian and Anna's for a big spaghetti feed. Everyone was going to be there and she couldn't wait for them to meet Jean. Connie was on cloud nine even though she was exhausted. Between making love with Jean most of the night and spending the rest of the time waking up every hour or so to make sure she was still there, she hadn't had much sleep this past week. For her part, Jean had no intentions of leaving, ever.

Lillian and Anna were busy preparing dinner and eager to see everyone. Cathy had called earlier to cancel out, saying "Anna I'm afraid we can't make it today. It's my fault, I thought we were going to Ronnie's family cookout next week, but it turns out to be this week. I'm sorry, we were so looking forward to seeing you." Anna replied, "You will both be missed, but it sounds like thing are progressing." "Yes they are." Cathy said, sounding very happy, "Ronnie is a terrific person and I'm crazy about her. Anna while I have you on the phone, we've talked to Carol a couple of times this week and she sounds like she is settling in okay, but what do you think?" Anna told Cathy she thought Carol was doing wonderfully and during the past week, while they were with her, she talked about her relationship with Liz, "She is trying to put the past behind her and focus on the future." "Yes," said Cathy, "she told us about the letter she'd written to Liz." "That's right," Anna said, "I think it gave her some closure." Before Anna could continue the doorbell rang. "Sorry dear, but I have to run…everyone is arriving now. We'll talk again later." And with that she headed for the door to greet their guests.

On the ride over to pick up her things, Jean was unusually quiet. Connie could tell she was nervous about meeting everyone. Reaching over and pulling her close she said, "Honey, just relax, they're going to love you." Jean wasn't so sure about that. She assumed they all knew the story about her walking out on Connie and she was ashamed and embarrassed about it. She thought, 'They must think I'm awful to have done something like that to Connie.

Pulling up in front of the boarding house where Jean had been living, Connie vowed to herself that this would be the last time that she would ever have to live like this. From now on she would love, protect and care for her and see to everything that she would ever need. Jumping out of the car in a flash she said,"Come on, lets' get your things out of there and bring them home where they belong!" Jean couldn't resist Connie's smile. Together they entered the house and packed up her few belongings. Connie took them down to the car while Jean said her good-byes. She had got to know the staff pretty well these past months and wanted to let them know that they had made a difference and she would be eternally grateful that they were there for her. She told them, "Thanks to everyone here and at the detox, I am employed, confident and sober and for the first time since beginning treatment, I truly feel that I am going to make it. 'Secretly, she knew it was because of the love she had found with Connie but she didn't voice that to anyone there. She did notice that Connie had received a few curious looks from the staff, which brought a smile to her face. She didn't offer any explanation other than introduce her as 'my good friend Connie.' Jean's only regret was that she took so long to be with Connie, but she knew she had to get herself turned around before she could accept her and realize just how much she meant to her. She thought, 'Absence really does make the heart grow fonder, at least in our case.' Her thoughts were interrupted as Connie came back upstairs and called out to her, "Jean, it's getting late, we really have to get going or we will miss lunch." "Yes, well I guess we have be on our way!" Jean said to everyone, giving hugs, and promising to stop by for tea. Once in the car she slid over as close to Connie as she could get and took her hand squeezing it hard causing Connie to laugh uproariously. All of her fears were put aside as they shared a kiss and then proceeded to head over to Anna and Lillian's place.

Carolyn and Julie arrived for dinner about the same time as Karen and Nancy. Carol was on everyone's mind and they were anxious to hear how she was doing. They all had talked to her on the phone and she sounded great, but they wanted to know what Lillian and Anna thought after being with her all week. They reassured everyone that Carol was doing way better than expected and then changed the subject to Connie and Jean. Carolyn let them know that Connie and Jean were finally together. Jean had brought Connie along with her to her weekly appointment and as to Carolyn's observations, "Jean was radiant and Connie was ecstatic. Things are looking good for those two."

While they were talking, a knock on the door announced their arrival. Anna swung open the door to find Jean standing close to Connie, holding on as tight as she could. "Oh dear," Anna cried, "Please come in and don't be intimidated by any of us, we're all harmless!" With that she threw her arms around her and gave her a great big hug. With that introduction, Jean's nervousness vanished as she was engulfed in hugs and greetings from everybody waiting to meet her. Gasping for breath she threw Connie a kiss as she was led away. Connie was grinning from ear to ear as she watched Jean being welcomed into the group. She just loved the way she moved, the way she carried herself. Jean had so much style and class, just the opposite of herself.

Amid stories and plans for their next get together in Maine, the afternoon went by too quickly, as it always did when everyone got together. The dinner was delicious, and yes, much to Connie's delight, everyone loved Jean. The only disappointment Connie felt was that Jamie wasn't there. She had really wanted her to meet Jean, but other than that it had been a perfect day. Anna and Lillian offered as an explanation for Jamie's absence, that since she had come back from Maine, she had become totally involved with Susan. Much to everyone's disbelief Jamie had fallen in love, but they weren't sure it was it a good thing for either one of them.

Carolyn and Julie were the first to leave, telling Lillian and Anna they would see them on Wednesday. They were meeting at the bank to pass papers on the cottage. Connie stood up then, taking Jean's hand in hers and said, "I think we better head home too. We still have to unpack the car and we both have to work tomorrow." Connie loved saying the word home; it had a whole new feel to it and Jean felt the same way.

As they were walking to their car, Jamie pulled up behind them. "Connie, hey, I hung around waiting for Susan to call, but..." getting out of the car she noticed Jean. Connie could see the appreciation in Jamie's eyes. Grabbing Jeans hands in her own, Jamie good-naturedly asked, "Now how did someone as beautiful as you end up with old Connie?" Jean blushed shyly and said, "I'm just lucky I guess." Jamie laughed with a wink to Connie, "Good answer!" Connie couldn't have been prouder. The three of them talked for a bit and then waved a goodbye. Watching them get into their car, Jamie was happy for Connie and a little envious, wishing her and Susan could be together like that. She was going to stop up to say hello to Lillian and Anna, but thought better of it, thinking they were probably tired. She would give them a call in the morning. The reason she was so late arriving was she had waited for a call from Susan, but she didn't hear from her. Jamie was in love with Susan, there was no denying that, but she wasn't used to being kept waiting and she wasn't sure how long she could put up with it.

Chapter Nineteen

Jimmy hadn't approached Susan since that night at his family's camp. It had been over a week now and he was working late every night. He hadn't wanted to wake her when he got in, but tonight would be different. He planned on being home early and surprising her with flowers. He had a romantic evening in store for them.

Susan woke up Monday and called Jamie to explain why she hadn't called on Sunday, "I'm sorry Jamie but Jimmy's family came by." As they were talking Susan's mother stopped in for a visit. Susan told Jamie she would call her later. Hanging up, she pictured Susan in a family scene with her husband by her side, 'Can I deal with this?' she thought, 'This situation is exactly what I have always tried to avoid and for good reason.' Jamie also knew it would be hard to walk away.

By the time Susan's mother left it was too late to go to Jamie's and she missed her. She hadn't seen her since Friday morning. She began thinking about a way to see Jamie that night. The thought came to her that Jimmy had been working late all week and tonight shouldn't be any different, so she began planning a rendezvous for that evening. She called Jamie and told her she had a plan to skip out and would be over tonight, adding, "I can't wait to see you." Jamie was thrilled and went right out and bought all the fixings for a romantic dinner.

Carrie and Jen had mentioned a movie they were dying to see. When they arrived home from school

Susan told them she would drop them off with their friends at the show and pick them up later, if they wanted. Of course they said, "Yes," and ran to the phone to let their friends know." When it was time to go Susan called upstairs to the girls, "Come on, it's time," she said. She had showered and spent extra time on her hair and clothes, hoping Jamie liked what she saw. The girls noticed right away how pretty she looked. Carrie asked, "Are you meeting Dad or something?" There was that jab of guilt, "Oh no honey, I just took a shower, that's all."

Backing out of the driveway Susan was chatting and laughing with the girls. She knew she would be with Jamie in about a half an hour and she was full of anticipation for the evening before her. Then she heard Jen say, "Hey mom wait, there's Dad!" Susan's heart sank. Jimmy pulled up along side of them and got out carrying the flowers he had for her, "Hey, where's everybody going?" Susan was in shock; this was the furthest thing from her mind. She couldn't speak or meet Jimmy's eyes, but no need, the girls filled him in. "Great," he said, looking at Susan, "Why don't I go with you and we can have dinner somewhere until the show gets over?" What else could she say but, "Yes, of course, that would be nice." Susan slid over as Jimmy got in behind the wheel, handing her the flowers, "Here, I thought you would like these." "Thank you, they're lovely." The girls started giggling at the show of affection. Jen said, "Dad doesn't Mom look pretty? She must have known you were coming!" Susan wanted to scream.

After dropping the girls off, Jimmy leaned over and hugged her as he asked, "Is Italian good with you?"

"Sure Jimmy that would be fine." Her voice came out flat, no emotion, no life, it caught Jimmy's attention, "Susan are you alright? You haven't said a word since I got in the car, in fact, you seem disappointed to see me." Susan still couldn't meet his gaze, instead rubbed the back of her neck, "I have a headache, that's all." He looked at her with a frown, "Well that came on pretty fast, when I drove up I saw you laughing with the girls." Susan told him, "Maybe I just need something to eat." Once at the restaurant Susan was anxious to get inside and keep Jimmy from paying too much attention to her. It was obvious what he had in mind, but she knew she wasn't going to sleep with him again. Some how she would have to deal with that later, but at that moment, all she could think about was Jamie. Somehow she had to find a way to let her know she couldn't make it. Susan's whole being cried out, 'Why did things have to go so wrong tonight?'

They were seated at their table and Susan, sitting directly across from Jimmy, was being closely scrutinized for a reaction, while he continued his questioning. He knew something was up and he wanted to know what it was. "Jimmy," Susan said as she got up, "would you order me a glass of wine when the waitress comes over? I have to go to the ladies room." She picked up her purse and left before he could say anything else. As soon as she was around the corner, she made her way to the phone booth. As Jimmy was ordering her wine, a couple they frequently socialized with, came over to the table to say hello, "Well, we haven't seen you in awhile," Jimmy said standing up to shake Tom's hand and to greet his wife Barbara. Then asked, "If you haven't eaten yet, why not join us? Susan's here with me and she should be right along." "Yes," said Barbara, "we just saw her using the phone."

Jamie hung up the phone and sat back in the chair, clearly disappointed, but if it helped any, she knew Susan was too. She couldn't help but wonder what Jimmy was around for. According to Susan she usually didn't see him much but lately he seemed to turn up a lot. Oh well, there was nothing she could do about it and rather then sit there feeling sorry for herself she poured a glass of wine and called Carol in Maine. They could talk cameras.

Once back at the table, Susan was relieved to see that Tom and Barbara were joining them for dinner. With a relieved sigh, she thought, 'That should keep Jimmy from paying too much attention to me.' By the time they had finished their dinner, she had drank more wine than she should have, but she didn't care. Jimmy tried to make a joke out of it, but she ignored him, talking kids to Barbara. When it was time to go get the girls, Jimmy had to help Susan walk out of the restaurant. He held her arm to keep her from stumbling as they walked to the car. When they reached the car, his grip got tighter as she tried to pull away. Opening the door he shoved her inside. Susan assumed his anger was due to her drinking and she really didn't care until he swung her around in the seat to face him. "Who did you call?" Susan just shook her head, not understanding at first. This time his voice grew louder, "Back in the restaurant, who the hell did you call?" Susan's face went white and her head felt like it would explode. She opened her mouth to speak but instead she threw up all over herself, barely missing Jimmy.

He let out a yell and raised his hand as if to strike her, then thinking better of it, he walked away, leaving her sitting there. By that time she didn't care what was happening, she slumped back in the seat with her head thrown back. Disgusted and confused, he got in the car and drove home, not saying another word to her.

Once they arrived home, he half carried her into the house and snarled at her as he pushed her into the bathroom, "Go clean yourself up! I'm going to get the girls and I sure don't want them to come home and see their mother drunk on her ass!" With that he stomped out to his car and left. He was gone long enough for her to take a shower and regain some composure. By the time the girls saw her, she was feeling a little better and sitting up in bed. They were anxious to see if she was all right. Jimmy had told them she had a stomach virus. They stayed with Susan for a while telling her about the movie before going to bed.

She didn't see much of Jimmy after that. He left for work early and came home late. When they did run into each other, he was brief and cold. It made her feel uncomfortable. She felt bad about the way things had turned out, but she couldn't change anything now, she was in love with Jamie and couldn't give her up. In three more weeks school would be letting out for the summer and the girls would be at the lake for couple of weeks with Jimmy's parents. She planned on spending every minute of that time with Jamie.

Chapter Twenty

Another weekend was fast approaching. Carolyn and Julie had met with Lillian at the bank and passed papers on the cottage. Now that it was officially theirs, they couldn't wait to start fixing it up. The first project to be tackled was the plumbing, then the wiring. The fireplace was also in need of repairs; they wanted it fixed-up right off so they could use it. At least the kitchen stove was okay and all it needed was a good scrubbing. At first they thought about replacing the old stove, but it belonged there. It was a part of the cottage and they would just have to learn to cook on it. Carol had found someone in the area to do the work for them and they were meeting at the cottage on Saturday morning.

Late Friday afternoon they packed their car full to the roof with cleaning supplies and headed to Maine. Lillian and Anna were leaving Boston as soon as they got out of work, so they all expected to arrive about the same time. Carol called earlier to see how many were coming, she planned on having dinner ready for them when they arrived.

Carol had accomplished quite a bit during her first week on her own and she couldn't wait to see what Lillian and Anna thought of her handy work. It was a little lonely up there by herself but the sisters next door were good company and the kittens, Micki and Maude kept her entertained. The elderly sisters had asked Carol if she would be interested in a job two or three days a week doing housework for them. They explained that they were getting too old to lift anything heavy and they couldn't climb up on chairs anymore to get at the cobwebs that were getting out of hand. Carol was more then happy to accept. Lillian and Anna had left her money in case she needed something, but she didn't feel right using it. They had given her enough already. As she busied herself in the kitchen, preparing the evening meal the kittens played between her feet, pulling on her shoelaces. They were such a joy, their antics kept her amused as they ran and played, following her everywhere. Liz still crossed her mind every now and again. 'It's strange,' she thought, 'after all I have gone through, that I still have feelings for her.' She didn't feel bad about leaving, she knew it was the best thing she could have done for herself. She would never go back.

When Lillian and Anna arrived, Carol and the kittens were on the porch waiting for them. They were both surprised and happy to see how well she looked. There was no sign of the bruises or the sadness that had surrounded her just a few weeks ago. Carol was ecstatic to see them and after hugs all around, she eagerly helped them unpacked the car, chattering non-stop.

It was six thirty and still light out, although the sky was beginning to darken as an approaching storm came in. No one minded, they could use the rain and it would be a good night to use the fireplace, which Lillian loved to do. By the time the fire was started, Carolyn and Julie arrived. It would be a while before they could stay at the cottage but they didn't mind, they liked their little room off the kitchen. They found Carol and Anna in the kitchen checking on dinner, "Oh Carol", Julie exclaimed, "you look so pretty!" Carolyn agreed. Carol blushed and thanked them. Julie and Anna picked up the kittens and went into the living room to enjoy the fire. Carol followed with a tray of crackers and cheese for everyone to snack on while Carolyn poured a glass of wine for each of them.

Cathy and Ronnie couldn't make it this time, but promised everyone they would be up next time. Karen and Nancy were arriving tomorrow, as were Connie and Jean. Jamie wanted to go up but she had a photo shoot to do and didn't know how much time it would take. Carol hoped Jamie could make it. She enjoyed their talks on the phone and wanted to pick her brain some more on photography. A cold rain had settled over the old farmhouse, but they didn't mind. They were warm and cozy in front of the fireplace, and were looking forward to the delicious meal they could smell cooking in the kitchen.

Dinner turned out to be awesome. Carol made homemade baked beans, baked ham and coleslaw. She was a wonderful cook, explaining that was all she had to do when she was with Liz. She spoke openly now, sure and confident in herself. Carol was emerging as a strong, self-sufficient woman. After dinner they settled down in the living room in front of the fire just enjoying each other's company. They all stayed up pretty late, talking and making plans until finally calling it a night. They had a lot planned for tomorrow and wanted to get an early start. Carol especially wanted Lillian and Anna to see the progress she had made on the chicken coop.

The next morning after breakfast, the rain stopped, but according to the weather report, it was only temporary as there was a tropical storm moving up the coast. It didn't dampen anyone's spirit; in fact it added a little excitement to the atmosphere. As they sat on the porch finishing their morning coffee and enjoying the balmy tropical air being pushed up from the south, Connie and Jean drove up. Jean came around the car as Connie got out, slipping her arm around her waist. Anna stood up to greet them, "My, we didn't expect to see you so soon!" Jean gave Connie's waist an affectionate squeeze, "She had me up at the crack of dawn!" Connie chuckled, "I know, I guess we should have come up last night. I don't know why we didn't," she said as she embraced Anna in a big hug. Anna liked Connie; there was something strong and comforting about her. As she received her hug from Connie, Anna asked, "Are you two hungry?" Jean answered, "Oh no, we already stopped for breakfast, but thank you anyway," Jean extended her hand to Carol, "Hello, I'm Jean." Carol took her hand in both of hers, "And I'm Carol, it's nice to meet you." Carol couldn't get over how attractive Jean was, and those deep blue eyes, it was hard to look away. Connie turned towards Carol, "Hey look at you! You look terrific Carol! I can't get over the change! I'm really happy for you." Carol laughed as she replied, "Thank you, my life certainly has changed for the better!"

Carol was anxious for everyone to walk around the farm to see the changes she had made and as soon as they finished their coffee she asked, "Well before the rain starts again, would anyone like to take a walk?" Lillian had to laugh, "Yes Carol, we would love to!" Then turning to Connie and Jean, she said, "Carol has been anxious to show us around. Would you two like to join us?" Connie answered, "That's fine with me."

Jean spoke up, "I would love a tour, its just beautiful here." Connie turned to Carol and said, "Okay, lead the way!" Carolyn and Julie followed along with them. They wanted to take the cleaning supplies down to the cottage before the rain started again, but couldn't resist Carol's persuasive smile. Jean was glad they were staying around for a while. Carolyn put her at ease with the others. She enjoyed being around Carolyn on a social level rather than just doctor/patient and she really liked Julie as well. She could see that they were a good match for each other.

As they left the porch, Carol took the lead and everyone fell in behind her. They were amazed at how much yard work she had done. All the old branches that had been lying around for years were stacked into neat piles for kindling. Everywhere they looked they saw Carol's touch. As they continued their walk the wind began to pick up and the tropical air was soft and caressing; it felt good. Jean kept putting her face up in the wind and taking in deep breaths of fresh air, she loved it and Connie loved watching her. Carol had accomplished a lot, but what she was most excited about was the chicken coop. Rounding the bend next to the barn, they came upon the coop. "Carol, I'm amazed!" Lillian said, and meant it. "I can't believe you did all this." Anna came up and put her arm around Carol's waist, "It's a miracle!" Carol was beaming. Everyone but Jean knew what it looked like before and they were all impressed. Carol had repaired the fencing on the outside, re-hung the doors that had fallen off and finished it off with a fresh coat of paint. The inside was just as much a surprise. Everything had been put back the way it had been in the past; with the nest boxes filled with fresh hay all lined up in a row waiting for the hens and clean cedar shavings covering the floor. "Well," Lillian said to Anna with a wink, "I guess all we need now are the chickens." Everyone laughed as Anna said with a knowing smile, "Carol, you wouldn't happen to know where we could get some baby chicks, would you?" Carol laughed out loud, "Yes, as a matter of fact I do." She had found some chicks for sale at the local feed and grain store. Anna said, "Well what are we waiting for? Let's go get them before the storm starts!"

Connie had planned on taking Jean into the village for some sight seeing and lunch. She felt they should get going if they were going to before the weather changed. Carolyn and Julie said it was time they got started as well. They got in their car and headed for the cottage to start unloading. Julie had made a picnic lunch for them so they could stay at the cottage for most of the day and get some work done without having to leave at lunchtime. They were meeting with the electrician at eleven o'clock, but the plumber wouldn't be in until next week. It was ten thirty when everyone went their separate ways, promising to see each other at suppertime.

Carolyn and Julie were just getting out of their car when the electrician pulled up. Carolyn went in with him while Julie started bringing in the cleaning supplies. The electrician looked the job over and gave them a price they were happy with, saying he would be able to start in a few days. After seeing him off they decided to take advantage of the blustery, balmy air and opened all the windows and doors to air the place out. With that done they began cleaning in earnest. The

179

rain held off a lot longer than they expected and at two o'clock they stopped for lunch and headed to the brook with their picnic basket. Julie spread the blanket as Carolyn began taking out the food. "And what's this?" she exclaimed, holding up a bottle of wine. Julie laughed saying, "Well, I thought we should celebrate, the glasses are on the side." Carolyn poured them each a full glass, while Julie set the food out. Sitting beside the water, they toasted each other, and their future in Maine.

Connie and Jean had a full day and by three o'clock, it was time to head back to the farm. Jean had enjoyed it thoroughly, especially the walk on the beach. For lunch, they bought a couple of take out dinners to eat while they sat on the rocks. The wind was electrifying as the storm came closer, hurling huge walls of water against the rocks. They stayed right where they were until the sky began to darken and they knew the rain was not far behind. When they got back to the farm they saw Jamie's car in the yard but no one was around. Connie figured she had arrived in time to hook up with Lillian, Anna and Carol leaving to get the baby chicks. The wind was intensifying but the rain still hadn't started. Taking Jean's hand Connie lead the way to the knoll on the hill. She wanted to introduce Jean to the old Oak tree she had grown so fond of. Sitting on the bench, Connie told Jean how she fixed the bench and brought it up there so she could just sit, hoping that one day they would be here together, "Just like this." Sitting with Jean nestled in her arms she could have stayed like that forever. Jean thought it was a beautiful spot and was overcome with emotion thinking about Connie, all alone with only the

Oak tree to help heal her broken her heart. The knoll, on which it stood tall, overlooked the farm and it's land. They could even see the roof on Carolyn and Julie's cottage in the distance. A light rain had begun falling, but they didn't mind. Turning to face Connie, Jean said, "I love you and I need to tell you how sorry I am for the way I walked out on you and…" But as before, whenever Jean would try to talk to her about that night, she would cut her off. "I've learned that anything worth having is never easy, and besides," Connie said as she stood up in the rain, pulling Jean to her, "All that matters to me right now is this moment."

As Lillian pulled the car onto their road, the wind had picked up dangerously. Lillian held tight to the steering wheel as she dodged the branches that were being blown around. The weather had changed in a matter of minutes. The rain was coming down so hard they could hardly see. Lillian pulled up to the porch to let everyone out, along with the new brood of baby chicks. Leaving the car in the barn and securing the door, Lillian ran to the house when she heard someone shouting behind her. It was Connie and Jean, "Hey, we're right behind you!" They all landed on the porch at the same time soaked to the skin. While they were changing their clothes, Jamie and Carol set up the baby chicks by the pot-bellied stove in the kitchen, (The nights were still too chilly for them to be out in the coop.) Anna checked the spaghetti sauce that Carol had left simmering on the stove. It smelled wonderful and inviting as they ran in from the storm. After Jean got into some dry clothes, she came out to the kitchen to see if she could be of help. She gave Carol and Jamie a hand getting the food and water set up for the chicks.

She was awed by the little balls of yellow fluff; she had never seen anything like them before. In fact this was a new experience for them all except Lillian, who had seen plenty of baby chicks when she visited the farm as a child. After Jean finished helping with the chicks, she gave Carol a hand with supper. Jean wasn't much of a cook, but she could cut up a salad. Connie and Lillian were busy checking the windows, making sure none had been left open.

Carolyn and Julie got caught up in the raw energy of the storm. Closing the windows in the cottage, they took out their blanket and set it in front of the big window. Knowing they weren't going anywhere until the storm passed, they nestled in each other's arms and finished the bottle of wine.

Back at the farm Lillian reassured everyone that Carolyn and Julie were safe at the cottage and not to worry. It was suppertime and the rain was still pounding on the roof but everyone was comfortable in the old house. Standing together in the kitchen doorway with their arms around each other, Lillian and Anna were enjoying the scene in front of them. The chicks were huddled together under the heat lamp peeping amongst themselves, while Carol was at the sink draining the spaghetti. Connie was setting the table as Jean finished the salad and took the biscuits out of the oven. Everyone was working harmoniously together like one big family. The only one out of sorts was Jamie who was standing alone staring out the window, probably thinking about Susan.

Susan had tried calling the farm around noon, but there had been no answer. She would try again tonight. In another week the girls would be out of school and leaving for the lake. She would miss them but she couldn't wait to spend some real time with Jamie. It was a windy, rainy day and the girls were upstairs with some friends playing a game. While things were quiet, Susan thought she'd get some housework done. She had let things go lately so she could spend her free time with Jamie. 'Oh how I miss her,' she thought. It was hard to concentrate on anything for very long before she would remember Jamie's touch on her skin. She relived all the times she had arrived at Jamie's apartment and quietly let herself in before she woke up. She remembered how she felt, slipping into the bed beside her and feeling Jamie awaken to her now familiar hands. Susan had to literally shake herself loose from all those memories to get the cleaning done. She threw some laundry in the washer then started cleaning the bathrooms. When she got to hers, she was still smiling with thoughts of Jamie running through her mind. She never imagined being in love could feel so good. As she open the cabinet under the sink to get the cleaning supplies, her hand picked up a box of tampons. Suddenly she had a sinking feeling in the pit of her stomach, her breath caught in her throat. Susan's mind began swirling with dates. 'How long, oh God, how long has it been!' her mind screamed trying to remember. She slumped to the floor when she realized she was two weeks overdue.

Carolyn and Julie saw that the wind was beginning to die down and they were losing daylight. It was time to go. They would stop by again tomorrow before they left to go back home. Holding each other's hands, they ran for the car then headed to the farm. Looking out the kitchen window, Carol turned to Jamie and said,

"Jamie, could you set up two more places, Carolyn and Julie are coming." Jamie gave Carol her full attention, "Sure thing." she said, amazed that this was the same woman that came stumbling in here a few weeks ago.

After supper they cleaned up the kitchen. Everyone was enjoying the antics of the kittens that were still caught up in the fluttering action of the baby chicks. Taking coffee and desert along with the kittens, they retired to the living room. Jamie sat down beside Carol on the couch, "I think I speak for all of us when I say that you have made a remarkable change. You should be proud of yourself." Carol looked a little embarrassed with everyone's attention focused on her, but she quickly regained her composure. "Thank you everyone, and I mean that. If it hadn't been for all of you along with Cathy and Ronnie, I don't know what would have happened to me." Carolyn said to her, "Carol, we're all happy we could help. Jamie's right, the change in you is remarkable. I wish I had that kind of result with some of my patients." That caught Carol by surprise, "There are other women in the same kind of situation as I was in?" "Yes," Carolyn said, "I'm afraid so. It's a long process for them to get back their self esteem, that's why we're so amazed by you." Julie added, "She's right Carol, it takes a lot longer at the clinic. I wonder what the difference is." Anna asked, "What do you think Carol?" Carol thought for a moment, "I guess I would have to say it's from all the support you've given me." "Yes, I'm sure that's part of it," Carolyn said, but added, "The clinic has a wonderful, supportive and caring staff, and still…?" Jean agreed with Carolyn on that and told Carol, "They do have a wonderful staff there. Although I was not there for the same reason, I do know they made it a lot easier for me." Julie knew the staff as well, but Carol's case was different. Having worked with battered women, Julie knew the strides Carol made were uncommon, "Carol just give it some thought, maybe sleep on it. There must be something more were not seeing." Carol agreed.

Connie and Jean brought everyone up to date on how things were going with them now that they were living together. Jamie was especially interested in how they handled things with Jean's kids. Jean told her, "To be honest with you Jamie, I haven't introduced them to Connie. I'm still trying to re-establish a relationship with them myself and…," she stopped to take hold of Connie's hand before continuing, "as much as I love Connie, I think things are better this way, for now. When I visit the kids, I go alone. Next weekend they're coming to spend Saturday night with me while Connie will be here in Maine visiting with everyone. It would be nice if things were different but right now they're not." Anna asked Jamie how things were going with Susan. "I'm not sure Anna. This is harder than I thought it would be. I love it when were together, but it kills me when she goes home. I just wish she wasn't married." Jamie finished with a shrug of her shoulders then changed the subject. Turning to Carol she asked, "I plan on being around for most of the day tomorrow, would you like to go for a drive and take some pictures?" Carol was delighted. Jamie told Lillian and Anna that they were welcome to come along but they declined. It had been a busy day and all they pictured themselves doing tomorrow, was working in their garden.

Julie and Carolyn were the first to say goodnight. They wanted to get up early so they would have more time to work on their cottage. Connie and Jean said they would love to see the place and lend a hand. Jamie was helping Carol in the kitchen with the supper dishes when the phone rang. They both jumped and then laughed at themselves. Carol picked up the phone, "Hello, yes, she's right here." Jamie knew who it was without being told and Carol left the kitchen, giving her some privacy. Jamie speaking into the phone as she sat down next to the stove said, "Hi, I was beginning to wonder if I was going to hear from you today." Susan answered, "I did try you sometime in the afternoon, but there was no answer," Jamie, sensing right away that something was wrong, asked, "Susan, are you alright, your voice sounds so flat." Susan cut her off reassuring her that she was fine, "I just miss you and wanted to tell you that I love you." They talked a while longer and Jamie filled her in on what was going on up there and what was planned for tomorrow. Susan let Jamie do most of the talking. It was comforting to hear her voice and she didn't want to take a chance on her finding out that things, quite possibly, may not be alright. By the time they hung up, everyone else had gone to bed and Jamie did the same. At first she laid awake thinking about Susan. She was happy Susan called but she still felt something was wrong. It wasn't long before the sound of the wind and the steady rain beating on the windows had its effect on her, lulling her off to sleep.

Chapter Twenty One

The next morning Carol was the first one up as usual. She had kept the kittens locked in her room last night to ensure the chicks' safety and with persistent mewing, they were demanding their breakfast. Scooping them up in her arms she took them with her to the kitchen and fed them while she started the coffee. Anna popped into the kitchen shortly after Carol to lend a hand with breakfast. As she worked, she couldn't help but notice all the changes happening around her. The kittens and baby chicks were certainly a welcome addition, and as she looked out the window she could see that the gardens were flourishing under Carol's nurturing hands. 'This place has really come to life since Carol arrived,' she thought, 'and just like the gardens she tends, she has blossomed under the spell of this old place as well.' As they worked along together it was apparent that they enjoyed each other's company. Anna appreciated Carol's quick mind and wonderful sense of humor. It was obvious to anyone that took the time to notice, that Carol was happy in her new life with her new friends.

Bounding into the kitchen with Jean right behind, Connie announced their arrival in her usual gregarious manner, "Smells good in here and am I starved!" And then graciously asked, "Can we do anything to help?" "Of course dear." Anna told her, "We could use some home fries." Grabbing a knife from the drawer, Connie started slicing and dicing with a flourish while Jean, getting out of her way before she was mistaken for a potato, got started setting the table. Julie arrived just in

187

time for toast duty while Carolyn and Jamie helped Lillian bring in the wood to have on hand for that night. It was warm enough during the daytime, but as soon as the sun went down, the Maine nights were chilly. They all sat down together and proceeded to polish off a big hearty breakfast. No one lingered long at the table, as they were all anxious to get their day under way.

As soon as they were finished cleaning up the kitchen, Carolyn and Julie took charge of their helpers, Connie and Jean, and led the way to the cottage. Jamie stuck around, helping Carol care for the baby chicks while Lillian and Anna kept the kittens out of the way. Afterwards, Carol went out to the porch while Jamie got her equipment. Finding Lillian and Anna playing with the kittens, Carol asked them if they minded her leaving with Jamie. "My dear child," Anna began with a chuckle, "we are not your ugly step sisters. You don't have to ask us, just go and have a good time!" Carol gave them each a kiss on the cheek and left to find Jamie, who was taking pictures of the baby chicks. Looking up, Jamie caught Carol in her frame and clicked. Carol laughed, "You didn't have to do that." Jamie was quick to say, "Oh yes I did! You look great and," she adlibbed, "being a professional photographer, I have an eye for beauty! Now, are we ready to go?" Carol blushed at the compliment, which was especially meaningful coming from Jamie, and then flashed her an excited smile, "Oh yes, I can't wait!" In the back of Jamie's mind she pondered the thought that it would have been nice and certainly less complicated, if it had been Carol that she had fallen in love with instead of Susan. On the way out, they stopped to say goodbye to Anna & Lillian. Jamie told them not to make supper as she was bringing back pizza for everyone. Lillian liked that idea saying, "Well that sounds good to me. Anna and I will make a big salad to go with it. Go on and have fun you two!"

Anna and Lillian enjoyed their day puttering around the gardens. They planted the flowers and shrubs they had picked up the day before at the feed and grain store. Around noontime Anna went in to make some ice tea and sandwiches for lunch and brought them out to the porch. She called to Lillian to stop working and join her there. It wasn't long after they ate and stretched out on their lounge chairs, that Lillian was fast asleep. Yesterday's storm had blown out to sea and was replaced by cool, crystal clear air coming down from Canada. It was just a beautiful day to be outside. Anna didn't feel inclined to doze right away, but rather, was content to sit and take in her surroundings. The trees seemed to be calling to her, wanting her to watch their leaves dance in the breeze. She was filled with a sense of well being, feeling fortunate that Lil and her really didn't have any problems. 'Life had been good to us both,' she thought. Carol crossed her mind; she was doing so well, maybe they could do more to help women like her. It wasn't long after, that Anna too, was sound asleep.

Jamie and Carol were having a grand time driving up the coast. Blessed with a beautiful sunny, clear day, they were finding incredible pictures to take. Together, they had gone through a couple of rolls of film and Jamie was sure she had a few quality pictures that she may be able to sell, but best of all, they were enjoying each other's company. Jamie especially enjoyed discussing her work with Carol. On the professional scene, it was men that dominated the world of photography and the general consensus among those that knew her was that she was just wasting her time. It really didn't bother her what they thought. Jamie knew she was better than just 'good' in her field, but it would have been nice to share ideas. Susan enjoyed going on shoots with her, liking the results when they were developed but it wasn't the same, Carol, like herself, had a real passion for it. Half way up the coast they stopped for lunch and Jamie treated Carol to a Maine lobster. They were having such a great time, laughing and poking fun at each other, Carol thought, 'it just doesn't get any better than this.' After they finished their lunch, they grabbed up their cameras and went for a long walk on the beach. The thought crossed Jamie's mind once again that if it weren't for Susan, Carol would have been nice to fall in love with.

It was almost three o'clock and time to put things away. Carolyn and Julie were grateful to Connie and Jean for all their help. The old kitchen looked wonderful. The only furniture they had decided to leave in the cottage was an old wooden table with some chairs that they just loved and couldn't part with. Just like the old kitchen stove, they just belonged there. With the weather cooperating, the invigorating air gave them a huge amount of energy and they had accomplished quite a bit. They planned next time they came up, to bring the necessary furnishings to finish the kitchen. Julie had measurements of everything, including the area under the sink, and knew exactly what she wanted for curtains. Carolyn thought that was a good thing, as she didn't have a feel for that. Feeling good about what they were able to get done, thanks to Connie and Jean's help, they headed back to the farm ready to meet up with everybody for supper.

Nancy and Karen closed the bakery at one o'clock on Sunday. They were both tired from the busy weekend. They wished they had gone to Maine with the others, but they were planning on going up over the Fourth of July. They were looking forward to taking the whole week off and just relaxing at the farm with everybody, and 'of course', visit the bakery in the village. On the way home they stopped for "Chinese" take-out and a couple of movies. That was all they planned on doing for the rest of the day. Unlocking the door to their apartment they could hear the phone ringing and Nancy ran for it and picked it up. It was Susan asking if they had time for some company, "Of course, we'd love to see you," Nancy told her. Susan said she was on her way. Karen set the table for the three of them and by the time they had everything set out, Susan was at the door.

They welcomed her with open arms. Karen noticed she held on tighter then usual. "Susan," Nancy said, indicating a seat at the table, "Pull up a chair and help yourself." Both Karen and Nancy dug right in; they hadn't had Chinese food in a while. Susan took some, but just enough to be polite. As of late, she didn't have much of an appetite. Sensing something wrong Karen was the first to speak up, "Susan, I'm beginning to think that this is not just a social visit. Did you want to talk to us about something?" Susan couldn't hold back the tears. Nancy and Karen were at her side in an instant. Taking a deep breath she began telling them

191

about the night at the camp with Jimmy and now she feared the worst, that she may be pregnant. And no, she hadn't said anything to Jamie. She had made up her mind that no matter what, she wouldn't let Jimmy near her again and she didn't. She didn't see any need to upset Jamie. How could she ever tell her now? She didn't know what to do. Speaking softly with a tremor in her voice, she continued, "We've been so close lately, it's been wonderful. I finally know what it's like to be in love and now this." Nancy was holding Susan's hand, "Susan, maybe you're late for another reason. You don't know for sure, do you?" Susan shook her head, "No, but I'm never late." Susan paused for a moment, "Maybe your right, my life has gotten so complicated lately, maybe, just maybe..." Neither Nancy, nor Karen knew what to say. Susan was in a real mess if she was pregnant. Nancy said, "Susan, listen to me. I know it's going to be hard, but you need to be honest with Jamie. Just explain it the way it happened, she'll understand, she's grown up a lot since she met you." Karen reaffirmed that, "She's right Susan, Jamie has changed. You need to tell her, you don't want her to find out on her own."

Back in Maine, the pizzas that Jamie and Carol brought back with them were quickly devoured, along with a big salad Lillian and Anna made. After coffee and desert on the porch, it was time for everyone to head home. Jean really enjoyed herself and promised they would be seeing a lot more of her. "More of us," Connie interrupted, putting her arm around her and pulling her close, "Now as much as we hate to, we do have to get going."

Carolyn and Julie were sadly leaving as well. They were both on call for the next couple of weekends but they would be up after that. They would definitely be here the week of the fourth, during their vacation. Jamie left at the same time. Carol said goodbye to her, telling her how much she enjoyed their day together. Jamie smiled saying that she felt the same, and then with a kiss on her forehead, she left. Lillian and Anna stayed awhile longer but finally had to leave too. Carol hated seeing everyone leaving, she really liked the camaraderie they all shared.

Susan didn't call Jamie that night. As much as she wanted to hear her voice she was too upset and confused and she knew Jamie would pick up on it right away. She could never talk about what was bothering her over the phone. She said a silent prayer that it was just stress that had caused her to be late, but instinct told her differently.

Jamie finally gave up on hearing from Susan; she hoped nothing was wrong but still had an uneasy feeling remembering how different her voice sounded on the phone last night.

Alicia Langley

Book Three

Alicia Langley

Chapter One

Anna had been preoccupied since they got back Sunday night and it worried Lillian. Taking her hand, she gently pulled her into her arms, "Anna, I'm starting to worry about you, is anything wrong?" "No dear, everything's fine but I've been wondering…why don't we sit down." Facing each other on the couch, Anna took a deep breath then began, "Lil, we've never talked about what we're going to do once we retire to the farm. Sunday, when we were sitting on the porch after lunch, I was thinking about how lucky we are and always have been. Really Lil, you and I have never had any real problems, our life together all these years has been wonderful!" Lillian nodded in agreement, "Yes Anna, you're right, we have been very fortunate. Now, do you have something in mind to change all that?" Narrowing her eyes in a mock glare, Lillian had just the hint of a smile coming to the corners of her mouth as she thought, 'I know her so well.' Anna continued, "Well then, don't you feel its time we gave something back, isn't that the way it should be?" Before Lillian could answer, Anna grabbed both her hands and held on tight, "I feel so good about Carol, couldn't we help more women that are stuck in a predicament like that?" Anna's voice was filled with excitement. Lillian could feel the passion she was caught up in, "Well, yes Anna, and just what have you been thinking about?" Anna began, "There's something spiritual about the farm. I have always felt it whenever we are there. It gives off a strength that makes me feel I can do anything, I really believe it's a healing place." Lillian shook her head,

197

not in saying no, just trying to absorb all that Anna was saying and feeling. "Anna, believe me, I'm not opposed to doing something to help but what, specifically, do you have in mind?" Anna had a determined look in her eyes, "Couldn't we open something at the farm, on a small scale I mean, nothing too big?" Lillian was so surprised it took her a moment to reply. "Anna, I thought we were moving to Maine to take it easy, do we need to take on that much responsibility just when we're going to retire?" Anna quickly answered, "Lil, it just feels so right." Lillian was quiet so Anna didn't say any more, giving her time to think about what she had said. After what seemed like forever, she turned to her and said, "My dear sweet Anna, it's not that simple! We would have to be licensed and hire a staff; we would need more rooms and another bathroom and that's just for starters. This a big responsibility for us, but I am willing to look into it if it's something you really want." Anna laughed with excitement; she knew Lil's wheels were turning, for she too, knew her so well. She scooted over on the couch and gave her a kiss, but Lil was not to be won over so easily, she held her off at arm's length and continued speaking in a serious tone, "Anna you must understand that we would be making an impact on the lives of many women seeking help, we need to be sure that it would be a positive experience for them and...", Anna interrupted her, "Lil, with all the women around us that are professionals in this field, that might not be as difficult as you may think. We can all get together talk about it and get their opinion." "Okay," Lillian replied, "I'll keep an open mind and we'll see what everyone has to say." They continued talking well into the night, discussing the pros and cons of such a venture, but Anna was not to be dissuaded, she felt it was the right thing to do. In the end they let the matter rest until they had a meeting with everybody in the group.

On Wednesday afternoon Anna got in touch with everyone and asked them to meet her and Lillian at Sally's Friday night. They were all curious as to what she was up to, but Anna remained very mysterious concerning the reason for the meeting. Meanwhile, it had been a few days since she had brought up the subject to Lillian. She was beginning to warm up to the idea, but Anna wanted to get everyone's input, and of course, more information about what this may entail, before discussing it with her further.

Chapter Two

After dropping the girls at school, Susan drove across town to Jamie's. All the way over she tried to rehearse what she would say. She had never been so nervous before, knowing she couldn't bare it if Jamie sent her away. She took a deep breath as she turned the key in the lock and let herself in. It was quiet inside, 'She must be still in bed,' she thought. On tiptoes she went into the bedroom, not wanting to wake her, delaying the inevitable. Afraid she was going to loose the woman that she loved so much, her eyes began filling with tears. She leaned over and kissed Jamie's bare shoulder. Jamie stretched, opened her eyes and sat right up, "Susan, what's wrong?" "Oh Jamie, I love you so much, I just wish things were different." Jamie pulled Susan to her and kissed away her tears. Susan couldn't bring herself to tell her what was really wrong.

Cathy came over as soon as Anna and Lillian walked into Sally's. She was happy to see them; it had been a while. Embracing them in a big hug she had to shout to be heard above the noise of the bar, "I've missed you guys, in fact I've missed the whole gang now that everyone's in Maine every weekend." "We feel the same way," Anna responded, equally as loud. "You and Ronnie need to come up with us." Cathy nodded in agreement, "We were talking about that last night. We are planning on coming up over the fourth and we may even be able to go this weekend." Anna said, "Oh that would be wonderful dear, I know Carol would love to see you both." Cathy smiled, "She's really doing great isn't she? We've talked quite a bit on the phone. She doesn't sound like the same person, she's so happy now. Thank you so much for letting her stay there, I believe it's made all the difference in her." Hearing that, Anna gave Lillian a knowing look. Just then Ronnie walked in and after a big hug and kiss for Cathy, she followed them to their table while Cathy went back to the bar for their drinks. It wasn't long before the rest of the group began trickling in, including a smiling Jamie with Susan by her side. Everyone was glad to see them out together as Susan often couldn't get away. Karen and Nancy figured everything must have been worked out all right with Susan's problem, she looked happy. Anna was quick to pull out a chair beside her for Susan, "Sit down my dear. We haven't seen much of you now that Jamie has you occupied every chance she gets," she added with a wink at Jamie.

Connie and Jean were the last to arrive. After Jean was introduced to Susan, Connie directed her attention to Anna and Lillian, "Alright ladies, we're all here and dying to find out what you have in mind." Anna explained that she and Lillian had been discussing the possibility of using the farm to help battered lesbian women like Carol, but wanted their opinion. Lillian added that they wanted to be realistic about it. "If we can start something like this, it would have to be on a small scale and of course it wouldn't happen until we moved in the fall." Julie jumped right in, "I think it's a great idea! It certainly helped Carol, but we thought you wanted to retire and take it easy?" Anna chuckled, "Retire doesn't mean roll over and play dead. Lil and I will always be involved in something. We've come to realize that we have had a good life these many years together with few, if any problems. This would be a chance to give something back to women who haven't had it as easy as us." Carolyn spoke up, "I think you two are amazing! You guys may be on to something good here. I'm not sure what direction you need to go, but if your thinking of opening a 'safe house,' we need to find out about a license and what regulations and restrictions there may be for such an operation. Maybe," Carolyn continued, looking at Ronnie, "if Ronnie wants to get involved, between the two of us we should be able to get the right information required for a license." Ronnie agreed, "It shouldn't be hard to find out." Jamie spoke up, sounding a bit negative, "Hey, slow down a bit! Are you two sure you want to do this…, not that I don't think it's a great idea, it just seems like a tremendous amount of responsibility. Some of these women may not recover as well as Carol has or for that matter, be as nice as Carol." Lillian answered, "We have thought about that Jamie, but we both feel its something we have to look into."

They discussed the possibilities in detail, even to renovating the top floor of the farmhouse to accommodate four more bedrooms. Maybe the sunroom off the kitchen that Julie and Carolyn use could be made into an office. The more they talked, the more ideas they came up with. The table was in a swirl of energy and animation! They brainstormed until they were all exhausted. As they were leaving, Carolyn and Ronnie promised they would find out more details on Monday and in the meantime, they would be in Maine for the weekend and would talk more about it then.

Anna and Lillian couldn't wait to tell Carol and find out what she thought of their idea. They could have called her but they wanted to wait until they got to Maine so they could see her reaction. It was going to be a great weekend; everyone, except Jean, would be there. She was having her kids over for the weekend and as planned, Connie would be going to Maine without her. Surprisingly, even Susan found that she would be able to make it. Jimmy had left with the girls for the weekend to help his father with some repairs at the camp. Needless to say, Jamie was ecstatic. She had plans and was looking forward to her and Susan finally being able to spend some real time together.

Chapter Three

The next morning Karen and Nancy were up at their regular time, only instead of going to the bakery, they were heading to Maine for the weekend. They were exceedingly curious as to what Anna and Lillian wanted to discuss last night at Sally's but they hadn't been able to go. They had a ton of extra work to do so they could be "closed" for the weekend. They would just have to wait until they got there to find out what was going on.

They were not the only ones getting an early start, Lillian and Anna were on the road early as well, full of excitement and ideas. They couldn't wait to tell Carol their plans for the farm! Julie and Carolyn were also getting an early start this morning. They had packed the car last night with everything they would need to furnish their kitchen. As much as they were looking forward to seeing the cottage again, they were both caught up in last night's talk about the "safe house" and couldn't wait to discuss it further with everyone.

Connie loved going to Maine but hated being away from Jean. She agreed with Jean's point of view that it was the best way to deal with the kids at this time so she kept her feelings to herself. Standing in the doorway they heard Jamie and Susan pull up in front of the house. Connie was riding up with them so Jean could use the car if she needed it. Jean promised to call after the kids went to bed and gave Connie a long kiss goodbye. She didn't like being separated from Connie either. She wished she hadn't taken so long to be with her, but she was here now and planned on them always being together.

Lillian and Anna were the first to arrive at the farm. Carol was out watering the vegetable garden when she heard their car coming up the lane. Dropping the hose, she ran to greet them. "I have really missed you two", she said, "I'll be glad when your here for good." Anna laughed, "We feel the same way dear, only three more months to go!" Lillian stood back to get a better look at Carol, "My God girl, you look better every time I see you." Carol blushed. She did look good. Her hair sparkled with red highlights and she had a healthy tan from spending so much time outdoors tending her gardens. She had gained a little weight and no longer had that gaunt appearance she had when she first arrived at the farm. All in all it agreed with her, she looked beautiful.

Karen and Nancy were the next to arrive. Still early, Carol put on a fresh pot of coffee, which complimented the coffee cakes they had made at the bakery last night. They were also surprised by Carol's appearance. What a change since that night she arrived at the farm.

Carolyn and Julie arrived shortly after and were more than ready for the coffee they could smell as they walked into the house. Carol asked if Jamie was coming. She usually heard from her a couple of times during the week, but she hadn't called at all. Julie told her that Jamie was totally involved with Susan now and they were spending a lot of time together. "In fact," Julie said, "You will get to meet her soon, she is coming up with Jamie for the weekend." Anna added that Carol would love Susan as soon as she met her.

Carol didn't let it show, but she was disappointed that Susan was coming. She enjoyed her time with Jamie. More than once since their afternoon together, she had caught herself wondering what it would be like to share a kiss. She knew Jamie was in love with Susan, but…Carol was abruptly brought back to the present when she heard Connie announcing her arrival in her loud boisterous voice as she usually did, "Hey, where is everybody?" Lillian yelled out, "We're in the kitchen." Connie appeared in the doorway with Jamie and Susan right behind her.

Amid hellos and hugs Susan and Carol met for the first time. Susan was quite surprised at meeting Carol. The way Jamie had described her, quiet, meek and "kind of mousy looking," was not at all like the attractive, confident woman that stood in front of her. Susan felt a twinge of jealousy when she saw the way Carol looked at Jamie. Anna said, "Susan dear, is something wrong?" "Oh, no Anna not at all. The place looks so different, you've done so much." "Yes we have," Jamie said as she came up behind Susan slipping her arms around her waist, "Actually Carol's the one that's made the difference around here," she said with a wink to Carol, "she's amazing." Lillian, noticing a little tension between Carol and Susan, thought it was time to change the subject.

Cathy and Ronnie arrived shortly after that. They gathered around the kitchen table talking about Anna and Lillian's idea. Carol was floored because the same idea had crossed her mind, but she was sure it was just wishful thinking on her part. She told them she was all for it and asked what she could do to help. The kitchen was a buzz of excitement and creativity as they exchanged their suggestions and plans for remodeling the house. Before they knew it, the morning was gone. Carolyn and Julie jumped to their feet and apologized for cutting out on them but they had a lot of work to do at the cottage. They said they wouldn't be gone long, and would be back in time to help Carol with the cookout that was planned for later. Jamie and Susan, along with Karen and Nancy, went with them for a tour of the cottage. Connie stayed in the kitchen getting the food ready for the grill. Lillian and Anna took a walk with Carol to see the gardens and baby chickens, which they thoroughly enjoyed.

About mid afternoon the smell of burning charcoal wafted through the air as Connie and Jamie started the grill, turning everyone's attention to the cookout. Before long they were all congregated in the yard. It was the first time they had all been together in quite a while. Susan was having a great time and let go of any bad feelings she had about Jamie and Carol, in fact she decided to make an effort to get to know Carol better. Finding her in the kitchen making a salad, Susan took a knife and sat down beside her. The conversation was strained at first, but the more they talked the more at ease they became with each other.

Jamie noticed that Susan had been in the house for some time, so she left Connie tending the grill and went looking for her. Finding her in the kitchen with Carol, Jamie smiling, touched Carol's shoulder as she walked by, and then bent down and kissed Susan. "Are you two ever coming out?" Returning Jamie's smile, Susan answered, "We're just finishing up." Then she turned to Carol and continued, "This is where Jamie and I met." But before Susan could go on, Jamie let out a groan. "Don't remind me, I was such a jerk that weekend." Susan laughed, agreeing with her. Karen popped her head in the kitchen, "Everything's done and we're ready for that salad!" With that they all headed outside for their meal.

The weather was perfect and remained that way until late in the night enticing everyone to stay outside by the fire long after dark. The conversation stayed focused on the future. As Carolyn and Ronnie were talking, Julie was pondering an idea of her own. Knowing if they went through with this and were licensed, the state would help cover the cost of a staff, including a psychologist, Julie began toying with the idea, 'Why not Carolyn?'

Jamie saw Anna get up and go into the kitchen. Removing her arm from around Susan's waist, she said "I want to see Anna for a minute. I'll be right back." Seeing Jamie leave, Karen and Nancy slid over to Susan. Nancy said, "We were surprised to see you at Sally's last night. I take it everything's alright?" Susan knew what they meant. Making sure she couldn't be overheard she told them, "I couldn't tell her. I tried but the words wouldn't come out." Both Karen and Nancy could see the anguish in her eyes. Karen asked in a hushed voice, "Susan, everything's alright, isn't it?" She whispered, "No."

Jamie found Anna in the kitchen getting a glass of iced tea, "Anna?" "Yes Jamie, what is it?" Jamie replied, "Can we sit and talk for a minute?" Anna, afraid something was seriously wrong, quickly sat down at the table. Jamie said, "Anna, I just want to ask if you're sure about this idea of running a safe house? I worry about you and Lillian. Please don't get me wrong, it sounds like a good idea. Women in that situation do need all the help they can get but…" Placing her hand on Jamie's, Anna stopped her flow of words, "Jamie, how sweet of you to worry, but it's not needed. This was my idea, but both Lil and I have given it a lot of thought. We can see, as you do, that these women are in need help, and we feel a need to be a part of that. It just feels right Jamie." Giving her a warm smile Anna continued speaking, "Thank you for caring, but I assure you that we will be alright. Now on another note, Lil and I have been concerned about you; are you alright?" Jamie was quick to answer, "You mean with Susan?" Anna nodded, "Yes, you've chosen a hard road Jamie, do you think you two have a future?" Jamie was wondering the same thing, "I don't know. We don't talk about the future. Right now we're just taking it 'one day at a time', as they say. I love her Anna and for now I can handle the fact that she has a husband. Knowing they aren't sleeping together certainly makes the difference, and we do get to see each other quite a bit. I have to go along with the way things are, I don't have a choice." Anna understood, "And what about Susan? I can see that she's in love with you but it must be hard on her trying to shuffle between two lives." Jamie looked at Anna, "Now that you mention it, she has been preoccupied this past month. Maybe it's getting to be too much for her. Thanks Anna, I guess its time Susan and I have a talk." Bending down, Jamie kissed Anna's cheek and taking her hand, they went back outside.

It was well after midnight when everyone went to bed that night. Connie gave her room to Jamie and Susan and slept on the couch. Jean called earlier, saying first she missed her and second she was having a good time with the kids. They talked for a while longer, then Jean surprised her by saying she had a special dinner planned for Sunday night when she got home. It surprised her because Jean couldn't cook. The few times she had tried were all disasters. Picking up on her thoughts, Jean told her not to worry and not to eat on her way home. Connie still had a smile on her face when she fell asleep.

The house became still as everyone fell asleep, everyone but Susan and Jamie. Cradled in Jamie's arms, Susan tried to keep her composure, "I'm really tired Jamie, do we have to talk now?" Jamie answered, "I just want to make sure your alright, you've been so preoccupied lately. Is our being together too much of a strain on you?" Susan didn't want to talk, afraid she would blurt out the truth; she would have to tell her soon enough. "I'm alright," she replied, "being with you is never a strain for me, I'm just tired". Jamie was tired too and didn't put up much of an argument before she fell asleep.

Sunday went by quickly. Everyone decided to take a break from making any more plans for the safe house until Carolyn and Ronnie came up with more information. Anna, Lillian and Carol spent all day working in the gardens while Carolyn, Julie, Jamie and Susan went to the cottage to put the kitchen in order. Connie had gone along with Karen and Nancy to visit the bakery that was still for sale in the village. She wanted to bring Jean something special for desert. It still brought a smile to her lips trying to picture Jean in the kitchen making dinner for them.

It was a short but enjoyable visit. The only disappointment was Carol not having time alone with Jamie. She knew she shouldn't let herself get caught up in that, especially after seeing her with Susan. It was obvious Jamie was crazy about her. Liz still crossed Carol's mind every now and again, after all, they had been together for five good years before things changed. It was just too bad things went sour. She wondered if she would ever find what everyone else in the group seemed to have.

Chapter Four

On the ride back to Jamie's apartment Susan's stomach was in knots. She had a doctor's appointment tomorrow, after that she knew she would have to face the facts. After they had dropped Connie off, Jamie wanted to talk about their relationship but Susan told her there really wasn't anything she could do about changing things right now. When they reached Jamie's apartment Susan got in her car and headed right home. She knew Jimmy and the girls would probably be getting in soon and she wanted to be there first.

It was late when she heard Jimmy's car in the driveway, late enough so they would expect her to be in bed asleep. 'Good,' she thought, 'one less problem.' She lay awake for most of the night. She already knew what the doctor was going to tell her and there was nothing she could do about it. She was sure Jamie was going to hate her, thinking she had been sleeping with Jimmy all along. What a mess!

When Susan got up that morning she called Jamie and told her she wasn't coming over. Jamie's voice was pleading, "I hated sleeping alone last night and now I won't see you today?" Susan had to laugh, "Yes you will, in fact I want to take you to lunch." Jamie just wanted to see her and would have agreed to just about anything, but she wondered what was behind the invitation. They stayed on the phone for a while until Susan had to get ready for her appointment. She hoped she had come across all right, and that Jamie couldn't tell she was dying inside. 'After today,' she thought, 'Jamie may not want to see me ever again.' In the shower Susan tried to find an answer but there didn't seem to be one. Under different circumstances she would have been thrilled to have another baby, but that was another time and another Susan.

Jamie knew the restaurant where Susan wanted to meet. She also knew there was going to be a dedication of a building going on in that area. Thinking if she left a bit earlier, she could get some good shots and finish up in time to meet Susan, 'Life is good!' she thought. Showered and dressed, she gathered up her gear and headed out the door with an obvious bounce in her step. She spent about an hour at the photo shoot, using up a couple of rolls of film. She was sure she had a couple of quality pictures to sell to the local media. Checking her watch she saw that she still had an hour to go before she met Susan. It was such a nice day, she decided to take her time and walk the few blocks over to the restaurant.

Susan felt numb when she walked out of the doctor's office. True she had expected it but there had been that glimmer of hope, that maybe, just maybe it was something else. As fate would have it, Jamie, with her camera bag slung over her shoulder, was at that moment, walking on the opposite sidewalk, on her way to the restaurant. She was lost in thought about how good her life was to have a great job and to be in love with someone so special when she spotted Susan coming out the clinic. Realizing that Susan was so close made her heart skip a beat and she felt lucky that she had decided come this way. Calling out her name she dodged traffic and jogged across the street, stopping just in front of her. Before Susan could react, the door to the doctor's office opened and the receptionist came out calling Susan's name, "Mrs. Chase, you left your purse." Susan gave her a nervous smile, trying to move on. Jamie saw that Susan was shaking but before she could ask if she was alright, the words the women was saying to Susan began ringing in her ears, "And again Mrs. Chase, congratulations. And don't worry, I know it's been awhile since you had the girls, but you're in good shape, you'll do fine dear," she then nodded to both of them and went back inside. Jamie was stunned; Susan could see it on her face. Jamie's expressions changed from confusion, to disbelief, to realization. Shaking her head, "Pregnant?" she was saying over and over as she stepped back away from Susan. Susan cried out "Jamie please, don't go, please just listen." Jamie couldn't hear her. It was a busy time of day and as she stepped back, the void between them filled in with people. Susan wanted to scream Jamie's name, but all that came out was a whisper. Jamie turned and walked away, hoping she would wake up soon and everything would be right again.

Later that evening there was a demanding knock on Jamie's door, "Jamie, it's me, Connie, open the door." As the door opened Connie walked in past Jamie and spun around to face her, "Are you alright? I tried calling but..." Connie got cut off by the ringing of the phone, Jamie made no attempt to answer, "Look Jamie, its probably Jean, I'll answer it." Jamie walked into the kitchen, she couldn't hear what was being said, but it was brief. Connie came out to the kitchen and sat at the table with Jamie, who had already taken out a couple of beers. She looked awful. She was pale and drawn, definitely hurting. Connie asked her, "Do you want to talk about it?" Jamie just looked at her for a moment then asked, "How did you know?" "Susan called, she's really worried about you." Jamie's face was expressionless as she replied, "Then she must have told you." Connie answered, "Yes, she did. Susan wanted to tell you but you left before she could explain. She feels awful that you found out that way. In all fairness to Susan, she just found out herself." Jamie looked at Connie, shaking her head, "Fairness! How can you talk about fairness?" Connie remained silent as Jamie vented her anger. "Connie, you just don't understand. She told me they had separate bedrooms, that they hadn't slept together in a couple of years!" Jamie was pacing the room, "How in hell did she get pregnant, answer me that…God I feel like such a jerk! There I was, just hanging around, not seeing anyone else, only her, when and if she could get away. I can't believe I bought the whole thing!" Jamie stopped pacing; Connie could sense the anger was changing to hurt. Glaring at Connie, she continued, in a quieter voice, "You know, I promised myself a long time ago, I would never get involved with a married women. God Connie, this shouldn't be happening." "Jamie sit down," Connie said as she pulled the chair closer to her resting her hand on Jamie's arm, "Just keep quiet for a minute and listen to me, Susan's been trying to call you to explain what's been going on." Jamie cut her off with a wave of her hand, "Explain? Explain what? I'm not living in a cave somewhere; I know how women get pregnant! She is pregnant, right, or did I miss something?" Connie just looked at her, "Well yes, you know she is." Jamie shrugged her shoulders, "Then there is nothing to explain."

215

Connie sat at the kitchen table with Jamie until one in the morning. Connie's heart went out to her. Putting her arm around her she said, "Jamie I know your hurting but there's more to it, believe me. It's not my place to say anymore but I can tell you this, Susan is hurting just as much as you are. She loves you!" Jamie just shook her head and replied, "I'm sorry Connie, I don't want to talk anymore." She stood up, speaking more to herself than to Connie adding, "I just need to lie down." Indicating the door to Connie, she said, "Thanks for coming by but don't worry about me, I'll get over it."

When Connie got home Jean was up waiting for her. She had talked quite a while with Susan and told her that Connie had found Jamie at home and would be staying with her for a while. Before hanging up she let Susan know that she would be calling her in the morning to see if she needed anything. Jean felt so bad for Susan she told Connie that she wished she could do more to help. Connie reassured her that she was helping in a big way by giving Susan someone to talk to.

After Susan hung up the phone she went into the kitchen to make herself a cup of tea. It was almost two a.m., but she couldn't sleep. She knew she should have told Jamie when she first suspected she was pregnant, but it was too late for that now. All she could see was Jamie's face as she realized what the receptionist was saying. Susan had stood in the crowd, unmoving, until someone bumped into her and brought her out of her daze. She didn't know how she got home, but by the time she did, she had made up her mind to see Jimmy in the morning before he left for work. She wanted a divorce! She was tired of living this lie. Whether things worked out with Jamie or not, she knew she needed to do this for herself. When he got up that morning Susan was waiting for him. They had a heated argument with him accusing her of having an affair, "I'm not stupid!" He snarled at her, "I figured out long ago you were seeing another man!" Finally he threw some clothes in a bag and walked out. She never said anything to him about the baby.

Word got around about Jamie and Susan. Connie called Anna and Lillian the next morning telling them what happened. Knowing they had a special bond with Jamie, Connie felt they could help. Connie was going to call Jamie before she left for work but it was too early. If Jamie was able to fall asleep last night, she didn't want to wake her. Jean decided to stay home. She called work explaining she had a close friend that needed her help. Her boss, Ted, was disappointed he wouldn't be seeing her, but told her he understood and would handle things. Hanging up he felt a void thinking about her not being there; he didn't like it when she wasn't around. He was growing very fond of her.

Lillian tried calling Jamie all morning, but she was either out or just not answering. At lunchtime she drove over to her place. After knocking on the door a couple of times, she called out her name and Jamie let her in. She couldn't stay long, but she told her that she would be over with Anna as soon as they got out of work, and to make sure she was here. She told Jamie that Anna was beside herself with worry about her and she needed to see her. Jamie didn't say anything, just nodded okay. Lillian felt bad leaving her, but she had to get back to work and call Anna to let her know how Jamie was doing.

Connie had stopped at Sally's before heading over to Jamie's last night, just in case she was there. She saw Cathy and told her what was going on. "Oh how terrible for Jamie!" she exclaimed in shock and then added, "I feel sorry for both of them, what a mess! They were so happy this weekend, how could this happen?" When Ronnie stopped in that evening, Cathy told her what was going on. Ronnie's first response was anger towards Susan for deceiving Jamie like that, but upon hearing what she had gone through with her husband, she soon softened towards her. It made her thankful that her and Cathy didn't have any problems in their relationship. They spent the rest of the night just holding onto each other, fearing that something unknown might come between them when they least expected it.

Ronnie was meeting Carolyn for lunch the next day to discuss the information they had gathered concerning the license for the safe house. When she arrived she had Jamie and Susan on her mind instead and told Carolyn what had happened between them. Carolyn was shocked, "Susan is pregnant?" she replied, not believing what she was hearing. Ronnie told her as much as she knew about the situation. Carolyn felt terrible; she knew how much they cared for each other. "I'll stop by Jamie's tonight after work, but I don't know what to do for Susan, I don't even know where she lives." Ronnie thought for a moment, "Karen and Nancy will know, I'll stop at the bakery on my way back to work. I'm sure they'll get in touch with her." Neither of them had much of an appetite;

they just had a quick cup of coffee then left. Ronnie headed over to the bakery and Carolyn went back to her office and called Julie. It touched them all, reminding them how vulnerable relationships could be, and how quickly things can change.

At the bakery Ronnie wasted no time telling Karen and Nancy what had happened. Neither of them were surprised, they knew it was just a matter of time before this came to light. Nancy told her, "We knew about the pregnancy, Susan told us about her suspicions as soon as she realized it. We were hoping she would tell Jamie before she found out from someone else, but she was so afraid of loosing her, she couldn't bring herself to tell her. She loves Jamie so much, she must be crushed!" Karen added that they would go over to Susan's as soon as they closed the bakery for the day. Ronnie replied, "Good, I'm sure she needs some one to talk to and she seems to be able to confide in you two. Let me know if Cathy and I can do anything to help. We are so sad to think that anything like this could happen to any of us in the group. We need to do something to help them." They assured her that they would stay in touch and let them know how Susan was doing.

When Jean spoke to Susan in the morning, she sounded tired and sad, "Susan, you sound like you could use some company, can I come over?" Susan said yes, and told her how to get there. On the way over Jean stopped and picked up a couple of sandwiches, sure Susan hadn't had anything to eat. When she arrived, Susan made them some tea and Jean placed the sandwiches on the table but she wasn't interested. Jean told her, "Honey, I'm sure you didn't eat yesterday and you haven't had anything today. You need to put your feelings aside for a moment and think about the baby." Susan didn't say anything, but she did eat her sandwich, and had to admit she felt a little better afterward. Susan and Jean really didn't know each other very well, but they felt connected. Susan began talking, telling Jean about asking Jimmy for a divorce. Now she was having second thoughts and was wondering if she had done the right thing. "I don't know what I'm going to tell my girls when they come back home Sunday. I've messed up a lot of lives and I'm sure they're going to hate me." Jean tried to reassure Susan that her daughters would not hate her, "Of course they're going to be upset Susan, but believe me, they won't hate you." Jean felt so bad for her, what would she do if something happened between her and Connie? She shook the thought out of her head, they had been through their bad times and she didn't want to think of anything coming between them ever again. She stayed with Susan all afternoon and was there when Karen and Nancy came by after work. They had also brought food with them, wanting to make sure Susan was eating. The three of them stayed with Susan for the rest of the day. Karen wanted her to stay at their apartment for a few days, feeling she shouldn't be alone. Susan thanked them both, but felt she needed time alone so she could think and plan what she was going to do from here on out. Jean was the first to leave; she had the car and needed to pick Connie up from work. She told Susan they would be home all evening and if she needed anything, Connie and her were there for her no matter what, so do not to hesitate to call. Susan thanked them all for their offers to help her, but said she was getting tired and wanted to lie down for a while. Reluctantly they left, but they reminded her again to call if she needed anything at all.

Lillian and Anna arrived at Jamie's after they picked up a couple of pizzas and some beer. Jamie wasn't hungry but did have a beer. As they were talking, Carolyn and Julie came in. They all understood how Jamie must have been feeling. None of them had known anything about Susan being pregnant and it was a shock; they couldn't believe she was the type of person that would lead somebody on, as it appeared that she had done to Jamie. There had to be more to it than that. Anna said, "Jamie, I know your hurting but I also know that you're in love with Susan and any fool could see that she is in love with you. Shouldn't you at least let her explain her side of this? Who knows what the circumstances were? I am a pretty good judge of character and I believed Susan when she told me they weren't together anymore. There's not a devious bone in that girl's body, besides, what reason was there for her to lie?" Carolyn spoke up, "Jamie, she's right! Karen called me just before I came over and there's a lot more to this than you think. You should talk to her." Jamie stood up abruptly, pacing the floor, "Look guys, I know you all mean well, but I'm just not ready for this." Jamie looked at the faces surrounding her and said, "Susan has two kids and a husband that she's obviously been sleeping with, and now she's pregnant. Now please, someone tell me, where do I fit in?" No one had an answer for her.

Susan didn't try calling Jamie again after that first day. As much as she yearned to see her to right the

221

wrong between them, she had to step back and take care of her own situation. She called her parents the next day and told them most of the truth. She explained that she and Jimmy hadn't been together for some time and she wasn't happy, and for that matter, neither was he. They were pretty upset at the news, wondering what in the world she was going to do and on and on and on. Susan didn't say any more, waiting until her mother stopped telling her all the reasons she should stay married, until finally she asked "Susan, are you sure about this decision?" Susan answered firmly, "Very sure." Deep down her mother knew they hadn't seemed happy together in a long time, but still, they had the girls. They talked awhile longer. Her parents were well off financially and she told her if she needed anything…Susan interrupted saying, "Thanks Mom, I appreciate that, but all I need right now is a lawyer. I want to get the divorce underway as soon as possible." She didn't say what she was thinking; that she wanted to start living her life as the person she now knew she truly was, regardless of what happened between her and Jamie. Her mother said she would make her an appointment with their lawyer. Susan thanked her again and added, "Don't worry about the girls and me, we're going to be alright." With that taken care of, Susan decided she would drive up and pick up the girls at her in-laws camp instead of them bringing them home. It would be a good time to talk with them. Now she just needed to figure out what she was going to say. With those decisions made, Susan began taking control of her life.

Jamie, on the other hand, felt as if she had lost control of hers. She couldn't concentrate on anything, she felt lost. With Susan gone from her life, nothing mattered anymore. Everyone felt terrible about the breakup between Susan and Jamie and a cloud of despair had settled over them all. As much as they felt it would help if Jamie knew everything, including Susan asking for a divorce, they knew it wasn't their place to tell her; it had to come from Susan. They could only hope that once Jamie got past the anger, she might be ready to listen. But Jamie was beyond hearing anything that would absolve Susan from being the cause of the pain she was feeling. It appeared that nothing anyone could say was going to change Jamie's mind about how she felt about Susan now.

Chapter Five

The week of the 4th was finally here and they had all planned to be in Maine for a whole week. Susan wouldn't have been able to go anyway, even if things were right between her and Jamie, but they still felt bad leaving her behind. Everyone was in touch with her before they left, telling her they would call during the week to see how she was doing. Connie talked Jamie into going with them, "There's no point in you sitting around, cooped up in this apartment, all by yourself." Jamie agreed.

Once in Maine, everyone came back to life. Carolyn and Julie spent their days furnishing their cottage. Karen and Nancy were seriously considering buying the bakery that seemed to be waiting there just for them. Jean arrived with Connie, but only for a couple of days as her kids were coming for a visit. She would have to leave on Tuesday but would be back on Friday for the rest of the weekend. Connie hated to see her go, but she was happy for her. She was rebuilding a strong relationship with the kids and it was something Jean needed. Connie and Jamie spent a lot of time together making minor repairs around the outbuildings. Lillian, Anna and Carol were meeting with the carpenters for an estimate to finish off the upstairs and add a bathroom. Evenings were spent going over the requirements needed for a licensed facility. Carolyn and Ronnie had brought a lot of information with them for everyone to look over. During the week Cathy and Ronnie went around visiting safe houses in the area to see how they were being run. One thing they found out for sure was the need for more facilities. All in all, as the week wore on, they all got caught up in the idea. Everyone in the group had something special to add to it.

Julie was still harboring thoughts of Carolyn taking the position of resident psychologist. She knew that she would be able to get a job up here in her own field as well so that wouldn't be a problem. She had it all figured out in her head, Carol would cook and Anna and Lillian would be the housemothers. She had to laugh at herself, it was a little far fetched, but wouldn't it be nice? Julie was wide awake and her thoughts were going a mile a minute, 'Maybe its not such a joke,' she thought. Turning to face Carolyn, she whispered, "Hon, are you awake?" Carolyn stirred and opening one eye, she could see Julie looking back at her, smiling. Carolyn asked, "Oh oh, what's going on in that mind of yours?" Julie told her, "Well I can't sleep, I keep thinking…" As Julie's rush of words began to penetrate Carolyn's dozy mind, she exclaimed "Are you crazy?" "No," Julie answered, "I don't think so. I know it sounds that way, but it seems like we're all here, we all have something to contribute and we all love it here." Carolyn was waking up and pushed herself up in the bed, leaning on her elbow, "Oh, I don't know Jul, it really sounds a little nutty, I mean, to think that we all would pull up roots and move to Maine, just like that?" Looking down at Julie, she conceded to herself that she was just a little bit interested in what she was saying, but not really believing. "Jul, I really think you've gone over board on this one, but I suppose it wouldn't hurt to think about it." While Carolyn didn't all together agree with her idea, Julie could see she was smiling as she considered it. She laughed with delight and threw her arms around Carolyn's neck, pulling her back down into the bed with her.

Jamie lay awake too, only she was thinking about Susan. During the day she kept herself busy, leaving little time to dwell on anything else, but now…at night, she couldn't keep her out of her thoughts. She was still angry and hurt, disappointed that she hadn't been honest with her, but she knew she was still in love with her.

Susan said goodnight to the girls and got ready for bed herself. It had been a very busy, stressful week. The girls were upset by her news, as were her in-laws. Susan knew it would be that way, but she also knew that in time everyone would adjust, they would have to. She missed Jamie, there was no denying that, but she knew right from the beginning, keeping house with a bunch of kids wasn't Jamie's style. Sobbing into her pillow to keep from crying out, she thought about the all the good times her and Jamie had shared together and in a fit of despair she asked herself why things had to turn out this way?

Connie woke up early. She hated turning over and not finding Jean there, but today was Friday and Jean's kids would be going home early this morning, then she would be on her way to Maine. "I can't wait to see her," she said out loud. Getting up, she headed to the kitchen where she found Jamie already pouring herself a cup of coffee. Connie looked at her, "God Jamie, you look like hell this morning, couldn't sleep?" Jamie shook her head, "No, I guess it's going to take awhile." Connie thought that was a good sign, she didn't sound angry anymore, just sad. Connie told her, "I never stopped thinking about Jean. I can only thank God she came back or I would still be thinking about her." She paused for a moment, pondering whether to tell Jamie about Susan's separation, but decided against it. That would be up to Susan. She fixed her coffee and sat down with Jamie, "You know it wasn't easy with Jean. I felt the same way back then as you do now, only worse. I didn't know what had happened to her and I had no idea of how she felt about me. But she came back and when I found out she was in love with me, I vowed that nothing was going to keep us apart again." Leaning over closer to Jamie, Connie continued speaking, "I know Jean's kids don't live with her, but even if things were different, I know, together we would have found a way to work things out. It's worth the effort Jamie. I've never been happier and I believe you and Susan could be too." Jamie just looked at her for a minute, and then said, "Connie it's different, very different. Jean is all yours; Susan has another life, completely separate from mine. I wish it wasn't so but…" Jamie shrugged her shoulders and changed the subject.

It wasn't long before everyone was up and ready to start the day with a big breakfast. They were all talking excitedly about what lie ahead. Julie, seeing everyone in a positive mood, decided to bring up her idea. Getting everyone's attention, she began, "Carolyn thinks I'm crazy, but here goes anyway," Julie explained what she had on her mind. Lillian, Anna and Carol, thought it was a great idea, but the others?" Carolyn spoke up, "At first I thought she was crazy, but now I'm not so sure. It would be a drastic change, but you know, I'd like to give it some serious thought," Looking at Julie she continued, "I'm not promising anything, but I do think we should talk more about this. I am open to change, if we can afford it." Seeing Carolyn taking this seriously put a new light on it. They all agreed to at least think about it. After breakfast, they all split up. Connie went outside and puttered around while waiting for Jean to arrive.

Lillian and Anna had a busy week so far and decided to just relax and enjoy the farm. Carolyn and Julie went back to an antique store where Julie saw an old four-poster bed that she fell in love with and just had to have. Carol asked the sisters if she could borrow their pick up truck so they could bring the bed back to the cottage. They were more than happy to let her use the truck anytime she wanted it. In addition to being a big help to them, they had grown very fond of her. Carol tried to get Jamie interested in going along for the ride, but she said she was tired and just wanted to take it easy for the day. At first Carol was secretly pleased to hear about the break up; but seeing how much Jamie was hurting, she knew that she must love Susan very much. Maybe in time she would forget, but something told her that wasn't to be.

Karen and Nancy were going back to the bakery in the village once more before deciding whether to buy it or not. They were pretty sure they wanted it, but they had to figure out if they could swing both places until they could sell the one in Boston. They knew they could stay on at the farm until everything got straightened out and they found a place of their own, it was just a matter of committing. They both liked Julie's idea and were sure they could find a way to help. In fact Karen already had an idea brewing in her mind about giving some of the women 'on the job training' at the bakery.

Cathy and Ronnie hung around for a while then went for a drive. Cathy wanted to go to the shore and take a walk on the beach. The traffic was horrible and after what seemed like eternity, they managed to find a good parking space. They were both quiet during the ride, which was unusual for them. They each seemed to have something on their mind. As they walked along they came across a beautiful place to stop. They sat on the rocks and watched the waves lapping at their feet. Ronnie said, in an off-handed manner, "Cath?" Cathy looked at her with raised eyebrows and a soft smile, "Yes?" Ronnie seemed to be putting the words together, "What do you think about Julie's idea? I mean, do you think it's crazy, or do you think she might have something?" Cathy answered, "Well, to tell you the truth, I have been thinking about it. It would be nice to do something more meaningful with our lives. It really felt good to be able to help Carol, but it would mean moving and I'm not sure about that." Ronnie asked, "You mean leaving your son?" "Cathy reached over and took her hand, "No, it has nothing to do with Tommy, he has his own life now, and Maine is not that far away. You're the reason I wouldn't move," Cathy added with a sly smile, "I couldn't live up here without you. I've become used to having you around!" Ronnie laughed, "That's the same reason I wouldn't move, I love being around you too." Cathy looked surprised, "You mean you would consider it?" "Only if you were here." Ronnie answered, pausing to taking a deep breath before she went on, "Cath, you must know by now that I'm crazy about you. You've added so much to my life. I can't ever picture myself being without you. What I'm trying to say is…would you consider moving in together?" Cathy answered right away, "Yes."

Jamie was sitting in the shadows on the porch, just quietly observing Lillian and Anna working together in their garden. All the years they've been together and you could tell they still loved each other very much. They couldn't pass each other without touching and they didn't need words to let their thoughts of each other be known. Jamie had hoped she had found that with Susan. She was still sitting there observing them when Jean drove in. Not noticing her, Jean went straight over to Lillian and Anna asking where Connie was. They told her she had gone up to her special place by the oak tree to wait for her. They said that Connie had bought a seedling oak at the feed store to plant as a friend for the big oak. They talked a few minutes longer and Jamie heard Susan's name mentioned, but couldn't hear what was said.

Jean found Connie on her knees patting down the ground where she just planted the baby oak tree. Jean smiled to herself, 'She is so sweet and caring, not wanting the oak tree to be alone.' She came up quietly behind her and wrapped her arms around her and whispered, "I love you." Connie jumped up, grabbing Jean in her arms, she swung her around in sheer delight, "I have missed you so much." Jean laughed, "I can see that!" Connie found Jeans lips warm and inviting.

Saturday night turned into a night of celebrations. Karen and Nancy finally committed to buying the bakery and moving lock, stock and barrel to Maine. Ronnie and Cathy made a commitment to each other and also were planning to look for a home together in Maine. It was going to be a fun evening. Connie set up the grill and Jamie went into town for beer and wine. There were a lot of laughs and many toasts to new futures for everyone. Now that Karen and Nancy, as well as Cathy and Ronnie had decided to move up to Maine, Carolyn and Julie were thinking more seriously about making the move also. Of course money would be the deciding factor, but it would be a challenge and they were up for it. Relocating meant they would need to look for jobs right away, but they didn't see that as a problem. Both Carolyn and Ronnie were confident they would find positions at the local hospitals and Julie said she would get in touch with the social services, knowing they were always looking for help. Cathy said she could work anywhere. Being a resort town, there were a lot of good restaurants around the area and she was sure she would find something that she liked. All of them felt the safe house was a worthwhile project and while they would be doing their own thing, they were glad to be a part of it. Connie and Jean said that they wouldn't be moving up because of Jean's kids, but they assured everyone that they would get points for being frequent visitors. Jamie surprised every one by saying she was going to give it some serious thought. She knew she could earn a living anywhere, and she didn't feel she had any ties in Boston anymore.

The week of the 4th had flown by and reluctantly it was time for everyone to head back to Boston. Ronnie and Cathy were anxious to get started now that they had made a commitment to each other and their future. Ronnie owned her own home and wanted to get it on the market as soon as possible. They planned on living in Cathy's apartment until the house was sold, then with money from the sale and Cathy's savings, they would be able to buy their own home in Maine, hopefully nearby the farm. Karen and Nancy were also taking steps to make their move. They put the bakery up for sale and began looking for a home in Maine. Carolyn and Julie planned on sending out inquiries about jobs available in the Portland area. Lillian and Anna were excited to say the least by all the changes that were taking place and had to stop and pinch themselves to make sure they weren't dreaming. Leaving their friends behind when they moved to Maine was the only downside to leaving Boston, now they had the best of both worlds. They reminded themselves again how good their life together always seemed to be. Carol was surprised by everyone's ideas. She was in for an exciting and worthwhile life, something she always dreamed of, but never could have realized while she was Liz's partner. She hated seeing them leave, but this time, she knew they wouldn't be gone for long and set her sights on helping to make it happen.

Chapter Six

Once they were back in Boston, no one lost their enthusiasm. They all went to work on making the necessary changes for their move. Karen and Nancy called Susan as soon as they got back to see how she was doing and to let her know of their plans to sell the bakery and move to Maine. Susan was glad to hear from them and invited them over for coffee after work. She had missed everyone when they left town and was dying to hear news about Jamie. Jean had called Susan a few times during the week just to talk. Susan told her there was a lot of tension between her and Jimmy when he came over to visit the girls, but she just stayed out of his way. She hoped they would get past that some day and be more civil to each other, for the girl's sake. She was more interested in finding out how Jamie was feeling towards her and asked Jean if she knew anything. Jean told her, "According to Connie, she's past the anger. She said if you still wanted to talk to Jamie, now might be the time." Susan wasn't sure she could bring herself to face Jamie ever again. She still remembered the way Jamie had looked at her when she realized that she was pregnant.

All week Jamie had been in and out on photo shoots. She had decided while she was in Maine over the Fourth, that her relationship with Susan was a lost cause and she needed to get over it. Instead of sitting around thinking about her any longer, she threw herself into her work as soon as she got back to Boston. But being back in familiar places, she was finding out that it was easier said than done. In the short time that they

233

were together, her whole world had revolved around Susan. Well, she'd learned her lesson, no more married women for her, she decided to put her old life behind her and stay away from all women for a while. Breaking the ties and moving to Maine, away from Susan, was sounding better and better.

Karen and Nancy told Susan the good news about selling the bakery and moving to Maine, and also what Lillian and Anna planned on doing with the farm. Nancy also told her, "I think you should know Susan that Jamie's thinking about moving too." Susan felt her heart sink, that would make it final. Karen reached over and took her hand, "Susan, believe me, we spent all week with Jamie and she's miserable without you. You should try to talk to her and explain." Susan wasn't sure, "If I thought it would matter, I would, but it doesn't change the fact that I'm pregnant." Then Nancy asked, "What did your husband say when you told him?" Susan shook her head, "I haven't told him yet, I haven't told anyone but you guys." Both Karen and Nancy were surprised, "Why not?" She took a deep breath before answering, "I want to get past the divorce first. I don't want anything to get in the way of that. My lawyer is working on it and as soon as it's final I will tell everyone. That's the way it has to be for now." "Even so," Karen spoke up, "I would still try to explain it all to Jamie." Susan remained seated in her chair after they left. She couldn't believe everyone was moving to Maine and that Jamie may be moving with them. Deep down inside she had always held out the hope that they would be together again. For the first time since the breakup, she felt an urgent need to try and make things right between her and Jamie, not being able to bare the thought of loosing her forever. She thought, 'Would my talking to her really change anything?' She didn't have the answer to that, but she knew she had to see her again.

Jamie was unlocking the door to her apartment when she heard the phone ringing. Running into the room, "Hello,...hello," Jamie figured whoever it was must have hung up. Ready to put the phone down, she heard a faint, "Jamie?" She instantly knew who it was and started to hang up, but couldn't, "Yes, what do you want?" she asked, trying to sound indifferent. Susan forced herself to talk, "Jamie, will you meet me for lunch? I need to talk to you." Jamie was hesitant at first, she wanted to tell her to go to hell..., but couldn't. She could hear the relief in Susan's voice when she said "Yes." They agreed to meet at a coffee shop not far from Susan's house in about an hour. Jamie had to sit down after she hung up the phone to pull herself together. Susan's voice had really thrown her. Her anger told her not to show up, but her heart said she had too.

It was a hot, humid day and Jamie, in an emotional turmoil, hoped the coffee shop was air-conditioned. Entering, she ordered two cups of coffee and found a place in the back to sit and wait for Susan. Thankfully it was cool in there and she had been the first to arrive, giving her time to regain her composure, or so she thought. Susan came in just moments behind her. As she walked toward her, all the emotions Jamie had been trying to bury these past weeks came bubbling to the surface. Angrily she told herself, 'Get over it now!' Jamie could see Susan was as nervous as she was and that helped her gain control again. Sitting down across from her, Susan gave her a shy smile, and said "Hi." Jamie couldn't help but soften when she looked into her eyes. She missed the sensation of falling into those eyes and all of her resolve to be big, bad and indifferent melted away. Instead, she said nothing, just nodded her head hello. The waitress came to see if they wanted to order anything else but they said they were both fine with their coffee. After the waitress left, Susan reached across the table for Jamie's hand, but she pulled it back, out of her reach. A little flustered, Susan started talking and told Jamie everything that had happened between her and Jimmy, from him wanting to renew their relationship right up to the night he made love to her. "Jamie, I didn't know how to stop him without telling him that I was in love with someone else. Believe me, if I had to do it all over again, I would have done just that. It was the only time it happened, I swear to you!" Jamie could see the tears in Susan's eyes, but she wasn't quite buying it. "So, if that's all there was to it, why not come to me and tell me?" she asked, somewhat sarcastically. Susan answered, "I know I should have, but things were so good between us, I didn't want to take a chance on ruining what we had. I was afraid you would think I lied to you about my relationship with Jimmy. I knew it was never going to happen again so I felt it was better to forget about it and just go on." "He has never bothered you again?" Jamie asked. "No, and he won't, we don't live together any more. I told him I was getting a divorce!" That surprised Jamie and a little less defensive, she asked, "What did he say?" "Well," Susan answered, "we argued for awhile. He said he'd known all along I was seeing another man. When I

didn't say anything, he packed up his things and left."
Jamie was confused by this turn of events. It was the
last thing she expected to hear. She continued, "What
did he say about the baby?" "I haven't told him yet."
Susan went on to explain why she hadn't, that she want
the divorce finalized first. Jamie was quiet, Susan
leaned towards her, "I'm sorry Jamie; I know it's a lot
to take in all at once. I wasn't going to bother you
again, I know you must hate me, but when I heard you
were thinking about moving to Maine…I just didn't
want you to go still thinking I had been sleeping with
Jimmy all along. Jamie, I'm so sorry I hurt you, can
you ever forgive me?" Jamie, still trying to keep her
cool, just nodded her head yes, not meeting Susan's
eyes, "Thanks for telling me," she murmured, "I guess
I don't know what else to say right now." Susan took
the last sip of her coffee hoping Jamie would continue
talking, but she didn't. "Well," Susan said, "thanks for
meeting me…I've got to get going, the girls will be
home soon." As she got up, she took out her car keys,
paused for a moment and removed the key she had to
Jamie's apartment. Setting it down in front of her, she
turned and left. Jamie sat unmoving, just staring at the
key. 'Well, now what?' she asked herself; she didn't
have an answer.

Jean was on the phone when Connie got home.
Connie leaned over and gave her a kiss as she passed
by her and headed into the kitchen to put the groceries
away. When Jean hung up the phone she said. "That
was Susan, she talked to Jamie today." Connie turned
to her with raised eyebrows, "She did? How did that
happen?" Jean repeated what Susan had told her.
Connie asked, "Jamie didn't say anything?" Jean

shook her head no, "I guess Susan did all the talking." Connie wanted to know if Jamie was angry. "I don't think so," Jean replied, "Susan just said she was quiet. You know Jamie pretty well, what do you think?" Connie paused a moment, then shook her head, "I have no idea, but I think I'll take a ride over there before supper. Do you want to come?" "No I don't think so," Jean answered, "she would be more at ease with just you. You can fill me in when you get back." When Connie arrived at Jamie's apartment, no one was home.

After Susan left the coffee shop, Jamie just sat there starring at the key on the table. When the waitress came over to see if she wanted to order anything else, Jamie shook her head no and paid for the coffee. Standing up, she reached for the key and started to put it on her key chain but changed her mind. Outside the heat and humidity were unbearable. Jamie was not ready to go home yet. Instead she got in her car, opened all the windows and went for a long drive so she could think about all that Susan had said. She knew one thing for sure, being that close to Susan made her aware of how much she longed to reach out and hold her close.

Carolyn and Julie got home from work about the same time. They were both hot and tired, neither one wanting to have to deal with cooking supper. They decided to go over to Sally's for cold beer and pizza. Walking in they spotted Ronnie at the bar talking to Cathy and went over to them. Cathy was surprised to see them, "What are you guys doing here, I thought you'd be getting ready to go to Maine tomorrow." Carolyn said, "I wish we were, but I'm on call this weekend and Julie's going to pick out the paint for the trim in the kitchen and bedroom." Laughing she added, "That will be an all day project!" Julie making a face, ignored Carolyn's remark and asked if they were going up, "Nope," Ronnie said, "we can't go either," "I'm putting my house up for sale next week and it needs a good cleaning." "Well," said Carolyn, "it sounds like we're all on the same track. Julie and I are going to order a pizza, how about you?" It was fine with Ronnie. They found a table close to the bar so Cathy could join in on the conversation when she wasn't busy. They had a nice evening, the place was crowded, but the air conditioning kept everyone cool and comfortable. They talked about the big move and the information Carolyn and Ronnie had come up with concerning the license. They also discussed what life would be like once they moved for good. Carolyn admitted, that as much as she was looking forward to the change, she had a lot of patients that she felt bad about leaving. She knew they would be in good hands, but for them, it would be like starting all over again. She hoped it would be a smooth transition for them all.

Chapter Seven

Everything seemed to be coming together and no one could be more excited then Carol. She was amazed by all the changes and possibilities. She was happy that something positive came from her situation. More importantly, she was to remain a part of it. She knew more than anyone the need for a safe house for women in her circumstance. It had helped her immensely. Just knowing that all the women giving her support and comfort were lesbians, like herself, made her feel connected and empowered. She knew she wasn't alone. She understood Anna and Lillian's need to give something back to women less fortunate than themselves. She too had reason to give something back. Knowing it would be awhile before this actually happened, she decided to seek out a safe house in the area and do some volunteer work. It would be good experience for her later on down the road. The only thing missing in her life now was some one to share it with. She already admitted to herself that she was attracted to Jamie, but she was well aware of Jamie's feelings for Susan. Even though they weren't together right now, Carol felt it was only a matter of time when they would be together again. She called Lillian and Anna that night and told them of her plans to volunteer at a local safe house. She planned on going there the next day to introduce herself. They thought it was a great idea and said they'd call her tomorrow evening to see how she made out.

The next morning Carol was up early and fed the kittens and chickens and turned on the water sprinklers in the gardens before going next door to do some vacuuming and light chores for the elderly sisters. With that finished, she borrowed their pick up truck and headed out. Arriving at the shelter, she went to the front desk and introduced herself to the woman in charge, asking if they needed any volunteers. The woman eyed her for a moment and then smiled as she held out her hand, "Hi Carol, I'm Donna, and yes, we can always use help around here!" She gave Carol a firm handshake and asked her if she'd like a cup of coffee. Carol replied "Great, I'd love one," and decided right away that she liked her. Donna poured them both a cup and sat down, "So Carol, have you ever volunteered before?" Carol had no reason not to be honest with her, "No I haven't, but I have been in the same situation as these women. I feel I have something to offer in the way of help." Donna said, "I'm surprised, you don't seem the type to take abuse from someone." "I'm not now, but at the time I didn't think I had any other choice." "Well," said Donna, "It sounds like you would have a lot of insight to share. I'm glad you're interested in helping." They chatted a little more while finishing their coffee, and then Donna asked, "Would you like me to show you around?" "Sure," Carol said, "if you don't mind I'd like that." They took a walk through the building that served as home for more women than it could accommodate. It was not at all what Carol expected, and to be truthful, she had no idea what to expect. All she knew was there was a great sadness about the place, brought there by the displaced, battered women who had no other place to go.

On the ride home, Carol felt depressed after seeing how many women were crowded into the small building. She had no idea there was so much battering going on. Donna had given her a brief general history about the women who were currently staying there. Most were married or had boyfriends that were the abusers, but the one that caught her interest was a young woman who kept to herself. Donna had some concerns about her. She told Carol that someone had dropped her off not quite a week ago. She was badly beaten but refused to go to a hospital and refused to say who did it. Carol thought it must have been a bad beating because she could still see the bruises. Donna went on to say she was a hard case and they knew as soon as she was well enough, she would be on her way back to the same situation. Carol had a strong feeling about her. Instinct told her the reason she didn't want to discuss the abuse or let anyone know who battered her, was because her partner was another woman. She tried to speak to the woman, hardly more than a kid, but she turned away from her, not returning her smile. When it was time to leave, Carol couldn't give Donna a definite time when she could come back, but assured her that she would return to help out. She still had the farm to take care of and her housecleaning job at the sisters, but she was going to be there as often a she could. She called Lillian and Anna that night and told them about her visit to the shelter and also about that one particular young woman that had caught her interest.

The next morning Carol was up bright and early, wanting to get her work done so she could visit the shelter again. She hoped she would be able to make some contact with the young woman she suspected of being a battered lesbian. When she walked into the shelter, Donna was the first one to greet her, "Well, good morning." Carol had to smile as she answered, "Good morning to you. You seem surprised to see me." Donna laughed, "Yes, well, we get a lot of inquires about volunteering. People have good intentions, but they usually don't follow through. I'm glad to see you have." Carol could understand that. "Thank you," she said, "I'm glad too. Now, tell me, what can I do to help?" Donna stood up and came around the desk and hooked her arm through Carol's, "Come, let me introduce you to Joyce, she'll be happy to have some extra help." Donna brought her upstairs to meet Joyce, a busy woman that hardly had time to look up from the pile of laundry she was sorting. After shaking her hand, Joyce got right down to business. She explained that most of the women coming into the shelter have just about given up. "They have lost pride in themselves, not caring how they look, or feel." Carol asked, "What do you do to help them?" Joyce told her, "Unfortunately not as much as we'd like. As you can see, we're always short handed, making it hard to have any real impact. As a result too many women just end up going back to the abuser." She followed Joyce around and met the women that were being sheltered there. Carol recognized herself in many of the faces, reminding her how lucky she was that Cathy cared enough to be there for her. She asked Joyce what the women did all day while they were staying there. "We try to keep them busy cleaning up, helping with the meals and of course, encouraging them to talk about what they've been through. Donna is constantly searching for jobs for them, and trying to get them interested in taking care of themselves." Carol asked, "Does it work?" Joyce gave a short laugh, "We don't have a very good success rate I'm afraid." Carol asked, "Why is that?" Joyce shook her head, as if she didn't understand, "Most of them don't stay around long enough for us to make a difference in their thinking. We don't understand why they go back, they just do." She stayed with Joyce, following her lead for the remainder of the day. She really didn't have anytime to interact with the women, but tomorrow would be different, she would be on her own.

That evening, Carol called Lillian and Anna telling them what she saw at the shelter. She told them she understood what had turned her around so quickly in comparison with so many other battered women who, after many tries to break with their abusers, go back to them. "Not only did I get the support I needed, but the farm gave me back my self respect. It gave me the opportunity to feel useful." After hanging up, Lillian and Anna talked about Carol's insight. They understood what she was saying. Anna was aware of that all along. Aside from the support Carol got from the group, working around the farm made the ultimate difference.

When Carol arrived at the shelter the following day, she walked in as if she'd always been there. She even remembered everyone's name. She looked for Joyce to see if there was anything in particular she wanted her to do. Catching up with Joyce, Joyce explained that someone had just arrived downstairs, "She's in with Donna right now, but when she's done I'd like you to show her where things are and just stay with her a while, okay?" Carol had no problem with that, she could see Joyce had her hands full with another woman that was obviously drunk and needed to be put to bed. On her way down stairs Carol saw the young woman she suspected to be a lesbian. She was standing in the hall staring out the window. Getting a good look at her, Carol realized that she was no more than 17 or 18 years old. She took the opportunity to stop and speak with her, "Pretty out today." The girl didn't say anything, just shook her head in agreement. Seeing a connection, Carol went on to say, "I just love this time of year, I get to spend a lot of time outside working in the garden." Carol caught her interest. In a quiet voice she asked Carol, "You have a garden?" Carol gave the young woman her full attention, "Yes we do, a big one." She didn't say anything for a moment thinking about what Carol had said and then asked, "What kind of garden is it?" Carol answered her questions, although she wanted to keep up the conversation she knew she was needed down stairs. Extending her hand, she introduced herself, "My name is Carol." The young woman took her hand, "I'm Kate." "Kate, there's a women being admitted down stairs, and I'm suppose to show her around, would you like to come with me?" Kate shook her head no, saying she wanted to go to her room. Carol said, "Alright, well I'll look forward to talking with you again. The rest of the afternoon went by quickly. Carol did the best she could to make the new woman feel comfortable and introduced her around. That night she couldn't get Kate out of her mind. Instinctively she knew her lesbian lover delivered Kate's beating to her. Donna had predicted she would probably go back to her as soon as her body healed. She continued to say that she hasn't had anyone come by or call to see how she's doing. That usually means she has nobody else to depend on." Carol knew she had to think of a way to help Kate from returning to that life.

Carol's first week at the shelter flew by. She was amazed at the numbers of women that came and went at the shelter. What surprised her even more was how few of them were actually looking for serious help. Most of them just wanted a place to stay until things cooled down and they could go home again. It was a lifestyle they seemed to be used to. 'My God,' Carol thought, 'I was just like them, relishing the few days after the battle when I went back and was doted on and loved, hoping the beatings were behind us only to have something trigger it off again.' During her first week, Carol had gained Kate's interest when she talked about gardening. She also sensed Kate was getting restless and wouldn't be here much longer. She had to think of something fast before she was gone.

The weekend arrived along with Lillian and Anna. They were loaded down with boxes full of stuff from their apartment. It was so nice to be able to escape the stuffy heat in Boston and come to Maine. True it was hot here too, but it was a different heat, one you could enjoy. After Carol helped unpack their car they took a break on the porch with a cool drink while getting caught up on everything. Carol told them all that was happening at the shelter making a point of saying she probably would have gone back to Liz if she had gone into a traditional 'safe house'. She went on to say, "The staff is wonderful, but they're always short handed. Besides offering a roof over their heads and three square meals a day, there's little time for anything else. The women need individual attention, a "big sister," if you will, to help them make decisions and changes in their lives. The way it stands now they are left to work it out for themselves, and quite frankly, if they were able to do that, they wouldn't be where they are now. It seems like a hopeless cycle. I've already told you about Kate." Both Lillian and Anna nodded yes, "Well the only time she shows any interest in anything I'm saying is when I mention the gardens we have here. I can tell she's not going to make it there but I'm sure it would be different if I could bring her here." "Well," said Anna, "is there any reason why you can't bring her out to see the gardens?" Carol thought for a moment, "Now why didn't I think of that? Yes Anna, that's a great idea! When I see her on Monday, I will ask Donna's permission to bring her here for lunch."

The three of them spent a leisurely weekend brainstorming ideas that would help battered women regain their pride. It went by all too quickly for them. It was only a matter of another couple of months before Anna and Lillian would be moving up for good. The carpenters had already brought in the materials they needed for the renovations upstairs. Hopefully it wasn't going to be too long a process.

Chapter Eight

Monday morning found Carol busy cleaning out the chicken coop. The chicks were all looking good. Their adult feathers were almost in and they were beginning to look like hens. She couldn't wait for the fresh eggs they would soon be producing. Finishing up, she headed for the gardens and set out the sprinklers. Her next stop was at the sister's place to give them a hand with their housework. Carol had wanted to stop by the shelter today, but, by the time she finished at the sister's, it was too late. She put it off 'til early tomorrow morning.

The next morning, stepping out of the shower and standing in front of the mirror, Carol towel dried her now, short red hair. She had decided to cut it last night, it was almost pixie style, framing her freckled face and showing off her hazel eyes. She had always wanted to have short hair but Liz had been against it. Now she was free to make her own decisions.

Drying herself off, Carol stood back, surprised at her reflection in the mirror. It was if she were looking at someone else's body. She had a nice shape with firm, well-defined mussels running down her chest and arms, over her flat stomach and down her slim legs. All she could think was, 'Wow, I look great, if I do say so myself!' Smiling at her thoughts, she slipped on a pair of shorts and tank top and headed out to get her work done so she could spend most of the afternoon at the shelter. Finishing up the chicken coop, she started weeding the gardens. It was a beautiful summer morning with just enough of a breeze to keep the bugs away. It was still early so she had plenty of time to tend her plants. Lost in her thoughts and the feel of the soil, it took a moment before she realized someone was calling her name. "Yes Mary, I'm over here," she answered as she stood up and waved, getting Mary's attention. Mary was one of the sisters that lived next door. In her late seventies, she was a strong, robust woman with a twinkle in her eye and a smile always tugging at the corners of her mouth. Carol met her half way. "Carol dear, would you be able to go to the drug store for us? Sister ran out of her pills and I don't want to leave her alone." Carol knew how much Sister suffered from back problems and was more then ready to help, "Of course Mary, I'll leave right now." Mary gave Carol the keys to the truck, then added, "Carol…seeing you use this old thing more then us, why not just leave it here? If I need it, I know where it is." Carol asked, not wanting to take advantaged of her generous nature, "Mary, are you sure?" Mary answered firmly, "Yes, yes, of course, it makes sense. Now, do you know where the drug store is?" Carol shook her head no and Mary explained how to get there, "On your way back would you mind stopping by the Farm Stand? Sister and I ordered some flowering plants and they came in yesterday. They're all paid for, all you have to do is pick them up." Carol said she would be glad to. She always wanted to stop there, just hadn't got around to it. Mary watched as Carol climbed into the cab of the truck and said, "I like your hair cut like that. You know Carol, you're much too pretty not to have a boyfriend." Carol laughed, "Well thank you for the compliment, but I like things just the way they are." Backing out onto the road, she called out, "I won't be long." As she drove off down the bumpy road, the old truck shook and rattled but she didn't mind, she was used to it, in fact she enjoyed driving it. She had to smile remembering what Mary said about a boy friend. She would love to meet someone, but certainly not a man.

After stopping in the drug store to get Sister's pills, she headed for The Farm Stand. Driving along clutching the steering wheel of the old truck, she suddenly became conscious of how her hands looked. They were rough and callused with stains from working the soil in the gardens. For an instant she flashed back to the way she used to be. As a youngster, she was obsessively neat, never letting a hair or apiece of clothing get out of place, or soiled. Feeling as she did now, it was hard for her to believe she was ever that person. 'Yes,' she thought, 'I am a very different person now, one that Liz would never have approved of.' The thought caused her to ponder what may be in store for her in the future.

The Farm Stand turned out to be very interesting. The place was a lot bigger then you could see from the road. Along with the vegetable stand, they carried everything in the way of plants and trees to gardening equipment. They even had a small coffee shop on the side where they sold baked goods. Walking in, Carol was greeted by an elderly man with a strong Maine accent and an even better sense of humor. Carol told him why she was there and of course he knew the sisters, "Known them for years. Ayah, seems to me, that order did come in yestahday, but I'll be dammed if I can 'member what I done with it," he said with a wink and a smile. "It's here somewhere though, gotta go look for it." Carol offered to help find it but he said, "That's alright, I'll get Patty, she'll know where it is, just follow me." He led Carol into the coffee shop where she was overwhelmed with the smell of fresh coffee and hot apple pie. "Patty honey, you in here?" A voice came from the back room, "I'll be right there dad." A young woman came through the door wiping her hands on her apron, "Patty, this young lady is here to pick up the order for the Sisters that came in yestahday but I can't for the life of me remember where I put it." He exaggerated the statement by scratching his head. The young woman rolled her eyes and winked at Carol before answering, "He has a way of not remembering things so someone else can take care of it for him." He just laughed and went back to work as Patty walked over to Carol holding out her hand, "Hi, I'm Patty." Carol took her hand, "And I'm Carol." Carol felt an immediate attraction to her. "Come on, we'll get that order." She followed Patty outside and around to the back of the building, paying close attention to the way Patty's jeans hugged her hips. "Here we go," Patty said as she bent down to pull the order sheet off the plants, "and they're all paid for. Now, if you'll just bring me that wagon over there, I'll load these up for you." Carol brought over the wagon and helped Patty with the plants. Patty said, "I haven't seen you around here before." Carol replied, "This is my first time here. I've been wanting to stop but...," Patty smiled as she interrupted her, "What I meant was, you're new to the area?" Carol chuckled, "Oh, yes, yes I am, I've only been here a few months." They filled the wagon with the plants then they both pulled it over a small rise to the pick-up truck. Patty passed the plants up to Carol in the bed of the pick-up; she arranged them so they wouldn't roll around as she drove. "There," said Patty, "your all set." Carol jumped down off the bumper, "Well thank you and its nice meeting you." Patty said, "Same here, do you have time for a cup of coffee?" Carol sensing the attraction was mutual wanted to say yes but, "I would really like that but I have a prescription I need to get back to Sister." "I understand, well maybe another time?" "Yes, I'd like that." She really didn't want to leave, but it was time. She was still smiling thinking about Patty, when she drove into the Sister's driveway. She told Mary, if she wanted, she would come over tomorrow and help with the planting. Mary thanked her and said it would be a big help if she could do that for them. Carol went back over to her gardens to get caught up on her work, but now she had something to keep her mind occupied as she worked. 'Yes,' she thought, 'I will have to spend more time at the Farm Stand.'

In spite of her good intentions of getting to the 'shelter' early, it was after lunchtime before she finished up. After taking a quick shower, she made herself some lunch then headed over there. She was looking forward to seeing Kate today, hoping she could peak her interest in seeing the gardens. Driving over, Carol passed by the Farm Stand and felt a little flutter in her belly remembering Patty in her blue jeans. 'I would like to stop by and get to know her better, but I can't right now. I hope I'm not imaging her interest in me.'

No one was at the desk when she walked into the shelter, so she went looking for Kate, stopping to say hello to everyone on her way. Carol met another new face. 'Funny,' she thought, 'a lot of these women seem to fit the same profile, their looks, their demeanor and their habits, all heavy smokers.' She would have to mention this when the group gets back together again.'

She was relieved to find Kate still in residence, but she could sense she was getting ready to leave. Kate was sitting outside on the back steps, "Hi," Carol said as she sat down beside her, "Beautiful day, isn't it?" Kate seemed surprised to see her, "Hi, yes it is." Carol said, "You look surprised to see me Kate," "Well, yes, I guess I am. I haven't been here long, but everyone says that the volunteers usually only last a couple of days." "Well I don't know why that is, but I plan on staying around for a while. Anyway," Carol said as she stood up to take an envelope out of her pocket. "I have something I wanted to show you, here." Kate took the envelope and removed the pictures, "Is this your garden?" "Yes," Carol told her adding, "I'm sure you think I'm a little crazy to be carrying around pictures of it, but..." Kate shook her head, "Oh no, if I had a place of my own, I would love to have a garden like this. It must be nice to work in it." Carol laughed, "Well it does have its moments, but it is a lot of work." Kate wanted to know what each of the rows of plants were. As Carol talked, Kate's reaction was more then she had expected. "When I get some time I'd like to put a fence around it but...," Kate interrupted excitedly, "I would help you with that, if you would let me." Carol jumped on it, "You would? That's great, how about tomorrow?" "You mean it?" Kate said, "I'd love to!"

Carol saw Donna on the way out and told her about Kate, "What do you think," she asked. Donna replied, "I think it's a good idea Carol. She may be more inclined to open up in that kind of environment." That was all Carol needed to hear, she really liked Kate and wanted to be able to help. When Carol got home she put a chicken in the oven to roast, planning on having it for lunch with Kate tomorrow. Then she remembered her commitment to help the sisters, 'No matter,' she thought, 'Kate would be able to help her with that. It wouldn't take long, then they could get to work over here.'

Carol made herself a quick supper, then called Lillian and Anna telling them how she made out with Kate. Anna was happy to hear it was going so well, "That's wonderful," she exclaimed, "I wish we were going to be there to meet her!" She went on to say that she missed the farm and the camaraderie they shared when they were all there together. "Everyone here has been tied up all week so we really haven't seen anybody. I hope you are not too lonely being there by yourself." Carol told her, "Anna, don't worry about me. I do miss everyone during the week, but between the work around here, helping the sisters and now Kate, I don't have time to think about being alone." Carol was about to ask her if she knew Patty, but didn't get a chance before Anna had to hang up to answer the door. 'No matter,' Carol thought, 'I'll just have to find out on my own.'

Chapter Nine

The next morning, Carol rushed through her chores and headed out to the shelter to pick up Kate. When she pulled into the shelter drive, Kate was already outside waiting for her. "I'll just be a minute Kate, I want to let Donna know we're leaving." Carol found her in her office. Donna remarked, "Kate was up early this morning, she's really looking forward to today." She continued to say that she was very surprised at the change in Kate's attitude, "I think this is going to do her a lot of good." Carol was hopeful, "I think so too Donna. I'll bring her back as soon as she's ready." Donna chuckled, "In that case, you may have her for a while." When Carol came out, Kate was already in the truck, ready to go. On the way out to the farm, Carol explained that she had promised her neighbors she would help them with some planting this morning, but it wouldn't take long. Kate didn't mind, as long as she could work in a garden.

Mary had everything needed for planting set out by the time they arrived. Sister's back felt good enough to sit on their porch and tell them where she wanted flowers planted. Both sisters had a hard time agreeing on the right place for each group of plants which brought a smile and a shared look between Carol and Kate.

After finishing up at the sister's place, they headed back to the farm. Carol wanted to get the chicken coop cleaned out before they started the fencing. She told Kate she didn't have to help with the chickens if she didn't want to, but Kate got right into it, saying, "This is fun!" Carol figured she would take advantage of the extra help and strip the coop right out. When they were finished, the chicks had a deep layer of fresh shavings on the floor and new sweet smelling hay in their nest boxes. Carol could see Kate was having a good time and she enjoyed her company. They worked well together and Carol had high hopes for her. Kate wasn't like the others; she just didn't fit the profile. She suggested they stop for lunch before they started putting in the fences. Walking into the old house, Kate was pleased with what she saw. Carol told her she would be glad to show her around after lunch.

After they washed up, Carol got out the cold chicken and potato salad, while Kate set the table on the porch. There she was introduced to Micki and Maude as the kittens were hanging onto the screen door, wanting to come in for their lunch too. Over lunch Kate began asking Carol questions. First she wanted to know if Carol lived here alone, "Not all the time." She answered, "The two women that own the farm are usually here on weekends with a bunch of their friends. They will be moving up here for good in October and I am so looking forward to it." Kate wanted to know how she came to be here, "Are you related to them?" Carol was ready and knew what she would say when it came time to answer this question. Taking her time, Carol started at the beginning, telling Kate about her relationship with Liz and how Cathy had brought her here that night. Kate didn't say anything for a couple of minutes; she was digesting everything that Carol was saying. Carol leaned forward taking Kate's hand asking, "It was the same with you wasn't it? It was a woman that hurt you?"

Looking at Carol, Kate answered, "Yes, I don't know what I did wrong, but…" Squeezing Kate's hand Carol interrupted her, "Kate, you did nothing that deserved being abused. Nobody has the right to hurt another person like that." Kate looked directly at her, letting down her guard. 'God,' thought Carol, 'she's so young!' Kate told her, "My parents caught me kissing a girl." She shrugged her shoulders and continued speaking, "They threw me out. They said something was wrong with me, I wasn't normal." Carol's heart went out to her, "Kate, believe me, there's nothing wrong with loving another women." Kate looked skeptical but continued her story. "I had no where to go. I was only sixteen and still in school. I didn't want to quit, but I had to. Trying to find a place to sleep and eat, took all my time." Kate took a deep breath before she continued, "I was in a store looking for a job. There was a woman at the register paying for her groceries. I could feel her looking at me as I asked the store manager about work. The manager just shook her head no, then nodded towards the door for me to leave. I couldn't blame him. I hadn't had a bath in a while and my clothes were all wrinkled and dirty. When I left I headed next door to another store to try again. The women I saw paying for her groceries, hurried out after me. She said she overheard me asking for a job, and she needed someone to help with housework. She said she worked a lot of hours and didn't have time to keep up with it. Part of my pay would be room and board. She seemed nice enough and it sounded perfect so I couldn't say no." Kate paused and picked up one of the kittens, holding it close to her, "At first I felt really lucky, but I would rather have gone home. I had tried talking to my parents a couple of times but they didn't want any part of me." Kate's eyes filled with tears. Carol moved closer, putting her arm around Kate's shoulders. Kate took a deep breath before she continued, "I guess I gave up on ever going back. I decided to do a good job for this woman and maybe I could get back in school and graduate. She did work a lot of hours and at first I didn't see too much of her. But things started to change; she became more affectionate toward me. I started liking her like, you know, as family. I missed my mother, that's all I was looking for. Outside of kissing, I had never really done anything with a girl. I wasn't thinking about doing anything with this women, honest, she was older, like my mother." Kate stopped again, looking a little embarrassed to go on. Carol told her, "Kate, it's alright, you can talk to me." Kate nodded and continued, "One night I woke up and she was in bed with me. I couldn't say no, I had nowhere else to go, so I did as I was told." Carol asked, "When did she start hitting you Kate?" Kate answered, "Usually the day after we had sex. She knew I was just pretending to like her; she would get cranky, and blame me for everything that went wrong. At first it was just a slap and then it just kept getting worse. The last time I was scared she was going to kill me so I had to leave." Carol asked her, "How did you end up at the shelter?" "I really don't remember. Donna said a friend brought me in, but I don't know who it was. I wanted to talk to someone about what happened to me, but...all they talked about was their husbands or boyfriends. I didn't think anyone would understand what was happening to me even if I had told them. I'm so glad you came around, it feels good to talk to someone." Carol took Kate in her arms, "I'm glad too Kate and from now on I am here for you."

The afternoon had flown by. Kate wanted to get started on the fences, but Carol said it was getting too hot outside and suggested they just putter around for a while. After supper, when it cooled down, they could lay out the fencing for tomorrow. Carol called Donna and told her she had a break through with Kate, "While Kate is in the mood to talk, I'd like her to stay over night." Donna sounded a little hesitant at first; she was still responsible for Kate whether she was at the shelter or with Carol. Donna liked Carol, but she didn't know her very well. Finally she said all right, "But call me in the morning and let me know how things are going." Carol hadn't said anything to Kate about staying overnight until after she talked to Donna. Kate was thrilled. She liked Carol from the start; she was so easy to talk to. She could finally be herself.

After supper they went out back and laid out the fencing they were going to use. Carol figured out where she was going to put the gates, she wanted one at both ends. When they were done, Carol took Kate for a tour of the house and decided to introduce her to the rest of the group. Bringing out the photo album that she and Jamie had assembled, she showed Kate the pictures of everyone. Kate couldn't get over all the happy faces looking back at her, she found herself laughing at some of the stories that went along with the pictures. Carol knew she was on the right track as she watched Kate changing right before her eyes, as if she was emerging from a cocoon.

Chapter Ten

Lillian and Anna had finished supper and were cleaning up when the phone rang. It was Carolyn asking if they were going to Maine this weekend, "Yes, no matter what, we miss it awful!" Carolyn laughed and had to agree, "Julie and I feel the same way. Do you know if anyone else is going?" "Yes," Lillian said, "Karen and Nancy are going. They're getting ready to take over the bakery, they're pretty excited." Carolyn agreed, "I'm sure they are! I hope everyone can go this time, we need to get caught up on this paper work and apply for a license." Carolyn and Lillian talked about Jamie and Susan. They knew about the meeting but hadn't heard anything since. "Well," said Lillian, "I'm going to call Jamie tonight and if there is any news I'll call you back." They talked for a few more minutes and Lillian told her about the girl, Kate, that Carol was trying to help. "I know Carol planned on having her over to the farm today, but that's all I've heard so far. I tried calling her before supper but there was no answer. I'll try again before I call Jamie." She finally reached Carol that evening and let her know that everyone would be there for the weekend and also to find out how it was going with Kate. She was glad to hear that things were still progressing on a positive note. After they hung up Lillian tried Jamie a couple of times but there was no answer.

Kate woke up the next morning actually looking forward to the day. It was the first time, in a long time that she had felt that way. She knew she would have to go back to the shelter later that day, but for now she was going to enjoy this for all it was worth. Carol woke as soon as she heard Kate get up and go into the bathroom. She stayed in bed a few minutes longer, still tired from a restless night, thinking about Patty. She knew this was probably not a good time to be thinking about a relationship, especially now that Kate needed her help, but she couldn't get Patty out of her mind. She wanted to know more about her and formulated a plan to meet her again. With everyone coming up for the weekend, she decided to call the Farm Stand and order a couple of pies, using that as her excuse to stop by and see her again. She would make the call before she left for the sister's place this morning.

When Carol came into the kitchen, Kate was pouring herself a cup of coffee, "Hi, can I get you one?" "Sure, that would be nice," Carol answered, then asked, "How did you sleep last night?" "Better then I have in a long time," Kate said as she set Carol's cup in front of her. She sat down and continued speaking, "Carol, I just want to thank you for taking an interest in me, I'm feeling so much better this morning." Carol smiled at her, "All this in one day?" "I guess so," she answered, "you helped me feel better about myself. I'm really happy you came along." Carol replied, "Thank you Kate, I feel good about it too."

They ate a quick breakfast. Kate said she would take care of the chickens while Carol went off to work. Carol was fine with that because Lillian was having a load of firewood delivered today and Kate would be here to show them where to dump it. Also Carolyn and Julie had a plumber coming by the cottage today and she needed Kate to show him where it was. As soon as

Kate headed out to the chicken coop, Carol set her plan in motion and made her call. "The Farm Stand, this is Patty." Carol's heart was doing flips when she heard Patty's voice but tried to stay cool and answer in a calm voice, "Yes, hi, I would like to order two of your apple pies for Friday, if that's alright?" "Well of course it's alright!" Patty chuckled, "Now what's the name on this?" "Carol Thompson, from the old "Hurley" farm." Carol could feel the pause as Patty realized who she was talking to. When Patty spoke again her voice was much softer, "Well hi Carol, did you want these for morning or afternoon?" "It will be afternoon, the women I live with are coming up this weekend and I thought it would be a nice treat for them." "Well, thank you for the compliment. Will you be picking them up your self?" Carol could feel her face go instantly red, thankful she was on the phone, "Yes, I will." "Good, then I look forward to seeing you again." "Yes, me too." When Carol hung up, she instinctively knew that Patty had more than a little interest in her also.

As soon as Carol's work at the sister's place was finished, she went home and had lunch with Kate. Finishing up the dishes, it was time to go to work on the fences. Carol wanted to have it finished before Lillian and Anna arrived on Friday. Luckily it was a cloudy day, keeping the sun at bay while they worked. It didn't take them long; they had already figured out everything and had the wire cut. It was just a matter of putting the posts in the ground and tacking the wire to the posts. Carol knew Kate didn't want to go back to the shelter and if it were up to her she would let her stay on, but she needed to ask Lillian and Anna first.

"Kate, can you hand me the staple gun?" Kate gave it to her and asked, "Carol, how do you know so much about everything? Is there anything you can't do?" Carol laughed, "Believe me, when I first arrived here I knew nothing. I had never really been in the country before or even had a backyard that I can remember. But around here, some things just seem to come natural." "Carol?" Carol stopped what she was doing, and looked up at the serious sound in Kate's voice, "Yes?" "Do you think I could stay here for awhile?" The tears in Kate's eyes reminded Carol of herself when she had found the peace and tranquility of the farm and had not wanted to leave. Standing up, she put her arms around her, "Oh Kate, if it were just up to me, I would say yes in a heartbeat, but I would have to talk to Donna first and if it's all right with her, I would still have to ask Anna and Lillian." Carol knew they wouldn't mind; she would call them as soon as they were done. But before she had a chance to call, Anna called her that afternoon to see if the wood had been delivered. Carol decided to ask about Kate right off. Anna's response was immediate, "Of course she may stay but will it be all right with the shelter? We're not licensed yet Carol, there could be a problem." She hadn't thought of that but somehow felt everything would work out for the best. She told Kate she had talked to Anna and that she was fine with her staying on, but they would have to go back to the shelter to see Donna and she wanted Kate included in the conversation.

Donna was not only surprised by the change she saw in Kate but she was relieved as well. Ultimately Donna wanted what was best for Kate and if this situation was helping her, she wouldn't interfere with her decision to stay with Carol, but she wanted to talk to Kate alone. Carol was fine with that and went off to visit with the other women there. After about an hour, Carol heard her name being called over the intercom and she went to Donna's office. Kate was beaming; things apparently went well. Donna said it was obvious Kate was making much more progress with Carol than she had at the shelter. After sending Kate out to pack up her stuff, Donna turned to Carol and said, "I'm amazed at the difference in her and she's only been with you for two days." Carol smiled, "I know, I'm happy for her." Donna told Carol that Kate had told her everything about being abused by a woman, "I can understand now her reluctance to talk to us. It's a good thing you were around for her Carol. I have to admit I don't know a lot about that life style but I want to be able to help these women as well as the traditional women we are most familiar with. May I call on you if a situation like this should present itself again?" "Of course you can," Carol said. "I was in the same situation once myself and being able to talk to women in a lesbian relationship really made the difference for me." Carol went on to tell her that the women where she lived were seriously talking about opening a safe house for battered lesbian women and they already had a psychiatrist and other professional women interested in helping them with it. Donna thought it was a wonderful idea and expressed an interest in meeting with them sometime. "Who knows," she said, "maybe we can all work together and reach out to help these women." When Kate came back in the office, Donna had her sign a release slip and gave her a hug wishing her well. Returning her attention to Carol, she said, "Now don't be a stranger, we have really enjoyed seeing you around here." Carol told her she would definitely be back, and she would probably be bringing a helper.

The rest of the week flew by. Kate was a big help to Carol. During the day she took over some her chores while Carol volunteered at the shelter and at night they discussed her future. Kate wanted to go back to school and get her diploma, but she wanted to get a job during the day. Carol could see how bright Kate was and thought it was a good idea. Kate felt once she was in school and working, it wouldn't be long before she would be able to find an apartment. In just one week, Kate was taking control of her life and planning her future.

Chapter Eleven

Before they knew it, it was Friday and Carol couldn't wait to see to see everyone and have them meet Kate. Kate, on the other hand, was very nervous. Carol reassured her there was nothing to be worried about; everyone was eager to meet her. Carol got an early start at the sister's house, leaving Kate behind to finish up around the farm. As soon as Carol was through helping them, she showered and headed over to the Farm Stand. When she pulled in, she was disappointed to see so many cars in the parking lot, but then, it was lunchtime. Walking in her eyes immediately found Patty, who yelled out over the noise, "Hi, I'll be with you in just a minute." Carol managed to find a spot at the end of the counter, close to where Patty was working. Looking up, Patty rewarded her with a smile. "Nice seeing you again." she said as she wiped the counter in front of Carol, "I guess I picked a bad time," Carol murmured. "No, not at all, we're just about caught up, I'll be right back," Patty replied. 'There's that smile again.' Carol thought. She liked the effect it was having on her.

It wasn't long before things quieted down and the counter girl working with Patty was able to handle things alone. Patty walked over to Carol with two ice-filled glasses of lemonade, handing her one as she spoke, "Angie's almost done and she'll box up those pies for you." "Thank you," Carol said as she took a drink, "This is so good, I didn't realize how thirsty I was." Patty asked, "So, how's things at the Old Hurley farm? I haven't seen it in quite awhile." Carol's eyes were bright as she answered, "A lot of renovations have been done, but there's still a lot of work left to do. We're still working on it though. I think it looks beautiful; I just love it there." Patty chuckled, "Yes, I can tell." Angie called to Patty saying the pies were all boxed and at the register. Carol wasn't anxious to leave but she knew she had to get back so she'd have plenty of time to prepare for Lillian and Anna. She finished her lemonade and followed Patty to the register, asking how much for the drink? Patty waved her hand, saying it was her pleasure and she looked directly into Carol's eyes, letting her know that she meant it. Carol, a little flustered by the show of interest, averted her eyes and mumbled her thanks as she paid for the pies. Regaining her composure, she continued speaking, "Well, I guess I should be going, but as they say, if you're ever in the neighborhood, stop in and I'll show you around." "Thanks Carol, I just might take you up on that and in the meantime, don't be a stranger!"

Back at the farm, Kate was glad to see Carol drive in. She had just finished opening the windows in the bedrooms and was freshening them up. Everything looked wonderful and now it was time to start the spaghetti sauce so it would be done in time for supper. It was so beautiful outside, they decided to clean up the porch and wash down the picnic table so they could eat supper out there when everyone arrived. "Kate, try to relax, they're all looking forward to meeting you," Carol said, hoping to reassure her. "I know," she replied, "I just need to keep busy." Carol had no problem with that, if everyone was coming, that would mean fifteen, including her and Kate, for supper. Now she had to figure out how to set it up so they could all sit down together. They removed all the lounge chairs from the porch, setting them on the lawn, making enough room to bring in the other picnic table. Butting them together, it made just enough room for everyone to sit down together comfortably. Turning to Kate she said, "Well, what do you think?" "It looks great," she answered, "but we need to cover the tables." Carol told her where the sheets were kept and suggested she pick out a matched pair with a flowery print to use as tablecloths. It was almost five o'clock before they were finished. "Wow, this looks great," Kate said as she set down the last place setting. Carol agreed, "It sure does. We have about an hour before they start arriving and I think we should take a couple of those lounge chairs over in the shade and relax until they get here." Kate was fine with that. It had been a busy day and they were both tired; it didn't take but a moment before the warm breezes lulled them to sleep.

The sound of a car door jolted Carol awake, "Kate, wake up, they're here!" Lillian and Anna walked toward Carol until she caught them both in her arms, "I have missed you guys." They shared each other's excitement, "It's good to be home," Anna said and then she saw the small figure standing behind Carol. Stepping around Carol, Anna held out her arms, "And you must be Kate," pulling her into a warm embrace, "Welcome to our home Kate." Carol saw the tears forming in Kate's eyes as both Lillian and Anna welcomed her.

"The place looks great!" Lillian said as she began looking around, and it did. The gardens were lush and green and flowers were in bloom everywhere they looked. They loved the fence Carol and Kate had put up, "Well," said Anna, "you two have certainly been busy, everything looks wonderful! And Carol, look at you, your all tan and your hair, you've cut your hair! I like it, it's very becoming." Lillian agreed and Carol blushed. The four of them went into the house. Anna and Lillian were anxious to see what the carpenters had done so far. Once inside, they were overwhelmed with the delicious smells wafting through the house. While Anna was sneaking a taste of Carol's sauce, Carolyn and Julie came in and gave her a big hug. During the next hour, one after another they arrived, except for Jamie. Everyone welcomed Kate into the 'fold' and by the time they all sat down to dinner Kate felt she had always known them.

The porch was a perfect setting for their dinner and as the wine was flowing, they talked for hours just getting caught up with each other. The only time it took on a serious tone was when Carol asked about Jamie. Carol already knew about Susan and Jamie's meeting, but didn't know if they had worked things out yet. Connie spoke up, "I hoped she might show up this weekend and maybe she will. The last time I talked to her was right before Susan told her what happened between her and Jimmy. I don't know if anything will come of it. She seems to have disappeared from sight. I have to respect the fact that she just doesn't want to talk to anyone about it yet, but I hope she's okay." Jean spoke up then, "I talked to Susan the other day and so far, she hasn't heard from Jamie, either." Anna said she would track her down when they get back if she doesn't show up here this weekend. She said," I suppose I shouldn't worry about her, she is more than able to take care of herself, but I hate to think of her going through this by herself, even if it is what she wants." Julie asked, "How's Susan feeling, is the pregnancy all right?" "Yes," Jean said, "she's doing fine, except for some morning sickness." Connie added, "I know Jamie's hurting and wants things to be the way they were before, but honestly, she can't see how she fits into Susan's life." Anna spoke up, "Jamie loves Susan, maybe in time they will work things out." "Well," said Karen, "I hope Jamie doesn't wait too long, Susan could use her support right now." Lillian said in a confident voice, "One thing I do know about Jamie, you can depend on her to do the right thing.

With good conversation and more than a few bottles of wine shared, the time flew by and it was almost midnight before Carol suggested desert and coffee. Nancy said, "Karen and I were going to bring something, but we just ran out of time." "Oh that's alright," Carol said rather nonchalantly. "I ordered a couple of pies from the Farm Stand." Anna always seemed to be able to read between the lines, "Carol dear, even in the candle light I can see your blushing, is there something we should know?" Carol had to laugh, "God Anna, you're good. Actually, I met someone I am definitely interested in getting to know better." Carol was immediatcly hit with questions from every direction. Holding up her hands, she shushed them with, "Wait a minute, let me get the desert and coffee, then I'll tell you about Patty." Kate, Jean and Connie went with Carol to help speed up the process. They were all dying to hear about who she met, including Kate, who was amazed by the natural openness of these women. She felt as if she had stepped into a whole other world, one where she belonged.

Over desert Carol told them about meeting Patty, "I've only seen her twice; and only for a few minutes. I don't know her other than to say hi and goodbye, but I'm working on that." Lillian spoke up, "Oh I remember Patty when she was a child. She was a pretty wild kid growing up, but then she went away to collage and I haven't seen her since. I didn't know she was back around these parts again." Carol replied, "You see, I don't even know that much about her, though I did invite her to stop by some time. I think she will, at least I hope she does." "Well," said Connie, "I think we should all make a trip to the Farm Stand tomorrow and check this babe out and make sure she is good enough for our Carol! How about it everybody, are you with me?" Jean laughed, "Connie we are not going to embarrass Carol!" Connie winked at Kate, "No, of course not, I just thought it would be a good place to visit tomorrow." Anna asked, "What are our plans for tomorrow?" Carolyn spoke up and said, "Julie and I have to unpack a ton of stuff we brought up but we should have things in order by early afternoon. Nancy and Karen said they had an appointment in the morning with a local realtor to see a couple of houses, but they'd be back fairly early. Cathy and Ronnie wanted to go for a walk on the beach, but could be back by afternoon. "Alright," said Lillian, "why don't we plan on all meeting back here at two o'clock, then we can all take that trip to the Farm Stand." Carol just shook her head.

The next morning everyone left to go about their plans while those that were staying at the farm waited to meet with the carpenters, who were planning to be there early. When they finally arrived, everyone followed them upstairs. They were all happy with their progress, it was really beginning to come together. Everybody was talking excitedly as they saw their future becoming a reality. They planned on sitting down with everyone after supper to discuss what was left to be done to get the safe house up and running. Both Carolyn and Ronnie had a lot of information to bring to the table.

MAINLY LESBIANS

Chapter Twelve

Jamie finished her photo shoot earlier in the afternoon than she had planned, leaving her more time on her hands than she wished for. Arriving home, she suddenly decided to pack some things and head for Maine. She had put off going because she felt like a fifth wheel and it brought back memories of Susan. She had tried putting Susan out of her thoughts, but try as she might, nothing was working. Being up there with everyone, without Susan, was definitely painful for her, but it was something she would just have to get over if she was going to move there. Half way up the Pike she turned her car around and drove back to Boston and to Susan. She needed to see her again and couldn't see a future without Susan in it. Pulling up in front of her house she didn't hesitate, she got out, walked up to the front door and rang the bell. A young girl, looking very much like Susan, answered the door. "Hi, my name is Jamie, is your mother here?" "Yes she is," then in a loud voice, "Mom, someone's here to see you." Jamie could here Susan's voice coming from the other room, "Who is it Carrie?" "Jamie." Susan came out wiping her hands on a towel. Jamie could see the disbelief in her eyes. "Oh…Jamie…come in," Susan said as she reached beside her to close the door. "This is my daughter Carrie." They said hello to each other then Susan said, "Carrie supper's almost ready, are you and your sister done cleaning your room?" Carrie rolled her eyes at Jamie, who couldn't help but chuckle, "Oh Mom, can't we finish it tomorrow? We don't have much left to do, honest." Susan didn't say

273

anything, just gave her a look she was apparently familiar with, "Oh all right," Carrie said as she turned and went up stairs. Jamie was smiling as Susan was shaking her head. Susan turned to Jamie, "Would you like a cup of coffee?" Jamie checked to see that Carrie was out of earshot and said, "I would rather have you in my arms right now, but I will settle for a cup of coffee." Susan took her by the hand and led her out to the kitchen asking, as she indicated a seat at the table, "Why are you here Jamie?" "I've missed you and I needed to see you," she replied, adding, "you look great, are you feeling okay?" "I'm alright," she answered as she put Jamie's coffee down in front of her. Jamie grabbed her hand and held on to it as she spoke, "Susan I don't know what to say, I love you and some how we…" Susan cut Jamie's words off as she bent down and found her lips.

Jamie stayed and helped with supper that night while the girls kept her entertained with dramatic stories of their, 'boring everyday lives!' After supper Susan sent the girls upstairs to pack their clothes for their trip tomorrow. They were going to their grandparent's camp for the weekend with their father. Susan asked, "Can you stay for a while Jamie?" "Yes, I'd like that." As soon as the girls went to bed, Susan made them each a cup of coffee. They talked well into the wee hours of the morning. Jamie didn't know how she was going to fit in with Susan, her two girls and now a new baby, but she knew now, that she couldn't just walk away. Looking intently into Susan's eyes she said, "I don't know where this will lead, but I do know I need to be part of your life and whatever lies ahead we will deal with it together."

Chapter Thirteen

Carol and Kate rode in the car with Lillian and Anna, while the rest split up in two other cars and drove to the Farm Stand. Much to Carol's relief, it was decided they wouldn't all line up at once to meet Patty. Everybody had something in mind to buy and felt they would run into her here and there while looking around. Patty's father saw Lillian walk in and came right over, "Well Lillian, hello, I haven't seen you in ages, how have you been?" Lillian took his out stretched hand, "Good Jake, and you?" Winking at her, "Oh, I'm still kickin', just a little slower now. My daughter Patty moved back this past spring and it's made a big difference. She's been a lot of help to me." Jake saw Patty out of the corner of his eye, "Patty honey, can you come over here for a minute?" Patty had just come from out back after seeing all the cars out front; she thought he might need some help.

Coming around the corner, Patty saw Carol and gave her a big smile. "You need something Dad?" He didn't, he just wanted Lillian to meet her. Patty recognized her right away, "I remember you! You used to come into the store when you visited your grandparents." Lillian was surprised she remembered, "Yes that's right. But even before that, when I was a teenager, I spent a lot of time up here. I knew your mother pretty well back then; she was such a good friend." Patty voice took on a softer tone; "I was pretty young when she died. I didn't really know her. Maybe you could share some stories some time?" Lillian told her, "I would like that Patty. Now let me introduce you to my friends, this is Anna and Kate and I guess you've already met Carol." Patty said hello to everyone, including Carol again. Anna, seeing the way Patty looked at Carol, spoke up, "Patty dear, we're planning to cook out tomorrow, would you be free to come by, I'm sure Lillian would like to talk with you about your mother." Lillian spoke right up, "That's a great idea Anna! How about it Patty?" "I'd love too, but I have to work until four o'clock tomorrow," Carol heard the disappointment in her voice, as did Anna, "That's not a problem dear, some of our friends will be leaving about that time, but we'll still be there for a while. Plenty of time to visit." Patty laughed and said, "Great, then I'll be there!" Looking at Carol, she gave her a small wink. Carol felt that flutter in her belly again. By the time they made all of their purchases, Patty had ample opportunity to meet everyone. It was not lost on her that they were all couples.

Over dinner that night, the requirements to obtain a shelter license were discussed. Carolyn and Ronnie had gathered a lot of information, along with the necessary forms to be filled out for the State of Maine. There was more to it than they had expected. While it was not necessary, it would benefit them to have a non-profit status; and they would need to appoint a Board of Directors. They also needed a mission statement and would have to draw up the by-laws. It was obvious they were going to need the help of a lawyer. On and on it went, but they weren't discouraged, they would just deal with each issue until it was completed. They were determined to accomplish their goal. Their first "official meeting" broke up around ten o'clock. They were all exhausted from a full day at the farm. Carolyn and Julie were going to spend their first night at the cottage and didn't want to be up too late as they had other plans in mind. As tired as every one was, they couldn't fall asleep right away. Their minds were still active, thinking over all they had talked about at their 'meeting.' but eventually the house settled down as everyone drifted off into a deep sleep.

Walking along the path to the cottage, Carolyn and Julie let the glow of the flash light lead the way. As they got closer to the cottage they became excited. Opening the door and stepping inside, they were greeted by the dim lights they had left on for their return. Both felt the warm, comforting sensation of coming home. They stood still and absorbed the presence of their new surroundings. Carolyn turned to Julie saying, "Hon, we're home."

Sunday morning found Susan waking up in Jamie's apartment. She smiled as she felt Jamie curled around her, 'This is the way it should be,' she thought. They had talked about it last night; Susan wanted Jamie to move in with her and the girls. Jamie was afraid it would cause problems for Susan. She knew she could loose her kids if Jimmy found out she was involved with a women. She said, "Let's give it some time Susan. Things might change, but for now I'll never be more then a phone call away." Susan knew she would have to settle for that, but now that things were right between them, she felt she could move on and deal with anything that came her way. She felt Jamie's lips on her shoulder, turning over to face her she said, "Good morning." Jamie smiled back at her. Slipping her hand under the covers, Jamie gently touched

Susan's now swelling belly. Susan pressed Jamie's hand firmly against her, "Are you alright?" Jamie asked. "I've never felt better, except for one thing, I'm starved," she replied. Jamie laughed and pulled her closer. After making love they headed out to the kitchen and she made her a breakfast fit for a princess.

Susan still had the rest of the day before she had to go home, the girls weren't due back until six. An idea formed in her mind and she asked excitedly, "Jamie, do you want to drive up to Maine?" "Sure," Jamie said, "if you'd like." Susan put her arms around Jamie, "I would love to. I have really missed everyone. We can leave as soon as we finish breakfast, we should be there around ten o'clock before everyone takes off to go somewhere!" Jamie caught her excitement, "Great, let's get going! I can't wait to let everyone know we are together again."

When Carol woke up she was looking forward to the day. Patty was coming over! Just the very thought of her brought a smile to her lips. She felt it was the beginning of a new chapter in her life; one she was looking forward to with great anticipation. Getting up she went to the kitchen and put on the coffee before heading for the shower. The smell of coffee brought everyone to the kitchen and by the time she had finished dressing, breakfast had been cooked and was taken out to the porch to be devoured while they planned their cookout for this afternoon.

At the cottage, Carolyn and Julie weren't in any hurry to get up but they knew everyone would be having breakfast early and they didn't want to be late. Carolyn whispered in Julie's ear, "The next time we come, we'll have to remember to buy some food."

Julie laughed, "I know, I'm famished. We should get over there before there's nothing left to eat." Carolyn paused for a moment, "Julie, would you consider moving sooner then we'd planned?" Julie sat up, giving Carolyn her full attention. Carolyn continued, "Why wait, I don't think it will be hard for us to find jobs." Julie was surprised, "Your serious?" Carolyn nodded her head yes, "Let's see if we can get away for a couple of days next week and see what's available at the local hospitals and Human Services Departments. What do you think?" Julie agreed immediately. They had been coming up here for so long now, it didn't feel like it would be a major change, as long as she could find a job in her own field. With that settled, they walked quickly up to the farm ready for breakfast.

After breakfast, Connie, Jean, Kate and Cathy elected to get things ready for the cook out, while the rest of the group tackled the job of filling out the forms and putting everything in order to apply for their tax exempt status. Outside the day was beautiful. Connie began cleaning out the fireplace while Kate brought out the lawn chairs from the shed. Cathy and Jean began preparing the food. After feeding the chickens, Carol went over to the shed she'd just seen Kate go into, "Hi, I haven't had a chance to see you alone this weekend, how's it going?" Kate set down the chairs she was holding. "If your talking about how things are going with me and your friends, I think they're all great. I am really happy to be here. Carol thanks again for taking an interest in me." Carol told her, "Cathy did that for me once, maybe you'll be able to help someone else along the way," Kate nodded her head yes, "I definitely will, but back to you." Kate added

279

with a grin, "I didn't know you were interested in anyone." Carol laughed, "Well I just met her last week but I liked her right away. I can't believe how fast Lillian and Anna worked to get her over here, but I'm glad they did." Their attention was diverted when they heard a car in the driveway. Coming out of the shed Carol saw Jamie getting out of her car. Kate saw her too, "Wow, who is that?" Carol chuckled, "That my dear is Jamie. Come on, I will introduce you." Carol could hear Connie as she got closer, "Hey, look who's here!" she said as she walked past Jamie and took Susan in her arms, "We've been thinking about you," Connie stepped back to get a good look at her, "How are you feeling?" "I've been thinking about you guys too," Susan said and then added, looking at Jamie, "I feel wonderful." Everyone came out, all excited that Susan and Jamie were together again. Anna cut through the crowd and found Jamie, "Well it is about time my dear; she needs you." Jamie gave her a hug, "I know Anna, I need her too." They all took a break from what they were doing and spent time visiting with Susan. They wanted to know all about her, how she was and how her daughters were doing. Susan told them, "It's not what I had planned, but I am glad it's over and I can be myself. As far as the girls go, they're handling things better then I thought they would." Taking Jamie's hand she said, "Believe me, being pregnant was the last thing I ever thought would happen, but now that I don't feel so alone, I know everything will turn out fine."

Around one o'clock, Connie and Jamie went out to start the grill. Connie said, "Hey Jamie, I'm happy for you, I think Susan's terrific." Jamie answered, "Thanks

Connie, I think so too. I wish things were different. I feel I should be there to help her, especially now, but I don't want to end up causing her any problems." Susan came up beside Jamie slipping her arm around her waist, "Can I help?"

Susan and Jamie left around three o'clock. Neither one wanted to go, but it was time. Jamie wished Carol good luck with her new friend Patty, "Call me and let me know how things went." Carol said she would. Everyone else began leaving shortly after, except for Lillian and Anna. They told Patty they would be there when she came over, but they didn't plan on staying too long after. They had eaten very little with the others so they could save their appetite for later when they had supper with Patty.

Anna noticed Carol seemed nervous. Walking over to where she was standing, she took her hand, "Patty seems like a nice person, I'm sure there's nothing to be nervous about dear." Carol raised her eyebrows, "Thanks Anna, but I've only been with one other person and I don't have much practice dating. I just hope I don't freeze up and not be able to think of anything to say." She replied, giving Carol's hand a gentle squeeze, "I have a feeling you'll be just fine. Now Patty should be here any minute so let's set up the table on the porch. It will be too buggy to sit outside." Lillian got the grill started again for the chicken while Kate cleaned up the kitchen and made a fresh salad. Carol continued to pace nervously, looking at her watch.

Lillian was just putting the chicken on the grill when Patty arrived. "Patty, I'm glad you could make it, I hope your hungry." Patty told her, "You don't have to worry about that, I always have a good appetite." Lillian laughed, "Good, then you'll fit in perfectly around here. This will be done soon; we're eating earlier then usual. Anna and I have to head back to Boston soon, but Carol and Kate will be here to show you around after supper." Patty wanted to know the relationship between Carol and Kate, but couldn't ask, "I brought a pie for desert, what would you like me to do with it?" Lillian said, "Wonderful, you can take it into the kitchen. Go right through the porch and down the hall and its on your right, Carol should be in there. She found both Carol and Kate there and they happily received the pie. Patty was so easy to be around that Carol immediately relaxed.

During dinner, Lillian told Patty some childhood stories involving her mother and the way things were back then. Everyone, including Anna, sat quietly as Lillian transported them all back to another time. Patty was grateful; it brought her mother back to life. After desert Lillian and Anna got ready to leave, but told Patty they would be back and hoped to be seeing more of her. Patty told them, with a side-glance at Carol, "I have a feeling you will." She helped clear the table and offered to help with the dishes. Kate stood back and said with a big yawn, "This has been a full weekend for me, if you guys don't mind I'd like to skip the 'tour' and just go to bed." She added laughing, "I'm exhausted!" Both Carol and Patty laughed telling Kate to go ahead, they would clean up. After they were done, Carol poured them each a glass of wine, which they took with them on the tour. Patty was impressed with all the changes they had made, but was more impressed with Carol and the women she'd met the day before. Arriving back at the porch, they sat on the porch swing together while Carol poured them another glass of wine. She began telling Patty about everyone, including how she came to be part of it all. Patty was impressed by Carol's frank admission to not only being a lesbian, but also being in an abusive relationship. Carol explained she had gone through a lot of changes since she came here and went on to explain about Kate. Patty felt bad for Kate, but was relieved to hear they were just friends. Carol continued talking and filled her in on their plans turn the farm into a safe house for battered lesbian women. Patty was amazed at what they were trying to do. She offered to help in any way she could. Sitting beside each other on the porch swing, Carol was very aware of her attraction to Patty, but still unsure of herself, she kept things light.

The evening flew by; they were having a good time getting to know each other. Around eleven Patty reluctantly had to say goodnight. She had to get up early the next morning. Facing Carol she said, "I hate to end the evening, but I have to get going." Carol could have stayed up all night. "I'm glad you came by Patty. I've really enjoyed talking with you. You're welcome to stop by anytime." Patty stood up, "It has been fun…Carol would you like to take in a show with me sometime?" Carol said, "Yes I would, I haven't been to a show in ages." "Good," said Patty, "Then it's a date?" "Yes, it's a date." Carol walked Patty to her car, wishing she had the nerve to kiss her goodnight. Standing by the car Patty stopped and took both of Carol's hands in her own, Carol felt her breath catch in her throat as Patty moved closer, giving her a quick but tender kiss.

Chapter Fourteen

As summer moved into fall, everything began coming together at a fast pace. The rooms upstairs were just about completed. With the help of a lawyer they finished making out all the forms needed for their non-profit status and the State of Maine. They were just waiting for a final inspection and hopefully, their license. Karen and Nancy fell in love with a place not far from the farm and put down a deposit. Carolyn and Julie had some good job prospects, but needed to decide what was best for them. Julie would be taking a full time job, while Carolyn wanted part time. She planned on spending her off time at the shelter as soon as it was up and running. Lillian and Anna were really excited about the move. Only six more weeks to go and they would be year 'round residents of Maine. They could hardly wait to 'begin the rest of their lives' as they liked to refer to the move. Cathy and Ronnie were also eagerly looking forward to the prospect of a new life together. Ronnie already had a couple of job interviews lined up at the hospital in Portland. They both decided to take a week off from work to line up jobs and find a place to live. Ronnie's house in Boston already had a buyer interested. Things were moving fast.

Connie heard Jean answering the door welcoming Jamie and Susan for dinner. Susan was really beginning to show. "Hi, come in." It was a hot and sticky day, but their apartment was air-conditioned. Susan said, "Oh, it's nice and cool in here Jean." Jean answered, "I know, it would be unbearable otherwise.

Let's go to the kitchen and see how Connie's doing."
On the way to the kitchen they stopped to admire
Jean's paintings that were hung on the walls of the
hallway. Jamie said with awe, "Jean these are
incredible! Connie told me you painted, but I had no
idea you were this talented!" Jean liked hearing that,
"Thank you Jamie, I really appreciate that." Susan
agreed, she knew quite a bit about art; her parents were
collectors of fine art. Susan asked, "Do you sell
these?" Jean smiled, "Oh no, I'm just learning right
now. But it is something I would like to pursue. My
boss has given me a lot of encouragement," Connie
could hear them talking in the living room. She didn't
let it show but she was a little anxious about Jean
pursuing a career in art. Connie didn't feel she would
fit into that lifestyle. She wasn't comfortable with
Jean's boss either. The few time she met him, he just
seemed a little too familiar with Jean.

Jean told them, "Connie is making her famous
spaghetti sauce." The kitchen smelled wonderful and
of course Jamie insisted on a taste right away, "Connie
this is great, where did you ever learn to cook like
this?" Connie laughed, "Believe me, this is about all I
know how to do, just ask Jean." Jean laughed, "She's
right, we eat a lot of spaghetti around here! I'm not
much better, but I am trying." Susan and Jean sat with
their tea while Jamie and Connie had beer. Connie,
always with the direct questions asked, "So, how are
things going between you two?" Jamie answered,
giving Susan's hand a squeeze, "We're doing alright.
I'm staying low key until the divorce is final." Jean
asked how long before that happens. Susan answered,

"Less then two weeks. Then I'll tell Jimmy about the baby. I'll just have to deal with what ever happens."

The four of them had a lot in common. Jean already knew her children were happy with the way things were. Her relationship with Connie wasn't going to affect that, "I think it's time Connie met my kids," Jean said and added, "I don't feel there's anything to hide anymore." Susan asked if Jean meant she was going to tell them about their relationship, "No, I don't see any need to. I think things will go along smoothly if we don't make an issue out of it, just be ourselves." Connie spoke up, "Well I hope your right, I don't want to come between you and your kids." Jean gave Connie a look; it was apparent they had this conversation before, "Connie, that's not going to happen, you don't need to worry about it. My time with the kids has grown to be a wonderful experience. They are a big part of my life and I need you to be a part of that too." They had a nice evening together until Jamie reminded everyone, "You know, pretty soon its just going to be the four of us." Connie replied, "We're well aware of that. Thankfully they're not that far away." "That's true," said Susan, "We can still go visit everyone." They all knew that, but they would still feel the void. A sadness came over them as they contemplated what it was going to be like with out the others. They were a close, tight knit group and had gone through a lot of changes together. It was easy to see that this move was going to be harder on the ones left behind.

Chapter Fifteen

The week before Labor Day, everything fell into place. Carolyn and Julie accepted the positions they had been looking for. The upstairs of the house was finished and the State of Maine approved the shelter and they were granted a license. In addition, their non-profit status came through, so they would be able to hold fundraisers and accept donations to help with the financial liability that they were sure to incur. Nancy and Karen passed papers on a little house not far from the farm. They planned on moving in right away and opening their bakery soon after that. Things worked out for Cathy and Ronnie as well. Ronnie got a good price for her house, enabling her and Cathy to buy a house in Maine. Ronnie also landed a job she felt she would be happy with. Cathy was going to take a couple of weeks off after they moved in. Ronnie would be working a lot of hours at first and she needed the time to unpack and do some minor fixing up. They couldn't have been happier with the way things were turning out. Kate also had good news. Not only did she find a job but she was starting classes in adult education a few nights a week. Everyone was proud of her.

Jamie stayed at Susan's for supper and was just starting the dishes. She had drawn the short straw and was exclaiming, "I think this was rigged!" Carrie laughed, adding with an innocent look, "Oh come on Jamie, would we do that?" Susan agreed with Jamie, giving her a wink, "Well I suspect the same thing, so it looks like it's just me and you for ice cream tonight." That did it. Carrie and Jenny said okay they would help

Jamie, adding, "Even though we are completely innocent"! Jamie looked over at Susan and shared a smile, family life was agreeing with her. Jamie felt different, something in her seemed to settle; she didn't know what it was, but everything just felt right.

After they came back from having their ice cream, it was late, time for the girls to go to bed. Coming down from upstairs, Susan looked tired. Taking her hand, Jamie said, "Come, sit down and relax, do you want anything?" Susan sat on the couch and put her feet up, "Thanks, I would like a cup of tea." Jamie got right up and went out to the kitchen to get it for her. She liked taking care of her. Susan, resting her head on the back of the couch with her eyes closed, was listening to Jamie busy in the kitchen. It brought a smile to her lips. She had found what had been missing in her life. Coming up behind Susan, Jamie gently kissed the top of her head, "Here's your tea." Taking a few sips, she said, "This is good, just what I needed." Jamie asked, "Are you okay, do you want anything else?" Setting her cup down, Susan turned to face Jamie sitting beside her. Taking her hand, she pressed it against her cheek. Jamie now understood how powerful those touches were, like the ones she had seen between Lillian and Anna, when words weren't needed.

Lillian and Anna were up most of the night packing the last few items in the apartment. They were more then ready to start their new life in Maine. Caught up in the excitement of moving, neither one had realized how sad they were going to feel leaving the apartment that had been their home for so long. Anna looked around and said, "Its like leaving an old friend isn't it

289

Lil?" Standing beside Anna, Lil could see the tears in her eyes. Taking Anna in her arms neither one spoke. There was nothing they could say.

Patty took the day off from work to help Carol set up for the big celebration planned for tonight! Kate would have taken the day off too, but she just started her new job and didn't think it was a good idea. She would be there as soon as she got out; it was going to be a great time!

Carolyn and Julie were up early, ready to help with the party! They moved in last week and loved it. They still had another week before they were to start their new jobs, giving them plenty of time to get settled in to their new home. It was an exciting time! Carolyn was heading to the car when Julie caught her in her arms giving her a big hug. Laughing Carolyn returned the gesture. Not letting go, they leaned back looking at each other and Julie said, "God I feel good, this is the best move we could have made!" Carolyn agreed, "I know we are going to be very happy here." They finished packing the car with the food they had made for the party and drove to the farm.

Susan was up stairs in the girl's rooms helping them pack some clothes. They were staying with friends while she and Jamie were in Maine for the big party. It had been a couple of weeks since Susan announced she was pregnant. After the initial shock, the girls began feeling excited. They surprised Susan by being concerned about her condition, and helping out around the house without being asked. Jimmy had been another story. Susan told him as a matter of fact, she was pregnant, and that it was his. "You really don't expect me to believe that do you? I knew all along you were having an affair! What happened, did he dump you?" Susan didn't let his ranting go on for long. Leaving, she told him it didn't matter to her what he believed, she just wanted him to know. They hadn't spoken since, but she was sure she hadn't heard the last from him.

Looking out the upstairs window Susan saw Jamie's car pull up. Leaning out, she caught her attention, "Hi, they'll be right down." Jamie was taking the girls over to their friend's house. Getting in, Jen told Jamie, "Mom said she was running a little late but she would be ready by the time you get back." Jamie asked if she was feeling all right. Carrie said, "Oh sure, she's fine. She's just packing the cooler with some food she made to take to Maine." Coming back for Susan, Jamie had a smile on her face, this certainly wasn't the life style she expected, but she loved it. She too was getting excited about the baby.

Connie and Jean were still in bed. Jean had started to get up earlier but Connie reached up pulling her back down, she had other plans. "Well" said Jean, "that's a nice way to start the day." Connie held her tight; "If we weren't going to Maine I'd keep you here all day." "Jean laughed and jumped up, "I would love to take you up on that, but we are going to Maine and I need to take a shower!" Jean turned around at the bathroom door and smiled at Connie, "I wouldn't mind a little company though."

Carolyn and Julie spent the day helping Carol and Patty get ready for the big party. Everyone else had arrived just before noon loaded down with stuff to add to the cook out. The grill was started about one o'clock and didn't shut down until almost nine that night. That didn't mean the party was over, not by along shot. It was coming close to one am. and Jamie noticed Susan was looking tired. Getting everyone's attention, "Hey everybody, I can see Susan is ready for bed, but before we call it a night, Connie and I brought a couple of bottles of champagne. We want to make a toast!" They were all ready for that. Connie uncorked the bottles and poured out the drinks as Jamie and Jean passed everyone a glass. Julie looked around but didn't see Carolyn, "Wait a minute," said Julie, "Carolyn was on the porch earlier, she must have fallen asleep, let me go get her." When Julie went out on the porch, she found Carolyn in the same spot as earlier, "Carolyn are you awake?" "What? Oh Julie, yes I'm awake. I guess I lost track of time. I've been remembering how we all came to be here." "Well that must have been interesting, you should write it down sometime. But right now everyone's waiting to make a toast." Taking Carolyn's hand they went inside and joined the others.

They were all gathered in a circle with their drinks in hand. Jamie stepped forward, raising her glass and indicating to Susan, Connie and Jean, "We just want you to know that as much as we are going to miss having you all close by, we're proud of you and what you are doing. Monday you will be officially opening a 'safe house' and we want to wish you all the best." Anna stepped forward and Jamie could see the tears in her eyes as well as everyone else's. Anna said, "That was wonderful dear, thank you. Now I want to include all of us in a toast. We may not be taking the same paths, but we have all made some serious changes in our lives and I would like to raise my glass to all of us and our futures." Standing in a tight circle with arms around each other, glasses raised, Anna said, "To new beginnings." In one voice, they repeated, "To new beginnings!"

Alicia Langley

Epilogue

Sunday breakfast went on longer then usual. Connie, Jean, Jamie and Susan weren't in any hurry to leave, especially Jamie, who had been a part of the 'group' for so long. Before leaving Jamie wanted a picture of everyone standing around the shelter's new sign that read, 'New Beginnings.' Finally, they had to go. With promises of lots of phone calls and visits, the four of them headed down the road. The ride home was quiet. It was the same for the others back at the farm. Watching them drive down the road and knowing they weren't going to follow, they all felt it, the change was real, there was no going back.

'New Beginnings' held a big open house the following Monday for the directors from other area safe houses in southern Maine and New Hampshire. The goal was to make everyone aware of the unique problems lesbian women had receiving help while in abusive situations. They planned to hold seminars throughout the fall and winter to discuss ways to work together. It turned out better than they hoped it would be. The shelter was well received along with their ideas and a lot of new ideas were brought to the table during the day as well. It wasn't long after that they began receiving calls and residents. It was a good start, easing them slowly into their new life. Lillian and Anna were very comfortable with their new roles as 'house mothers'. True it was more then they expected, but they felt they would handle it easily, as they had done with everything else throughout their life together.

Ronnie spent one evening a week taking care of the books and paying the bills. Cathy was scheduled two days a week to help out with anything and everything that needed to be done. She helped the residents with everything from writing letters to taking one or more of the women to a job interview, shopping or doctors appointment.

Patty became a familiar face at the farm. She and Carol were seeing each other as much as they could, enjoying their new relationship. She stopped by often in the evenings to help Carol with dinner. Carol started taking a course in photography two nights a week. She loved it and was becoming very good at it and took over the photo journal Jamie had started long ago.

Kate was doing well in school and her new job. She was concentrating on getting herself together and planning her future. She did get in touch with her mother, but it wasn't a good meeting. She was going to keep trying to mend their relationship and hoped someday things between them would change for the better.

Karen and Nancy loved their little bakery. They didn't have much time to be at the farm to help with the women residing there; instead they set up a workshop for any of the 'house' residents that would like to learn a trade. It was a wonderful idea, one everybody was sure they would be using.

Carolyn was working part time in order to spend her afternoons at the farm. Julie's job at Human Services turned out to be very demanding, leaving her little time for much else.

Back in Boston, life went on. Over the winter holidays Jean introduced Connie to her children, so far, things were going well. Jean was also taking her art more seriously; she had a goal. Connie gave her all her support, but secretly felt uncomfortable and uncertain about how she would fit into Jean's new lifestyle. She also wondered what role Jean's boss would have in the future.

Just before Christmas, Jamie gave up her apartment and moved in with Susan. Things were a little cramped with Jamie's photo equipment taking up a lot of extra space. It was decided in the spring, after the baby was born, they would look for a larger place. Jamie was happy with that, she just didn't feel comfortable in the house Susan had shared with her husband. They needed a place of their own. But for now they were all adjusting and waiting for the baby's arrival. By the end of the year, everyone settled into their new roles, and they were all looking forward to what the New Year had in store.

"Watch for the second book in this series...

'NEW BEGININGS'

Alicia Langley

About the Author

Ms Langley resides in a small coastal town in southern Maine. She is a 50 + year old feminist and has been in a committed relationship with the same woman since 1974. Relocating from Boston Mass in 1976, she and her partner purchased a 1700's antique farmhouse on three acres of beautiful, pastoral land. While writing and art make up a large part of the many facets of Langley's background, her first love has been animals and she has worked in the pet care field most of her life. In 1979, realizing a need for a safe haven for abandoned and lost animals in the area, Langley and her partner co-founded and operated a regional animal rescue shelter on their property. Drawing from her unique experiences while working in her chosen field, as well as her own relationship with her partner and friends, Langley incorporated her love and interest in women's issues into a beautifully written, easy to read, fictional novel. Mainely Lesbians reveals Langley's sensitive nature to the downtrodden and her intuitive ability to find the silver lining in most situations. Langley still resides in southern Maine with her partner and is currently working on her second novel in a series of books chronicling the everyday lives of lesbian women.

Ms. Langley may be contacted via e-mail; alimar@maine.rr.com